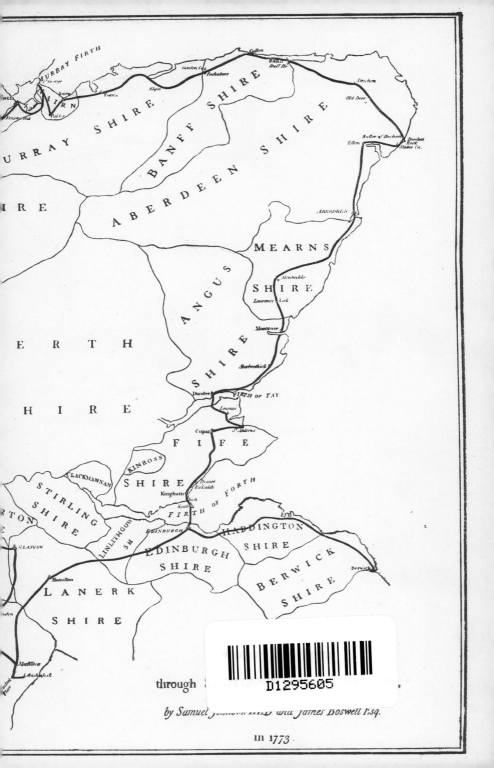

through

by Samuel Johnson LL.D. and James Boswell Esq.

in 1773.

THE HIGHLAND JAUNT

The Beginning of the Jaunt, or "I smell you in the dark". Samuel
Johnson and James Boswell walking up the High Street of Edinburgh
on August the 14th, 1773. An engraving by Thomas Rowlandson
from a set of satirical prints issued shortly after the publication of
Boswell's *Journal of a Tour to the Hebrides in 1785*

THE
HIGHLAND JAUNT

A STUDY OF JAMES BOSWELL AND
SAMUEL JOHNSON UPON THEIR
HIGHLAND AND HEBRIDEAN
TOUR OF 1773

MORAY McLAREN

JARROLDS PUBLISHERS (LONDON) LTD

Jarrolds Publishers (London) Ltd
London   Melbourne   Sydney   Auckland
Bombay   Cape Town   New York   Toronto

First published in June 1954
Reprinted in October 1954

Printed in Great Britain
by The Anchor Press, Ltd.,
Tiptree, Essex

CONTENTS

LIST OF ILLUSTRATIONS

FOREWORD

"Shall we ever have another frolick like our journey to the Hebrides?" So wrote Johnson at the age of seventy-three to Boswell nearly ten years after the Scottish tour which the two men had made in 1773. Boswell called his first seriously intended literary composition (an account of an autumn journey which he made in Ayrshire and South-West Scotland in 1762) *Journal of my Harvest Jaunt*, and jaunt was a word he often used. As this book is primarily a study of James Boswell during the Highland and Hebridean part of the famous journey he took with Doctor Johnson, I have named it *The Highland Jaunt*.

The Highland jaunt may, in a sense, be said to have started on 14 August, 1773, when Boswell and Johnson met on Scottish soil for the first time in Edinburgh. I have, therefore, devoted two chapters to the Edinburgh of that classic meeting. Thereafter I have moved directly to Inverness, the Highlands and Islands. This is not because I consider the Lowland part of the tour through St. Andrews, up the East coast, through Aberdeen, Elgin and Nairn uninteresting, but simply because the Highlands and Islands were the prime object of the journey which Johnson and Boswell undertook.

In these observations on Boswell on his native heath, on that native heath itself, on Johnson and on other *dramatis personæ* of the tour, I have, apart from the usual sources, relied mostly on the admirable edition of Boswell's *Journal of a Tour to the Hebrides* made by Robert Carruthers of Inverness, and, of course, on the original MSS. of the unrevised Journal in Boswell's own hand which was so miraculously discovered in a croquet-box at Malahide Castle as

9

late as the 1930s. Though Carruthers' edition first came out just over a hundred years ago, it remains, from the internal Scottish point of view, one of the most informative and certainly most interesting of all the many editions of Boswell's book. Carruthers was a Scot, a Highlander and a scholar. He was learned in Highland tradition as well as in Highland and Scottish history. He lived at a time when many more families than there are today were still surviving in the houses and lands which their forbears had occupied when Johnson and Boswell visited the Highlands and Islands. His comments and notes are informed not only by learning but often by first-hand personal knowledge. It is, of course, unnecessary to speak here of the incomparable value to all students of Boswell of the original or croquet-box version published amongst the Malahide papers.

I would like to thank Sheriff T. B. Simpson who corrected my MSS. on matters of fact, and often on points of style. This was a kind action on his part; for his opinions do not always march with mine. My thanks are also due to Miss C. Dickson of the Edinburgh Public Library.

For the rest, my information has come from Scotland where I live and from the Highlands and Hebrides where I have travelled much, but at no time with greater curiosity and pleasure than when compiling information for and thinking on the shape and content of this book.

M. McL.

I

THE ARRIVAL IN EDINBURGH

WHEN Doctor Johnson, accompanied by the eager James Boswell, stepped out of Boyd's Inn in the Canongate into the "effluvia" of the Royal Mile of Edinburgh, that ancient Capital was at the peak of its celebrated period of high thinking and high stinking. In 1773 the small, overcrowded, precipitously built city on the slopes of the Castle rock was the home of David Hume, Adam Smith, Principal Robertson, John Home, Robert Fergusson, Lady Nairne, Jean Elliot, Henry Mackenzie, Lord Kames, Lord Monboddo, Lord Hailes, Dr. Blacklock, and a number of other men and women then well known in literature, science, philosophy and learning. The boy Walter Scott had just been born in Edinburgh, and in a few years Robert Burns was to make his entry into the world of fame through the gates of the city. In the immediate past Allan Ramsay, the poet and playwright, Hamilton of Bangour and Robert Blair had added lustre to the town; and twenty-eight years earlier the last Stuart claimant to the throne of the United Kingdom, Prince Charles Edward, had held the last court of his line in Britain at the Palace of Holyroodhouse.

The names of some of these men and women endure, others once known internationally have now been all but forgotten save by the curious or the learned. A few, such as Robert Fergusson (Edinburgh's boy poet), are more widely known now than they were in their day. Never, however, has the reputation of Edinburgh stood higher in the world of learning and of literature. Soon that high midday of fame was to fade into afternoon, only to blaze up again before departure in the sunset glories of Sir Walter Scott. But in the 1770s Edinburgh was in her own world, the world of intelligence, secure. Her security showed itself in the even tempers, the happy dispositions of her greatest men whose characters shone with a peculiarly luminous sunniness in the dark little northern Capital. Their apparently effortless superiority of intellect, their superiority to the majority of other writers and thinkers in the United Kingdom of the time, put them beyond jealousy and beyond resentment of attack, even when that attack was spiteful and ill-informed. Edinburgh in 1773 was sure of herself in the way that only a capital city, however small, can be sure and secure.

"I smell you in the dark," the first recorded words of Dr. Johnson in Boswell's Journal, are an eloquent testimony to the high stinking that then also prevailed in Edinburgh. Johnson was not a cleanly man in his person. He splashed his food over himself, dressed in a slovenly manner and seldom changed his clothes. Even in his 18th-century literary circle (and men of books and newspapers have not been noted for their cleanliness at any time) he was regarded as "careless in his person". There is no record of him ever having had a bath during his adult life. If the "evening effluvia of Edinburgh", as Boswell describes it, were strong enough to penetrate the ambient *esprit de corps* of this great and good man, they must indeed have been powerful.

In few other towns in Europe can that puzzling 18th-century contrast of refinement in manners, art and thought with indifference to dirt have been stronger than in Edinburgh of the Golden Age. Only a few years before 1773 the "slops" of each of the many-storied households were hurled out into the street at night time to dribble away down the hill if they were liquid, to await the later arrival of the scavengers if they were solid. And by "slops", it should be remembered, were meant not only the dregs of the kitchen but the contents of the chamber-pot and the stool. When the warning bell for the nightly deluge and cascade sounded over the city, men in even the deepest taverns in the most secluded clubs would light brown-paper spills to fumigate the atmosphere against the all-pervading, the penetrating fetor.

By the time Johnson had come to Edinburgh, the Magistrates had put a stop to the worst of these habits, but the sewers were still open and in the street, and other conditions of disorder and uncleanliness remained unchanged from centuries earlier on—had even become more acute. Fine ladies would have to manœuvre their hooped silk dresses down winding narrow stone stairways, constructed as much to repel the attacks of swordsmen in past ages as to allow exit. Having managed this they would often have to squeeze themselves into sedan-chairs for even the shortest journey, so disgusting were the streets. Judges, noblemen, University professors and statesmen would descend to drink their often carefully chosen French wines and eat their delicious oysters from the beds in the Forth (now alas ripped up and sold to the Dutch) into underground taverns which never saw the light of day and seldom felt the touch of a broom.

One could go on almost endlessly recalling the conditions of squalor that did not so much penetrate to the private rooms but immediately surrounded the daily lives of some of the most intelligently refined, delicately minded, and, after their own Scotch fashion, charming people in Britain at the time. Let it be enough to say that the whole situation arose from enforced overcrowding, the overcrowding of the well-to-do as well as of the poor. Year after year, unable to break the city bounds, the houses piled upon the top of each other in "lands" or, as we would say, flats, until they reached nearly to the heights of the Castle far above the town, while far below them the Nor' Loch, hard by the steep rock on which they were built, breathed up its odours on the rising air of each summer and on the no less potent guffs of each calm autumnal zephyr.

It was intolerable; and even 18th-century Edinburgh

by the time it had reached the 70s was beginning to find it so. The way of escape, the New Town, had been planned, and was already being built in 1773, but no one of consequence, save Hume, had moved there; nor did Johnson visit it. He saw and stayed only in the old Edinburgh at the last gasp of its fascinating squalid existence. English and London readers may have some idea of what that old Edinburgh was like if they think of there having been no fire of London in 1666, and of all the citizens of the expanding town having been forced for another century to go on living within the narrow confines of what was then, and still is, the city of London. Then let them imagine that city of London perched upon a rock and surrounded by swamps, lakes, walls and hills preventing any expansion no matter how much the citizens wished for it.

Within a few years of Johnson's passage through Edinburgh, the Old Town was to burst its bounds into the then apparently limitless spaces of the Augustan New Town. The swamps and lochs were not only to be drained but cleansed, the stink and overcrowding of the black little city on the hill were to be, if not put an end to, relieved by one of the most gracious architectural experiments in Europe. Had Boswell stayed on in Edinburgh, had he lived to the normal age of many of his long-lived fellow citizens, he too would undoubtedly have joined in the great exodus across the Nor' Loch and would probably have enjoyed the space and the ordered beauty of George Street, Queen Street and the surrounding squares. He would have left the windswept yet smelly heights along with the Duchesses and the professors and the lords and the lairds and the ladies. He would have left those high-perched warrens of antiquity to the poor of Edinburgh who still inhabit them. He would have left them of necessity and perhaps with an eager curiosity—for James Boswell "catched new enthusiasms easily"—but I wonder whether that most companionable of men would not have left his old habitations with a certain amount of regret.

The present writer is a child of the New Town of Edinburgh; so were his father, his grandfather and his great-grandfather before him. It has been his home in boyhood and at times in youth, and now in middle-age. When he is absent from it the memory of its cool and ordered spaces come to him with the refreshment of a spring of water. Even now when he lives in it he takes a daily pleasure in its austere loveliness, yet if he feels the lack of one thing in it, it is something that James Boswell of all men particularly relished— the sense of open, easy and bustling companionship. If the Old Town with its overcrowding, its smells, its underground taverns, its high-piling "lands", its congregation of wit, learning and dirt had one large quality, it was its companionability.

When Johnson and Boswell walked up from Boyd's Inn to the top of the Royal Mile where the young Scots lawyer lived, they were passing through the main, indeed nearly the only, large street in the last truly democratic capital in Europe. Nowhere else could people of quality and of poverty, of learning and peasant ignorance, have lived so closely and so harmoniously together. Duchesses, or at least one very charming Duchess, the Duchess of Gordon, bargained with fishwives in the open street, Judges, often men of ancient lineage as well as of high position, would talk in court not only to poor witnesses but to all and sundry in the "common Scotch tongue"—imagine a London Judge at any time talking Costermonger cockney! Lords, lairds and men bearing great names either in history or in contemporary learning were on easy terms of familiarity with the poorer neighbours on their stairs—the milliners, the cobblers and booksellers; while all the time as a running current of intersocial life there existed the caddies. These were low-born messengers who knew everybody's business in the city, including their amours and their less openly advertised habits. Smollett in his *Humphrey Clinker* has a most amusing description of the caddies' annual dinner when the lords and gentlemen waited upon these humble Mercuries, these social scavengers of Edinburgh.

David Hume was one of the most famous men in Europe at the time, but when he got stuck in a bog by the Nor' Loch and appealed for help to a passing fishwife, she would not give it to "the atheist" (he was really a Deist) until she had made him repeat the Creed and the Lord's Prayer. For all its insanitary qualities it must have been an enchanting town, and not even 18th-century London's multi-coloured vivacity (so often and so well described) had quite the same human as well as aristocratic quality.

Today the Old Town is still in a sense companionable, particularly on Saturday nights, but it is less democratic just because it has lost its aristocratic quality. It is companionable but (though no one could blame its inhabitants for this) it is class conscious. They, the poor people, the abandoned, are the ones who have been left to hang on like bats in the rotting tenements, hanging on still speaking much the same language as the lords and ladies and their own forefathers spoke 200 years ago. But the lords and ladies have moved to easier circumstances and to the use of smoother, less forceful and perhaps, to judge from some of their pronouncements, a less articulate tongue. If the present-day poverty-stricken inhabitants of the Old Town feel that it is their own class territory and sometimes show class resentment at the presence of richer sightseers, they are hardly to be blamed. Still, even so, there are moments when something of the air of old classless companionability seems to stir in the centuries-old main street of the city on the hill. One sees tartan-shawled housewives lolling from high windows in the calm of the long northern summer evenings, or passes by the venerable lady who keeps the whelk stall in the Lawnmarket and listens to her clients, one watches the decrepit eccentrics fingering the books on the second-hand stalls; and in fancy they do not seem to be very different in style and manner from the inhabitants of the place 200 years ago. They are just authentic "antique Scotch" in the true style. The Duchess of Gordon or Davie Hume would know them and would be able to speak to them. And, more important, one feels that they too would "ken" the Duchess and the amiable "philosopher of doubt" and would not mind talking to them on their own level. But these moments of human continuity in the main arteries of the Old Town are fleeting and transitory, though none the less authentic for that.

If one should wish, however, to revive in fancy the scene of the Royal Mile as it was when Boswell received Johnson in Edinburgh, one should visit it as the present writer once did at four o'clock on a summer morning, when no one is about, and when the ghost of the skeleton, or the skeleton of the ghost of the place lies bare. With no one of the present time showing himself, and, what is equally important, with no wheeled traffic of this age to swell, congest and over-power the ancient thoroughfare, it is possible, standing at any place in it, to do two things. One can see the shape of the irregular, all but winding, now contracting, now expanding, main artery of the Capital of Scotland as it was not so much designed but rather as it grew—the shape that has not changed since Scottish Kings and Queens once walked, rode and drove in it. Also, it is possible to fill it in one's mind's eye with the folk who made it so vivid once upon a time.

Many of the buildings have, of course, disappeared or changed since 1773. Nineteenth-century Augustan or mock Augustan town and city offices have arisen; 19th-century breweries and tenements have overlaid old houses, but it is surprising, if one takes the trouble to walk leisurely from the Palace of Holyroodhouse to the Castle, to notice how many 18th, 17th and even earlier century buildings remain. Crapulous, decayed, or carefully restored, they are still there and provide a framework for the imagination to work upon; and the shape of that framework has changed but

B

little through the centuries. Within that shape one can recall the crowded thoroughfares, the goods-laden stalls of the Luckenbooths, the dark tavern doors with the lawyers and the lairds going in and out, the closes with the sedan-chairs standing by to lift the ladies when they came down from their stairs, the harlots lying back within the close mouths, the caddies clustering for custom by the Mercat Cross, and the colour of the multifarious crowds that jostled each other in this the highest man-built canyon of its time in the world. All this one can see in fancy on a summer morning by that wonderful pristine light that comes out of the sky in the North in which it has so recently died at twilight. One can, however, hear nothing, for the eye of imagination is quicker than the ear; and the sounds that these long dead people made have died with them beyond recall. Thus one can stand watching and dreaming in a primrose-coloured dawn—and then the first motor bus, the first 20th-century dust-cart arrive, and the dream is over.

No such sights, however, greeted Dr. Johnson when, having abused the waiter at Boyd's Inn for putting sugar in his lemonade with his fingers and having subsequently greeted and embraced Boswell, he emerged into the street to make the steep and, to elderly English legs, tiresome ascent up the High Street and Lawnmarket. No such sights greeted him, for the simple reason that it was a "dusky night", and the Edinburgh streets were then nearly as celebrated for their bad lighting as for their smell. The two men linked arms and, through the darkness and the "Edinburgh effluvia", mounted the hill to James's Court where Boswell lived and where the affectionate, but almost certainly slightly frightened, Margaret Boswell awaited her extraordinary husband and his extraordinary friend whom she was to meet for the first time.

It is possible over the century and a half to sympathize with her anxiety. For ten years Boswell had dreamed of this moment and must have chattered often to his wife about it since their marriage three years earlier. He had himself shown considerable anxiety as the great day of Johnson's arrival approached, and that anxiety must have increased her own nervousness. It was all very well for him to exult as he set forth "in the thought that I now had him actually in Caledonia", but it was not so easy for Margaret Boswell to exult in the prospect of acting as hostess to this celebrated eccentric and Scot-baiter who had so strange and strong an influence over her husband, and whom all literary Edinburgh was agog to meet. It was indeed a great occasion and one which has remained great, or at least highly remarkable even now as we look back at it over 181 years—Dr. Samuel Johnson in Edinburgh, Dr. Johnson emerging into the High Street and walking up it with his exulting young friend.

Indeed this leisurely, arms-linked noctambulation up the Edinburgh hill is amongst the most famous short walks recorded in our language. Only one remark, a growl in the darkness from Dr. Johnson, has been preserved for us, yet ever since Boswell first published his account of the Tour and of Johnson's arrival in Edinburgh, people have delighted to call up in fancy what it was they said to each other as they went up the way to Boswell's house. Imaginary dialogues, scenes upon the radio, descriptive essays have been put forth about it; and hundreds of Johnsonians and Boswellians have trod the modern paving stones of the Royal Mile in daytime, in dusk and at night in endeavours to recapture the atmosphere of an immortal occasion, an immortal walk.

It is important, therefore, to correct a mistake about the starting-point of this walk which has arisen from (of all sources) the pen of the great Birkbeck Hill. He makes out that Johnson lodged at the inn in Whitehorse Close which stands at the bottom of the Canongate, and by the gates of the town. He decorates this error by describing the picturesque remains of the coaching-horse inn that undoubtedly did stand in Whitehorse Close and, in his huge book on the tour, gives an illustration of the front of it. In fact, as Boswell clearly states, Johnson lodged at Boyd's Inn, a popular resort in the centre of the town, at the junction of the Canongate and the High Street. The whole point of Boswell's introduction of Johnson to Edinburgh is lost if one thinks of them walking up the Canongate from the fringes of the city instead of (as actually happened) emerging directly into the dark ravine made by the two high facing cliffs of the High Street. A London lover of *The Life* can get some idea of the quality of the mistake if he can imagine someone talking about the Mitre Tavern as if it stood not in Fleet Street but just west of Charing Cross. George Birkbeck Hill's researches into Johnsoniana are so scholarly, so luminous with correct intuition, that it is with hesitation that one points out this lapse on the part of the great Johnsonian editor. Nevertheless as Boyd's Inn was the starting-point of the tour to the Hebrides and as "I can smell you in the dark", the first recorded words of the tour were spoken in the high effluvial channel of the High Street, it is important to get that starting-point right. And should any future lovers and followers of *The Journal* wish to tread in Johnson's and Boswell's footsteps upon this memorable occasion, they should begin by placing themselves at the lower centre of the Old Town and march thence westwards and upwards to the heights just below the Castle where Boswell's house in James's Court stood, the court which George Birkbeck Hill describes so well.

James's Court in 1773 was the most salubrious and most respectable of domestic congregations within the Old Town. In its lofty and carefully preserved position above and slightly apart from the congestion of the main thoroughfare, it was socially a jumping-off place for the New Town which was then just being built. Once you had penetrated through the closeway the court was spacious and was guarded by a private porter who would conduct you to the doors of houses which were for the time and place ample and comfortable. It was a kind of 18th-century Albany cut off by height as well as by guarded entrance from the Piccadilly of Old Edinburgh. Old-fashioned aristocrats, Judges and lairds had not left their more congested town houses for it, but the smarter young advocates, professional men and ladies of quality were in the vanguard of fashion by inhabiting it. Even Johnson who had been disgusted by the slovenliness of Boyd's Inn and a little overcome by the towering squalor of the main part of the Royal Mile was impressed by the comfort of James's Court and found that Boswell was very well housed there.

Today James's Court is as decrepit as any other place in the Royal Mile that has not yet been renovated to modern use. Broken windows, peeling walls and sweating stones are all that remain of façades that were once thought elegant. Poor little Scotch children, shouting or fighting at their play like wild animals, as it sometimes seems that only Scotch children can do, fill the open spaces of the courtyard; and over everything there hangs that indefinable air of rancid decay so familiar to modern visitors to the Old Town. Decay and decline apart, there is for the modern pilgrim to James's Court another disappointment. Though the shell of most of the old houses still stand, Boswell's was one of the few that were completely destroyed by a fire some ninety years ago. Nevertheless, it is possible, just possible, as one turns into the low archway from the main street, to imagine something of the sense of withdrawal that James's Court once gave to its visitors, and particularly to Samuel Johnson as he came up into the cleaner heights of the Lawnmarket and followed his friend James Boswell to his home.

There he was to find the warm comfortable lights of a well-furnished spacious house. There was Margaret Boswell waiting, nervous but too well-bred to show it more than in a trifle over-stiff-lipped "Scotch civility". There was the best bedroom which she had vacated for her husband's friend; and there on the next morning was Boswell's four months old daughter Veronica who much pleased Dr. Johnson and who pleased her father even more by showing her own infant pleasure in Johnson's voice, face and movements and by wishing to be held close to him. There was tea and talk in plenty; there was the comfortable end of a long and tedious journey and the prospect of the beginning of a new and exciting one. And finally there was Bozzy, not only amiable and affectionate and sensible, but at his best—healthy and to all appearances well-behaved and most certainly happy.

Nor was it only the long-looked-for presence of his beloved mentor that had produced this state of affairs. To understand this we must recall Boswell's position in life, in Edinburgh society and in his work at the time of Johnson's visit. All too shortly the clouds were to roll over him again, but at this time and for many months past he had enjoyed and was enjoying one of the better periods of his life, and his happiness was increased by the thought that he was just on the verge of the long anticipated tour with Johnson. It is pleasant to think of him as he was then, and it is difficult not to believe that Johnson, who had so deep an affection for him, did not find pleasure too in contemplating James Boswell in Edinburgh in 1773.

There are those who regard Boswell's whole life and achievements as a half-ridiculous, half-incomprehensible freak of nature. They cannot understand how such a "sot, lecher and buffoon" could have held the affection of Johnson until the end of the great man's life. They profess to regard the enormous achievement of *The Life* and the little masterpiece of *The Journal* as two of those unaccountable outbursts of genius which are said to descend upon half-mad people; and amongst other incomprehensibilities they are astonished that any society, particularly the somewhat consciously intellectual society of 18th-century Edinburgh,

The Old Tolbooth in 'the Royal Mile' of Edinburgh near the
entrance to James' Court where Boswell lived

(Courtesy of the Edinburgh Public Library)

The Old Town and the beginning of the New Town of Edinburgh in 1773, the year of the tour

(*Courtesy of the Edinburgh Public Library*)

could have put up with him. They refuse to believe that his own merits in work or conduct could have had anything to do with it. The vague use of the word "amiability" is the nearest they approach to offering an explanation.

In fact, James Boswell, apart from his never-ceasing aspirations after goodness as well as after respectability and fame, was capable of oddly sustained and nearly successful efforts to achieve his ambitions. The world has recently been entertained by the ingenuous accounts of Boswell's drinking, fornications and toadying in his London Journal of 1762–63. It was less entertained by, though it might have paid more attention to, his papers from Holland immediately following the London year in which is chronicled an admittedly comic but none the less brave attempt at reform.

He made a second, longer and more successful attempt in the years immediately after his marriage in 1770. He drank considerably less: he was for the time faithful to his wife, and, upon his visits to London, even resisted the "invitations to amorous intercourse" of many pretty girls in the Strand "wearing the girdle of Venus". He confessed that they made him uneasy, filled him with "patriarchal thoughts of polygamy and concubinage", but he did resist and even resolved never to visit London again without his wife—a resolution, of course, which he did not sustain. Finally, in Edinburgh he was not the foolish, prattling, all but idle lawyer that some people imagine him to have been. Naturally well placed by his aristocratic connections and the fact of his father's seat upon the Bench, he took advantage of this by building up a tolerable practice as a Scots advocate. By 1773 and even in 1774, when he was backsliding badly, he had a decent amount of work, won a number of cases and could plead well. A well-known law officer of the Crown in Scotland and one of the wisest living authorities on Boswell and the 18th century has given it to the present writer as his opinion that Boswell might easily have become a Judge if he had stuck to it a little longer.

That he did not stick to it was due to a number of causes. These were his distaste for the Scottish Law which prevented his applying himself assiduously enough to its intricacies, and which led him to take the ill-advised step of being called to the English bar too late, his openly expressed dislike of certain high officials in Scotland, his melancholy which later induced excessive drinking, and finally his incurable good nature. Boswell frequently made himself unpopular in high places by espousing the causes of poor people in causes unpopular in those high places. Those who doubt this should read the extraordinary story of his partly comical, partly admirable, attempt to get John Reid the sheep-stealer acquitted—"Poor John" who the Crown was determined should hang. Boswell's fearless kindness to such creatures offended the mighty and weighed against him. To adapt a well-known *cliché*, Boswell through the better side of him was, in his profession, his own best enemy.

At the time of which we are speaking, however, he had not yet defended "Poor John", had not yet indulged in the wild debaucheries of 1774, and was regarded with favour (slightly tolerant and amused perhaps) as a lively young man who had sown his wild oats, who had cut something of a figure (according to his own accounts) in London and Europe, who was well connected and who had written a successful travel book on Corsica—though it must be admitted that this last was looked upon, for the son of Lord Auchinleck, as much a piece of eccentricity as evidence of talent. Still he was not negligible. In short, they in Edinburgh in 1773 did not know about him what we know now. They did not know what an incredibly pathetic ass the poor man could make of himself, nor did they suspect what depths of genius there lay in him.

For over 150 years the world has, in its varying fashion, recognized the fact of his genius. It is only comparatively recently, however, that we have had revealed to us through

the astonishing discoveries of his private papers the extent
of his weaknesses and folly as well as the pertinacity of his
private and better aspirations. These have been discussed at
length elsewhere in many books and journals clinically and
sympathetically, disapprovingly and humorously, but as we
are dealing here with Boswell on his native heath, it will
not be out of place, I suggest, to speak of them afresh,
particularly as they manifested themselves so violently in
Edinburgh the moment Johnson had left Scotland.

When he was not happy and not behaving himself
Boswell drank excessively. He drank to the detriment of his
health and spirits, to the distress of those who loved him
and to the deep distress of himself. His Journal for 1774 in
Edinburgh is full of records of huge drinking bouts, huge
protestations of reform and sad accounts of his wife's and
his own misery as a result. To one who has an ineradicable
affection for the man these records are more pathetic than,
as they are often regarded, contemptible. They possess,
however, for the student of the past a curiously statistical
fascination. On one occasion in 1774 he and five companions got through what would amount to nearly thirty
modern pints of wine made up of claret and hock, and what
was probably half a dozen modern bottles of brandy and
gin. And though this was one of his major debauches, there
is no indication that it was unique. He attended the kirk
next day and the court on Monday morning.

Against these staggering statistics and distressful records
of remorse must be set certain facts. For huge sustained
drinking 18th-century Edinburgh must have been difficult
to beat at any place, at any time, in the world's history.
Judges, advocates, Writers to the Signet, lords, some ladies,
country lairds, tradesmen and ministers consumed amounts
of wine and spirits to an extent that makes one think that
one is reading some saga of festivals in Valhalla. And the
remarkable thing was how little harm it seemed to do them.
One could go on almost interminably quoting further

statistics on this point. One example will suffice. Henry
Mackenzie, author of *The Man of Feeling*, in his anecdotes
has the following:

> It is dangerous to the health of an old man accustomed to
> drink hard to give up drinking suddenly. An old friend of mine
> shewed good sense in this. He was one of the hardest drinkers in
> Scotland in his middle-age, having prepared himself, however, by
> having tasted no strong liquor till past twenty. From that till
> sixty he drank more than any man in Scotland. I once saw him
> after he had drunk fourteen bottles of punch when he came to
> my father's to supper, and, feeling his situation, begged to lie
> down for half-an-hour while the company was playing cards. He
> was called when supper was served and behaved with perfect
> propriety like a gentleman. After sixty he reduced pint by pint
> until he had only a few glasses poured out by his wife. He lived
> to over four score.

In such a world in such a company how could poor
volatile Boswell refrain without heroic effort? He did not.
It should be noted, however, that despite his frequent lapses
and despite the fact that as he put it "No man is more easily
hurt by wine than I am", he never became a jerky, nervous
dipsomaniac of the modern kind. He drank mostly in
company, seldom alone, and was not a secret dram drinker
whose nerves cried out for alcohol at unexpected times. You
always knew when Boswell was drinking and when he was
going to get drunk, but alas! you could never be certain in
company when he was going to be sober.

Boswell's other weakness, folly, vice, anodyne or evil
inclination, define it how you will, was fornication with
street harlots. Despite his induced, exaggerated and worked-
up mental passions in his early days in London and on the
Continent, Boswell was no Don Juan, not even a Casanova,
largely, I suspect, because though well liked by some women
of his own class, he was romantically unattractive to them.
He was a little too ridiculous. Whenever his strong physical

feelings, his curiosity, or the mere vagrancy of his persistent desires were released from their inhibiting chains by drink, company or high spirits, he sought the nearest, easiest and probably often the only sexual relief he could find—the women of the streets. These he not only pursued and found in the streets but made love to in the streets. If Boswell's drinking was indulged in, seated in comfort indoors and soaking over long hours, his fornications were often vertical, abrupt and in the open air. This habit too, like his drinking, cost him dear in health and in distress of spirits amounting at times to mental anguish.

Ridiculous and pitiable though this may have been, I cannot find it in me to be as shocked as a number of his modern critics have shown themselves to have been after the recent publication of his Journals. After all, many other well-known men in the past have on occasions bought fleeting pleasure from harlots. Not many of them, however, have given themselves away so freely on the subject: and this, I suspect, is partly the reason for the critics' contempt. He gave himself away. This too was, in the popular eye, the fault of Oscar Wilde. At a time when, as every man of the world, and certainly as every Continental pimp, knew, English society contained a strong and persistent streak of active homosexuality, Wilde gave himself away, and consequently gave a number of other people away—to themselves as well as to others. The comparison, however, is not exact. Wilde gloried in his weakness; Boswell did not.

Another point of mitigation, at least as far as 1774 was concerned, is this. Edinburgh has always been a city of Jekyll and Hyde (it and not London has long been recognized as the true locale of Stevenson's story) and this was most certainly true of it in the 18th century. Boswell, like so many outwardly respectable Calvinists, sure of their predestined salvation, could have hidden away his lusts in the secrecy of the many bagnios of the town, or have used his position and his easy circumstances to procure and pervert youth in comfortable security. He did nothing of the kind; nor was he ever even tempted to those refinements of desire and cruelty so fashionable amongst libertines of the period in France and England. No, he merely practised his foolish, ridiculous, selfish, self-destroying lusts in the open streets and mostly under the shadow of the Cowgate.

I do not wish to be accused of sentimentalizing over Boswell, nor of condoning his squalid self-indulgences, but in conclusion I would say this. As I write these words there is published in the Press news of a man who has just procured his ninth divorce and who proposes to marry as his tenth legal wife the twin sister of the woman to whom he had been married the week before. Only recently there were published statistics of the frightening number of young people in the United States, some of them of seventeen and under, who are suffering from alcoholic disorders amounting often to Delirium Tremens, through the drinking of spirits. Such things would have been incredible not only to Boswell but to the age in which he lived.

To mention these is to take extreme instances. Nevertheless "There's just time for a quick one" is, in its sinister undertones, one of the grimmest adages of our time—a quick one and then another quick one before Doom. And I do suggest that an age which is infected by such a maxim, an age in which, *mariage en dixième noces* and childish alcoholics apart, an age in which the swilling of poisonous spirits in jerky succession is so prevalent, an age in which casual fornication is, in certain circles, so common that it amounts to no more than the small change of social intercourse—I suggest that such an age should pause before it condemns James Boswell. He destroyed no homes, seduced none of his friends' wives or sisters, was a loving husband and affectionate father who hated himself for the distress which he gave to those who loved him; and when he drank he did so nearly always in civilized company, leisurely and at ease. If he had had a better head, a less volatile temperament, he might have drunk just as much as did his companions and have behaved himself as well as most of them did.

On the night of 14 August, 1773, no such questions about Boswell's conduct assailed the private company at James's Court. Except for a slight nervousness on Margaret Boswell's part and perhaps a faint foretaste of the difficulties she was going to have in acting as hostess to the greatest Englishman then alive and one of the most personally slovenly men in the United Kingdom, all was warmth and light and happiness. The Doctor was affectionate. Little Veronica loved his rambling talk and heavy pock-marked face. Bozzy was not only exulting in the achievement of a near miracle (bringing Johnson to Scotland) but was on the tip-toe of expectation, looking forward to what were to be amongst the happiest and best three months of his life.

II

BOSWELL AS HOST

I CAME out of James's Court in the Autumn of 1952 and began that series of disjointed wanderings which, when strung together, would, I hoped, provide the theme for the present-day side of this book. Entering the Royal Mile at a comparatively unfrequented time my mind was full of the travellers of 1773. I decided to put my thoughts to the test and entered a public house, one of those infinitely remote and decayed descendants of the 18th-century howffs or clubs, which were then so prominent a feature of the Capital of Scotland, and having ordered a drink, asked the landlord if he had ever heard of Dr. Johnson. I was lucky; he had.

"Oh, yon was the auld Englishman that was always blethering against the Scotch."

I could not but agree that this was a fairly accurate description of a part of the great man's conversation: but I pointed out that he had many other claims to be remembered, that he had spoken a good deal of sense in his time, that many of his views on Scotland were sound, and that he had, upon his visit to Edinburgh, stayed but a few doors further up the street.

"Ay, so they tell't me: that's as mebbe, mebbe."

Later on, after a few failures I encountered one ordinary person in that winding old street, where Boswell was once a so-well-known figure, who had heard of him. Him too I questioned in the crapulous circumstances extended by a modern High Street inn.

"Ay, Boswell. Yon was the felly who was always going with whüres and pitting it doon on paper."

Again I could not but agree, but again I added that there was considerably more to be said about this notable fellow townsman of ours than this. The reason for my humble interlocutor's laconic dismissal of Boswell in this way was I think the recent publication of Boswell's London Journal. He had almost certainly never read it; for the price of it was far beyond the capacity of his purse. But faint references to the more "juicy" parts of the book rather than reviews had got into the public Press; and quite recently, cashing in on Bozzy's reputation, a popular Scottish daily newspaper had been serializing Boswell's Dutch Journal which, with its partly pathetic, partly comic, record of attempted reform must have proved a sad disappointment to those readers whose salacious tastes had been titivated in advance.

Descending into the presumably more educated quarter of the New Town I did not bother to cross-examine any of my acquaintances there. I merely recalled past remarks, and I reflected that, in more elegant language, the two judgments I had heard on these two men had often been expressed to me by my more comfortable, though not necessarily scholarly, fellow citizens. What a reflection on modern Scottish opinion! Or rather what a reflection on the way modern opinion is everywhere moulded by the popular Press!

Yet I could not help wondering whether there were not more reasons than that to account for the general Scottish attitude towards Johnson and Boswell. The Scots are a highly sensitive people on a question of manners; and despite Johnson's immense good sense on many Scottish problems of his time, despite his many generous and warm-hearted outbursts, he was often by modern, indeed by any, standards unpleasantly and crudely rude in Scotland, particularly in Edinburgh. Traditions live long in the Northern Kingdom and again particularly in Edinburgh. It may be that something of the traditions of Johnson's rudeness to a whole country may have lingered here

while his more personal and private rudenesses in England
(a country for which he patriotically glowed) have been
forgotten.

Leaving aside all that has been written about Boswell
seriously, popularly, salaciously and trivially, I cannot
help wondering whether the long traditions of Edinburgh
may not have something to do with the popular attitude
towards him. Boswell may have succeeded in concealing
some of his grosser follies in the larger city of London; he
did not, later than the period we are discussing, do so in
Edinburgh, the city where much of his family background
and where his work lay, the city that knew his circumstances
and thought that it knew all about him. Boswell was a
supreme giver-away-of-himself. He never gave himself away
with greater abandon than in Edinburgh. And the Capital
of Scotland has always, I regret to say, regarded this quality,
whether as a failing or a virtue, with contempt.

On the next day I returned to the Old Town, and,
wandering in it, allowed myself further reflections on
Boswell's entertainment of his great mentor in Edinburgh.
I know my native city fairly well, and have written much
about it. It was, however, strange to me to observe that
when I concentrated my thoughts upon one particular
moment of her past how much of that moment I usually
passed over in my wanderings in the city. Merely to walk up
and down the Royal Mile thinking of Boswell and Johnson
was to refresh my mind on a subject which I had so often
read about, on which I had so often pondered. I decided
then and there to extend this process of mental refreshment
by physical means further North and into the Highlands
and Islands. I had been to nearly every place Boswell and
Johnson had visited on their tour, but I decided to see them
all over again thinking of the great pair while I did so. I did
not conceive anything so ambitious as a reconstruction of the
Highland part of the tour, already so admirably done by
Birkbeck Hill 60 years earlier; I merely sought (I repeat the

word) refreshment on the theme; and I decided to take that refreshment sip by sip and as leisurely as possible.

Wandering in the Royal Mile of the Old Town, in some ways so evocative of the past, in some ways so different from it, I did not bother myself too much with noticing which buildings remained, which had gone or changed. Rather I pondered on Boswell's state of mind on these first days when he introduced the Doctor to Scotland. Clearly he was extremely anxious not only to be on his best behaviour himself but to show off his circumstances and his acquaintances in the most respectable light he could. Considering Boswell's position in Edinburgh, remembering Johnson's reputation as a Scot-baiter, and reflecting on the certainty that Boswell must have boasted in Edinburgh of his illustrious friend's arrival, one can scarcely wonder at this. One is grateful, however, that as the tour proceeded and as Boswell went further from home he threw off these restraints, and as a result we get, as his book develops, the more real Boswell upon his native heath, the real Boswell who was not only the Johnsonian recorder, the great man's foil, what is called in modern music-hall language his "feed", but the Boswell who was also the ideal companion for him on this extraordinary journey.

After the first candle-lit evening in James's Court, after the joyful and awkward meeting, the surrender by Mrs. Boswell of the best bedroom; and after the awkward but happy meeting with the infant Veronica on the next day, Boswell plunged his guest into a swirl of respectable Edinburgh society. That it was a swirl we learn from Johnson's letters to Mrs. Thrale in which he complains of the noise and confusion of some of the gatherings—though he is at pains to acknowledge the comfort of Boswell's situation. Boswell was quite clearly doing what many a modern Edinburgh or Dublin citizen does with a distinguished London visitor: he was overloading him with what he believed to be suitable company. That it got a little on the

c

Doctor's nerves is shown by his rather ill-natured reference
to the Duchess of Douglas, who spoke such broad Scots that
Johnson claimed she could hardly be understood by her own
compatriots. He added that her voice was "paralytick".
Johnson was no snob, but he was sufficiently of his age not
usually to speak of duchesses (even Scotch Duchesses) in
this way.

As I wandered in the Royal Mile I could see the crowded
little drawing-room in James's Court and hear in fancy the
babble of noise coming from it. Though long ago destroyed
by fire it must have been to look at not unlike the back
drawing-room in Gladstone's Land hard by James's Court
itself, the Gladstone's Land which of recent years has
been so admirably rescued and restored. The drawing-room
in Gladstone's Land is a cool quiet retreat panelled in the
gracious 18th-century fashion. From it you can look out on
to the swarming present-day slum. From Boswell's drawing-
room you could look out on to the steep decline into the
swamp of what remained of the "Nor' Loch", and to the
first experiments with the New Town, but you must have
been conscious that immediately behind you lay streets just
as swarming though not as slummy as they are today.

When the great English Doctor was being entertained
there it must, however, have been far from a quiet retreat.
Low ceilinged, narrow and possibly overloaded with chairs,
it may have seemed to Johnson, when he first saw it, commodious, after his original introduction to the Edinburgh
streets. It must, however, soon have lost that commodious-
ness when crowded by the chattering and eager respectable
Edinburgh gatherings which Boswell got together to honour
the occasion, crowds chattering for the most part in an accent
which offended Johnson's Lichfield-cum-Fleet-Street ears.

I could in imagination see the candle-lit, hot and over-
crowded room with the old man sitting in the corner and
Bozzy darting hither and thither as he led up the suitable
Edinburgh respectabilities to speak to him. I can hear also

Bozzy's distinctly anglified Scots as he did his best to draw his great guest out. That he succeeded in doing so on more than one occasion during the Edinburgh visit we know from Boswell's Journal. But from Johnson's deliberate refusal to discuss Edinburgh in his book on the tour, and from his slightly grumpy remarks to Mrs. Thrale in his letters, it is fairly obvious that the old man, while doing his best to be polite, and not always succeeding, looked upon the Capital of Scotland, the "Academy of Europe", as no more than a stepping-stone to the "romantick journey" which he had planned. At the end of the evening he must have retreated with a sigh of thankfulness to "the best bedroom" where he could make the candles burn better for reading by turning them upside down for a moment (thereby, to Margaret Boswell's irritation, spilling grease on the best carpet) and then dipping into Boswell's favourite volume, *Ogden on Prayer*, which his host had probably left beside his bed.

Boswell's frequent references in his tour to *Ogden on Prayer* must have made every Boswellian aware of his devotion to this book of sermons. Indeed, even Boswell's own contemporaries poked fun at him for it; and in the Rowlandson cartoons about the tour Ogden's book is seen sticking out of Boswell's pocket. It was with some curiosity therefore that I sought out this slim volume of long-forgotten sermons by the choleric, black-jawed, heavy-featured Anglican Divine, who was on account of the shortness of his sermons George III's favourite preacher. Ogden also did himself so well at the table that he is said to have been the original author of the saying that a goose was an unsatisfactory bird on the board, "not enough for two, but just too much for one". The volume that I consulted was the first edition, which is still preserved in the Advocates (now National) Library in Edinburgh. I do not suppose anyone had opened it for decades, possibly for over a century. Boswell himself may well have handled it; for he was no stranger to the Advocates' Library in his day.

I had expected to find the usual 18th-century set oratory of piety, rotund and long-winded. On the contrary I was surprised and pleased to discover that Boswell's favourite sermonizer wrote in crisp economical English not unlike Swift's, and that his arguments were clear, and directed to the head rather than being merely rhetorical. It is easy to see why they had caught Boswell's attention. Boswell was haunted by fears as well as by constitutional melancholy. He feared annihilation after death, he feared the consequences of his own sins. He feared the philosophy of Determinism; and these fears were constantly being excited by the "philosophical" French and Scottish literature which he read with fascination but equally with horror.

Ogden's taut, reasonable arguments in favour of the existence of God and of His interest in us and of our certainty of being able to solicit that interest by prayer must often have soothed the excitable young Scot in his hangovers from sin. Boswell was continually thrusting Ogden under Dr. Johnson's nose, and with what seems to us today a remarkable lack of self-consciousness would often read extracts from the sermons aloud in company when the Doctor was present. Once, upon a later stage of the tour he succeeded in getting the great man himself to give a reading of the sixth sermon. This combination of the powerful respected voice speaking the clear cold logic of the respected sermonizer must have lifted poor Boswell's spirits immensely.

For the lover of Edinburgh who is also an admirer of Johnson it is disappointing that the Doctor's visit to the Capital of Scotland seems largely to have been taken up with a few polite dinner parties and a few explosions of, one hopes, good-tempered rudeness on Johnson's part. He met Principal Robertson, leader of the moderate party in Presbyterianism and the nearest approach to an Anglican clergyman in the Church of Scotland. He met a number of University Professors, legal luminaries, country lairds and aristocrats, some of whose names are still remembered. He had also one touching meeting with Dr. Blacklock, the blind poet, in which Johnson showed himself at his best, affectionate and warm-hearted—but of the tang and taste of that fascinating late-18th-century Edinburgh he experienced little. One has only to read Smollett's account of the Edinburgh of the period in *Humphrey Clinker* to realize what Johnson, through Boswell's understandable caution, missed.

One of Johnson's outstanding characteristics was his curiosity about life in all circumstances. Boswell's full-length biography of him is crammed with instances of this gustful curiosity not only in Fleet Street, and London, but in the provincial English towns. What a pity it is that he could not have penetrated to the taverns and howffs and oyster-shops of the Edinburgh of the period! What a pity he was never allowed to meet the caddies, the eccentrics, the innumerable oddities who gave such a flavour to the place at the time!

What a pity too that no one read to him or introduced him to some of the poems of the Edinburgh boy poet Robert Fergusson, who was to die at the age of twenty-four in the next year, and who was already sinking! Johnson hated the Scotch accent. At the same time, however, he hated to see old customs, old habits and old languages disappear. He might have dismissed Fergusson's verses, if he could have understood them, as "crude jinglings in an outlandish dialect". On the other hand, if he had met the appealing attractive boy himself, if he had realized the gusto with which the tavern frequenters of the Edinburgh of the Golden Age repeated and relished his verses, that paradoxical and generous heart might have been warmed to some kind of sudden appreciation.

Fergusson was alive but dying in 1773. In that year, however, there was another Scots youth only fourteen years old living in Ayrshire. A few years later he was to come to Edinburgh and to set the place aflame by his poetry in the old tongue of Scotland. Having mentioned Fergusson it is impossible not to ask oneself the question what would Johnson have made of Robert Burns and his poetry if he had been born a little later and had come to 18th-century Edinburgh when the "ploughman poet" was the fashion of the Capital?

What a question! All reason, all deduction from what we know of Johnson's tastes incline one to believe that he would have been antipathetic to everything that Burns stood for. And yet, and yet, there remains an obstinate doubt in one's mind. Johnson's warm-heartedness towards the warm-hearted was and is acknowledged. His taste, so often twisted by the turns of his own tortuous moods, was sound at basis: he usually recognized beauty when he saw or heard it. Is it not just possible that he might have recognized in Burns's poetry the authentic note which we now recognize—which the whole Scottish nation is now inclined to praise often unthinkingly? And above all might he not have felt upon meeting Burns that generosity of soul which always pleased him in other and younger men and with which he himself was so well endowed? Finally in hearing that Burns was singing amidst the then anglified Edinburgh in the old Scotch manner might not his conservative heart have been kindled to a sympathetic glow— Scotch or no Scotch?

Probably not, but the question, though unanswerable, is open to endless speculation. One thing is certain: if the years had been kinder and if Boswell had managed to bring off a meeting between "the sage of Bolt Court" and the "ploughman poet" he would have achieved as big a scoop as the meeting for which he was responsible between Johnson and Jack Wilkes; and it might have been just as successful. But, though not as certain, it is highly probable that Boswell would have disdained to bring about such a meeting. Boswell, a laird in Burns's own county, lived through the first and most luminous part of Burns's period of fame; yet he does not seem to have paid the slightest attention to him. Unless Boswell's volatile spirit had somehow been caught by the Edinburgh fashion for Burns, unless, as might well have happened, his own generous heart had opened to his humbler countryman, it is extremely unlikely that he would have thought it worth while to introduce the greatest Englishman alive, the man whom he revered above all others, to someone whom he might, with the best intentions, have looked upon as the product of an ephemeral Scotch fashion. Boswell did not lack patriotism, but to have recognized the genius of Burns contemporaneously, and to have brought him into Johnson's company deliberately, might have been straining that patriotism too far.

There was, however, one figure which he almost ostentatiously did not bring to meet Johnson in Edinburgh; nor can one blame him for his restraint. That figure was "le bon David", David Hume the philosopher. Hume had been Boswell's neighbour in James's Court, but by 1773 had moved over into the New Town into that street which subsequently and ironically, yet affectionately, had been named "Saint David's Street" hard by St. Andrew Square. He had made the move into the easier quarters because he found the high narrow stairs of the Old Town too uncomfortable for his corpulent body. It is just possible too that his orderly mind may have been held by the fancy of living in the ordered plan of the New Town which was then being built. But, for whatever reason he had moved, he was not far away; and as evening fell Boswell could often have seen the lights in St. Andrew Square and its tributary streets below him and just across the North Bridge in the dusk. Hume in 1773 was one of the most famous intellectual figures in Europe; certainly in Edinburgh and Scotland. Yet Boswell did not take Johnson over the short journey across the North Bridge to see him, nor did he invite "le bon David" to the philosopher's old haunts in James's Court.

Not only does one not blame Boswell for this, but one recognizes the impossibility of his even attempting it, in view of Johnson's remarks about Hume while he was actually staying with Boswell in James's Court and when the philosopher's name cropped up.

> *Johnson:* And as to Hume—a man who has so much conceit as to tell all mankind that they have been bubbled for ages . . . is one to be surprised if another man comes and laughs at him? If he is the great man he thinks himself all this cannot hurt him; it is like throwing peas against a rock.

Boswell in his published version of the tour says "He added here something much too rough both as to Mr. Hume's head and heart which I here suppress." From the notes of the full Journal we now know what this was.

> *Boswell:* But why attack his heart?
> *Johnson:* Why sir, because his head has corrupted it. Or perhaps it has perverted his head. I know not whether he has first been a blockhead and that has made him a rogue, or first a rogue and that has made him a blockhead.

After this it would, even for a man of Boswell's celebrated social intrepidity, have been not only injudicious but impossible to bring Hume and Johnson together in Edinburgh.

Boswell throughout his volatile life was fascinated by many men; but only three during his or their lifetime sustained that fascination in him—Johnson, Wilkes and Hume.[1] The fascination which Johnson exercised over Boswell was the strongest but possibly the most complex. Boswell saw in the great Englishman not only a rock of goodness, of

---

[1] Boswell's admirable fidelity to Paoli was not due to fascination but a long-standing friendship tinged possibly by the recollection that Paoli and Corsica were the springs of his first literary success.

human warm-heartedness, a mass of common sense un-
commonly well expressed, but also something else. He
sympathized, in the true sense of that much misused word,
with those deep fears which tormented his great master, the
fear of doubt, the fear of annihilation, the fear of unworthi-
ness and Hell-Fire. Johnson supported Boswell's instinct for
goodness, yet was not too remote from Boswell's own
distress of mind and spirit to be inaccessible. If someone so
obviously, so fundamentally good as Johnson could suffer
these things was there not in the contemplation of the
greater man's difficulties and distresses some assuagement
for Boswell's own sufferings?

Boswell's attraction towards Wilkes sprang from quite
different reasons. Wilkes was a rake, a libertine, a heavy
drinker, yet quite without fear of the consequence of his
sins. He was also, as the Apostle of Liberty, a man of considerable influence in his time. In an odd and contradictory
way Wilkes also was a rock to which Boswell could cling.
Wilkes fornicated and drank and indulged himself in every
way except that of selling his political soul, yet he was not
in the least troubled by fears on account of all this. Wilkes
was Boswell's "gay companion" and could be relied upon to
relieve Boswell's fears in a totally different way from that in
which the company of Johnson did. Boswell (is it necessary
to repeat this at this date?) was no fool, and he recognized
in Wilkes an outstanding personality and intellect of the
time. If he could be a rake and a libertine without worrying
about it why then should Boswell worry?

Boswell's third lodestar, Hume, was again different from
either of the other two. He was a fellow-townsman and yet
was celebrated throughout Europe. Naturally the literary
lion-hunter in Boswell had made him eager to seek his
acquaintance, and circumstances had made it easy for him
to do so—he even once contemplated writing a life of him.
Having gained his friendship he at once fell under the charm
of this most likable and kindly of Edinburgh men. And,

deed, he would have been entirely at ease in his company
d it not been that Hume lacked two qualifications, either
which would have made him more comprehensible to
swell. Hume was not a religious man—indeed his fame
rested upon his attack upon religion, and he had no belief in
the immortality of the soul. On the other hand he was not
a libertine. He was in his life of the very essence of propriety,
and combined that propriety not only with charming easy
manners but with the placid fortitude of one who might to
all outward appearances have been a believing Christian
"sure in the hope of resurrection and eternal life". This
was a combination or (as it seemed to him) a paradox that
was too much for Boswell. He could understand a great and
good man like Johnson holding firmly to his religion yet
dreading eternity. He could also in his wilder moods understand and appreciate Wilkes laughing, drinking, wenching,
wasting his substance and being witty in the face of a
God in whom he did not believe. But Hume's patent
goodness combined with his patently expressed infidelity
attracted and at the same time repelled Boswell. Yet
he remained fascinated by him to the end of Hume's
life: indeed his celebrated near death-bed interview with
the great infidel is one of the biggest scoops in English
literature.

Another great scoop was Boswell's introduction of
Johnson to Wilkes at Dilly's dinner-table in 1776. Johnson's
aversion to everything that Boswell's "gay companion"
stood for was and is famous—his republicanism, his support
of the American colonists, his blasphemous libertinism, all
these would naturally shock and disgust Johnson. Yet, as
all the world knows through one of the most celebrated
passages in *The Life*, the meeting between Boswell's good
and bad angel came off with considerable success. There are
a dozen different reasons for this success. Johnson for all his
forthrightness did not wish to be grossly rude at a fellow
Englishman's table. He had, moreover, been caught off his

guard by the unexpected appearance of Wilkes in the house
of an honoured literary friend and allowed himself to be
exposed to that English form of charm which few could
exercise more effortlessly or more delightfully than Wilkes.
Johnson, for all the respectability of his own life, had a weakness for what he called "gay dogs" (his friendship with
Topham Beauclerk is an example) and, having surrendered
to the first battery of Wilkesian charm, the Doctor may well
have soothed his social conscience by saying to himself that
it was merely Wilkes's gaiety and doggishness that he was
responding to, and so on and so on.

To have attempted to have introduced Johnson to
Hume in Edinburgh of all places would have been a very
different matter. In Edinburgh, the home either of "Presbyterian bigotry" or of "philosophical infidelity", the great
English churchman was prepared to dislike and be rude to
anyone who differed from him in essentials. Had Boswell
brought David Hume into his crowded drawing-room in
James's Court when Johnson was there Johnson would at once
have recognized him as an enemy, a world-famous enemy,
and have been compelled to offer a challenge. It would for
Boswell have been a painful and embarrassing encounter.
Johnson would certainly have been rude and almost equally
certainly David Hume would have been urbane and
humorous and ironic in that homely Scottish manner which
was so antipathetic to the Doctor. The result would have
been that Boswell, who had gained so much prestige by
bringing Johnson to Edinburgh, would have lost face,
while the ordinary Edinburgh, folk (whether Presbyterian
or Freethinker) would have rallied to their beloved Davie
and have with Lord Auchinleck dismissed the great Johnson
as "*Ursa Major*".

No, the introduction would not have come off and even
over the years one is grateful for Boswell's good sense in not
attempting it. To have introduced this great and good
Christian Englishman to this great and good Scottish infidel

would have been like bringing together a bulldog and large marmalade and doctored tom-cat.[1]

Leaving the tempting divagation upon Fergusson, Burns and Hume on one side I do not wish to give the impression that I am interpreting Boswell's introduction of Johnson to Edinburgh as simply a succession of crowded dinner parties. Johnson certainly had some leisure, enjoyed meeting some of his young Scottish friend's acquaintances, and, as always, said some good things. He was also taken upon a tour of the sights of the Scottish Capital which, whatever he may have said about them, must have excited his ever-curious antiquarian mind.

It was during this tour that he indulged in one of those outbursts against the country in which he was being entertained as a visitor, which so frequently occur in the journey. However violent these outbursts may seem to us over the

[1] It should also be remembered that Hume loathed the English with a detestation beside which Johnson's heavy irascibility against Scotch manners, Scotch habits and Scotch pertinacity in London fades into a pale personal prejudice. Writing to Adam Smith he said: "Nothing but rebellion and bloodshed will open the eyes of that deluded people" [the English]; "though they were alone concerned I think it is no matter what becomes of them. . . . An Englishman is a man (a bad animal too) corrupted by above a century of licentiousness." This is more violent than the shrillest blast by a modern nationalist or the speeches of an Irish patriot in 1919.

David Hume was so amiable, placid and good-humoured a man that it is strange at this distance to recall the ferocity of his dislike of a whole people. David Hume had suffered from the English ruthlessness in the anti-Scotch feeling that pervaded London in the latter half of the 18th century. But it is strange to find him speaking with the accents of those who consider themselves inferior to or oppressed by the English—Hume certainly did neither. Something of the odd mixture of his amiability of character combined with this ferocious hatred of the English may be found in the following letter in which he actually regrets that he may not live to record the dissolution of England by revolution:

"I live for a twelvemonth in my old house (in Edinburgh) which is very cheerful and elegant, but too small to display any talent for cookery. I have just now a receipt for making *Soupe à la Reine* copied with my own hand. For beef and cabbage and old claret nobody excels me. All my friends encourage me in this ambition. . . . I am delighted to see the daily and hourly progress of madness and folly and wickedness in England" [he was certainly right about these qualities in the George III administration of the time]. "The consummation of these qualities are the true ingredients for making a fine narrative history, especially if followed by some signal and ruinous convulsion, as I hope will soon be the case with that pernicious people. He must be a very bad cook indeed who cannot make a palatable dish from the whole. You see in my reflections and allusions that I mix my old and new professions together."
This was indeed "ganging his dinger"!

years one or two things should be remembered. Eighteenth-century forthrightness or lack of polite hypocrisy was as much a mark of the period as was the practice of exquisite formal manners in polite society. Moreover on more than one occasion Boswell seems deliberately to have provoked the old man into speaking as he did. He certainly did so when he took the Doctor into the Laigh House where the Records of Scotland were deposited, and showed him in the presence of the Keeper the Treaty of Union between England and Scotland in 1707.

I here began to indulge old Scottish sentiments and to express a warm regret that by our Union with England, we were no more—our independent kingdom was lost.

Johnson: Sir, never talk of your independency, who could let your Queen remain twenty years in captivity and then be put to death without even a pretence of justice, without your ever attempting to rescue her; and such a Queen, too!—as every man of any gallantry of spirit would have sacrificed his life for.

Worthy Mr *James Ker*, Keeper of the Records: Half our nation was bribed by English money.

Johnson: Sir, that is no defence; that makes you worse.

Good *Mr Brown*, Keeper of the Advocates' Library: We had better say nothing about it.

Boswell: You would have been glad, however, to have had us in the last war, sir, to fight your battles!

Johnson: We should have had you for the same price, though there had been no Union, as we might have had Swiss, or other troops. No, no, I shall agree to a separation. You have only to *go home*.

Just as he had said this, I, to divert the subject, showed him the signed assurances of the three successive Kings of the Hanover family to maintain the Presbyterian establishment in Scotland. "We'll give you that," said he, "into the bargain."

This is an excellent example of Johnson at his best and at his worst in his anti-Scottish mood. His reference to the

Scots allowing Mary Stuart to remain in captivity ("and such a Queen") for twenty years was, is and will remain unanswerable. And any decent Scot can only blush for "worthy Mr. James Ker's" attempted apology. Johnson's jibe, however, about the Scots soldiers in the British army being no more than mercenaries was just a piece of rudeness which it is fortunate that no Highland officer of spirit was near enough to hear. But maybe it is ponderous to take these ponderous witticisms too seriously at this distance. Bozzy provoked them, and he got what he may have well deserved.

That he provoked them, however, is of interest. The London buck in London, the Scottish patriot in the Laigh House in Edinburgh, the romanticist over the '45 in the Highlands and Hebrides only twenty-eight years after that still tantalizingly immortal adventure—what a characteristic combination of contradictions! But how comprehensible to any Scotsman even of today! It is incidentally interesting that so politically respectable an Edinburgh citizen as James Boswell should have allowed himself such openly expressed Nationalist sentiments as late as 1773 when all but the most ancient and hidebound patriots had, so one is led to believe, accepted the fact of the Union with gratitude. It is all very well uttering these sentiments nowadays when National feeling and National discontent can take so many forms, but deep in the heart of Edinburgh's Golden and contented Age it was a different matter. However, Boswell was a creature of moods, each one (however contradictory of the last) felt genuinely. Even as a very young man in London he could at one moment glow with the "spirit of Bannockburn" and a little later be disgusted by the very sound of the Scotch accent and Scots words. Moreover he may have been partly trying to get a rise out of the Doctor by means of this perfectly genuinely felt if transitory mood: if so he certainly succeeded.

I had seen this copy of the Treaty of Union before, but I went to have another look at it in its present home in the Register House guarded over by a descendant of an acquaintance of Boswell's. I was familiar with the sight of this document, of recent years the subject of such hot debate, but with the thought of this Johnsonian outburst fresh in my mind I looked at it with new and personal, if not affectionate, interest. "Sir," I murmured in quotation, "never talk of your independency, who could let your Queen remain twenty years in captivity; and such a Queen too!" Worthy Sir James Fergusson of Kilkerran, present Keeper of the Records, smiled his recognition of the words but made no comment.

Wishing to raise my spirits I decided to do so by raising my body. I retired from the Register House and, crossing the North Bridge, went once again up the Royal Mile, across the Castle Esplanade and to the highest point of the Castle Rock. From there I looked down upon the noble if confused panorama of Edinburgh of the 1950s.

To the immediate North of me there lay the gracious outlines of the never-completed and now so frequently disfigured New Town which had just been begun in 1773, but which Johnson never visited. Beyond the New Town and away on all sides there was the sprawling mass of modern suburbs looking almost romantic in the slight autumnal haze. But in front of me uncompromising as ever, and as distinct as an old roadway seen from an aeroplane, there straggled and twisted the herringbone of the Royal Mile and the Old Town.

At this distance and from this height one could not see the differences between the Old Town of the 18th century and the Old Town of today. No changes in detail from this lofty and peculiar if perspectively elongated position could be observed. Only its general shape was visible—more visible than ever. I allowed myself a sigh partly from content, and partly from a recurrence of regret that Johnson had not been allowed to taste the true flavour of that Old Town in its most vital age. But in that sigh there was no hint of rebuke for my friend Boswell. I saw his difficulties perfectly and sympathized with him. And after all Johnson's passing visit through Edinburgh in its own way had not been so unsuccessful. "I smell you in the dark," I repeated to myself. If only he could have smelt a little more.

Ah, but it was to the North and to the West that one should look for the true glories of that immortal journey. And in obedience to that thought it was to the North that I turned. The haze, too light to be called a haar, that lay over the Forth all but obscured the Fife coast, and completely hid the Highland hills. There was little, even from this height, that one could find to refresh one's memory, to lead one's imagination forth on the journey the two of them had taken 179 years earlier.

Then, with one of those happy accidents which occur more frequently in real life than in fiction, a sword-like ray of autumnal sunshine cut through the haze and illuminated a heap of grey stone surmounted with a white building standing well out in the Firth of Forth. It was the island of Inchkeith, with its lighthouse upon it, the guardian of the Firth of Forth, of Leith and of Edinburgh, the island where there still stand the last crumbling stones of Queen Mary's fort. It was the island which Johnson so characteristically insisted on visiting when the boat was taking him and Boswell across the Forth from Edinburgh at the beginning of their northward journey.

The travellers had visited Inchkeith. Thence they had gone on through Fife, St. Andrews, the East Lowlands and Aberdeen. But their object all the time had been those hills to the North and West and the islands that lay beyond them. This sword-like ray of sunshine appearing so suddenly and unexpectedly, illuminating the first step of their journey, seemed to me a clear and definite pointer. I too would go northwards through the autumnal haze in pursuit of those two ghosts whom I felt I knew so well. As soon as possible! Why not on the next day?

III

THE BEGINNING OF THE HIGHLAND JAUNT

"WE were now to bid farewell to the luxury of travelling, and to enter a country upon which perhaps no wheel has ever rolled." With this characteristic, reverberating, yet surely joyful sentence, Johnson announced the travellers' departure from Inverness. With it he announced the beginning of that part of the Scottish tour to which he and Boswell had especially looked forward ever since they had first discussed the project in London in 1763—the entry into the Highlands.

Johnson, though he had been slightly on his guard in Edinburgh, cannot fail to have been interested by his stay in the Scottish Capital. He had been made a little melancholy by the ruins of St. Andrews and the 18th-century desuetude of the University there, but had been gratified by his reception. He had been even more gratified by professors at Aberdeen and by the burghers who had made him a freeman of the city. He had been well received all the way up the East Lowlands of Scotland, and had shown his appreciation. But all this had been but a preparation for, an approach to, the true object of the Scottish tour—the Highlands and Islands. When the travellers swung westwards from the North Sea and the Moray Firth by Elgin, Nairn and Fort George, and entered the Gaelic part of Scotland under the hills and by Inverness, they were coming to that object. "This," said Johnson on a happy occasion later on in the tour in the middle of the Gaelic song and dance and festivity, "this is truly the patriarchal life. This is what we came to find." In coming into Inverness they were entering the doors to that patriarchal life which was awaiting them.

From Inverness the accounts of the tour both from Johnson and from Boswell gather not only in interest but in a sense of excitement. At Inverness, Boswell, who had hitherto been understandably restrained by Lowland circumstance, gives the impression of beginning to let himself go for the first time. He seems to have got rid of his awe of actually "having Johnson in Caledonia". He goes calling upon Highland society in Inverness upon his own. He suffers from and sets down his account of his first, and one of his few, fits of melancholy introspection upon the whole tour. But he consoles himself quickly and characteristically: "A sentence or two of the Rambler's gave me firmness; and I considered that I was upon an expedition for which I had wished for years, and the recollection of which would be a treasure for me for life."

Johnson had seen "a few women with plaids at Aberdeen", and had heard a whiff of the Gaelic language at Nairn, but he notes with approval, and probably with some degree of anticipation of what was to follow, that at Inverness the Highland manners were common to all and that there was a church there in which the services were in Gaelic. At the supper party at the travellers' inn on the evening before they set out for what Boswell calls their "equitation" into the Highland country, Johnson tasted roast kid for the first time. He relished it much and was in high spirits. One of the guests, a Mr. Grant, used to tell afterwards an extraordinary story of Johnson's behaviour on this evening. Carruthers passes on Grant's own account thus:

In the course of conversation he mentioned that Mr. Banks (afterwards Sir Joseph) had, in his travels in New South Wales, discovered an extraordinary animal called the kangaroo. The appearance, conformation and habits of this quadruped were of the most singular kind; and, in order to render his description more vivid and graphic, Johnson rose from his chair and volunteered an imitation of the animal. The company stared, and Mr. Grant said that nothing could be more ludicrous than the appearance of a tall, heavy, grave-looking man like Dr. Johnson standing up to mimic the shapes and motions of a kangaroo. He stood erect, put his hands out like feelers, and, gathering up the tails of his huge brown coat, so as to resemble the pouch of the animal, made two or three vigorous bounds across the room.

Mr. Grant was a well-respected clergyman of the Church of Scotland who lived until 1828, dying as the minister of Cawdor. There is no reason to doubt his story. Boswell, it is true, did not include an account of this remarkable performance of Johnson's in his Inverness pages, but it should be remembered that this was still fairly early in the tour, and Boswell, for all his increased sense of liberty in his approach to the Highlands, had not yet quite acquired the full freedom of his journal. Had this episode occurred some weeks later, at Coll for instance, Boswell would probably have put it in.

I was able to do no more than guess at the site of Mackenzie's inn where this joyful and absurd supper party had taken place. The old inn, and all the houses round about it, had long been pulled down by my great-great-grandfather's brother, who had been Provost of the city at the end of the 18th century, shortly after Johnson and Boswell had visited Inverness.

I do not know Inverness nearly so well as I know my native city of Edinburgh, but I never approach this delightful little Highland capital without a tug not only at my heartstrings, but at some unconscious memories within me. I have, on my maternal side, pre-natal connections with Inverness which go back long before any family connections with Edinburgh or the Lowlands.

Three hundred years ago my forbears held distinguished places in Inverness as merchants, chief burghers and the owners of ships which traded directly from the Highlands to the South—not only to London, but to the Low Countries and France. One of them was concerned in gun-running for Prince Charles Edward Stuart in 1745. We once had a tall black walking-cane presented to this ancestor of mine by the Prince in gratitude for his services. Alas! it was lost in some house or furniture removal in London, and if it still exists is probably in the back room of some junk shop off the Fulham Road, or is used as a "prop" in some repertory company's belongings.

This same ancestor was deeply involved in a plot to bring back from London to the Highlands, and by sea in one of his own ships, the severed head of the Lord Lovat of the '45. His son was Provost of the city when the new town (in imitation of Edinburgh's Augustan expansion of the same time) was built near the end of the 18th century. My mother's family had existed until recent times as lairdlings in an estate on the borders of Inverness. It was in the policies of this small estate that the last fugitive from Culloden was cut down and massacred by Cumberland's troops. What my Jacobite forbear was doing at that moment I do not know. It is for me interesting to note that Boswell and Johnson passed not only by the field of Culloden (about which they said nothing) on their way to Inverness, but also by this small Inglis estate, and by the little mill lochan with its island in the centre of it, and the great 300-year-old trees overhanging it—the little lochan on which I have spent so many happy hours fishing for little brown trout.

I always approach Inverness with a mixture of curiosity and an undefined feeling that I already know something of the place. Both these sentiments were sharpened in me when I came once again to Inverness to set out upon the Highland part of my own tour. I had gone to Inchkeith in the Firth of Forth, had followed the travellers to St. Andrews and Aberdeen, but, like them, I felt that when I got to Inverness the true part of my journey was beginning.

I had decided to imitate the travellers of 1773 by taking horse from Inverness, not only to recapture as far as possible the atmosphere of the leisurely journey of the 18th century but also because it would allow me to wander off on the old roads and the hillsides as I wished. I had also persuaded a companion to come with me on this part of the journey. While I awaited his arrival and that of the hill ponies that were being "floated" up, I had ample leisure to explore Inverness again.

Inverness is now described as the Capital of the Highlands; but before my Inglis ancestor of the 1780s and 1790s had moulded it after his heart's desire in imitation of the New Town of Edinburgh, it was, as Carruthers put it, "a little old-fashioned town or emporium for the country North of the Spey". And not even the most imaginative antiquarian could reconstruct from its present appearance the shape of the antique jumble of stone houses when Boswell and Johnson visited it. It was then a quiet little cut-off northern city where smuggling was practised by all political parties, and where the Christmas and New Year festivities were leisurely kept up for three weeks. We can, therefore, only guess from the new town the whereabouts of Mackenzie's inn where the travellers stayed.

I was, however, pleased to find the site of the Episcopal Chapel where they worshipped. Boswell calls it "the English Chapel" and describes it as "mean", the altar "a bare fir table covered with a piece of thick sail-cloth doubled by way of a cushion". He goes on to say that Mr. Tait the clergyman read the prayers "with much of the Scotch accent" and preached on the text of "Love your enemies". If it should seem that this was a strange text for Inverness Episcopalians so soon after Culloden, it should be remembered that Mr. Tait was the official Chaplain at Fort George. Mr. Tait went on to say that "some connected themselves with men of distinguished talents, and since they could not equal them, tried to deck themselves with their merits by being their companions". With a characteristic touch of self-consciousness, Boswell adds, "It had an odd coincidence with what might be said of my connecting myself with Dr. Johnson."

Boswell's complaints about the "meanness" of the little chapel are understandable; for it was a shabby place in 1773. From my enquiries about it when I was in Inverness I learned something about it, however, and could have informed Boswell as to how that meanness had come about. No religious community, not even Catholics, were then so persecuted as the non-juring Episcopalians. And Inverness was a particular haunt of non-jurors. No Episcopalian "minister" was allowed to hold a service whereat more than five people were present. This particular chapel in Barony Street had, until just before the travellers visited it, been ministered to by a non-juring clergyman called Mr. Stewart, and the chapel was his own house. He held the Episcopal service in his living-room in the presence of his family (which was not more than five); the rest of the congregation huddled in the loft and gave their responses through an open trap-door. When there was any warning of military or police approach, the trap-door was closed, the congregation, literally aloft, remained silent, and Mr. Stewart went on reading prayers to his family.

Upon Mr. Stewart's death, his wife, unable to support the house, surrendered it to the "qualified" worshippers, that is to say those who were prepared to take the oath in support of the House of Hanover. And in recognition of this fact the Chaplain to the English Garrison at Fort George (despite his Scotch accent which so displeased Boswell) was allowed to come and officiate. By 1773 there was no need of a trap-door to conceal hidden worshippers; but the meanness, I cannot but think pathetic and creditable meanness, of the hidden place of worship still clung about it. I also feel that had Johnson, whose Episcopal and Jacobite sentiments were so much a part of each other,

'Setting out from Edinburgh.' From the set of eighteenth-century
Rowlandson satirical prints

(*Courtesy of the British Museum*)

Inverness. An eighteenth-century view of the 'capital of the Highlands' about the time Boswell and Johnson stayed there

(Courtesy of the British Museum)

known the circumstances, he himself would have been touched by the story.

I know that my Inglis forbear had been in the old days before 1773 a worshipper above the trap-door. I know also that his son the Provost secretly attended the qualified chapel in Barony Street. It pleases me to think that he may well have been there when Boswell and Johnson worshipped in the "mean Chapel" of Inverness that Sunday of 29 August, 1773.

Johnson mentions with that generous approval which was so characteristic of him the services held in what he called the "Erse language" in Inverness in his day. And at this point it is worth remembering that Johnson's support for the translation of the Scriptures into Gaelic was one of the most valuable in bringing about that worthy project. Alas! the last regular service in Gaelic in Inverness has ceased three years ago.

There is, however, one Gaelic prayer meeting which is a direct survival from the days after Culloden. It is a survival today, and was, of course, a survival in 1773. Had Johnson known about it his curiosity might have led him to make Boswell take him to taste of it.

On the Tuesday night of Culloden and during the first debauches of cruelty practised by Cumberland's troops there was an interdenominational prayer meeting held to pray for all sufferers in the battle on *both sides*. This prayer meeting continued regularly on Tuesday nights until the end of the 19th century, but as the years went by it became less and less associated with Culloden and more and more an occasion for those who spoke Gaelic in Inverness to pray together. When in the last years of the last century the building in which this Gaelic prayer meeting was held was pulled down its last faint acknowledged connections with the battle of Culloden were severed. However, the Free Kirk lent their vestry for the continuance of this interdenominational prayer meeting; and it still continues on every Tuesday night, because that is Culloden night. Today there can be only a few of the worshippers left who consciously connect this day of their Gaelic prayer meeting with a momentous event in Gaelic and Highland history.

In 1773 however the Gaelic orisons at the Castle Raat had a distinct flavour of Culloden about them. Johnson's tenderness towards Jacobitism coupled with Boswell's much less practical romanticism about the '45 would have certainly led them to the Castle Raat if they had known about what went on there and if they had lingered till the Tuesday.

It was, however, on a Monday that they were to begin the Highland part of their journey. On Monday, 30 August, 1773, on three horses, Johnson, Boswell and their Bohemian servant Joseph Ritter set forth from Inverness down the Great Glen. They were accompanied on foot by two Highland guides, John Hay and Lauchlan Vass, who were also responsible for a fourth horse carrying the travellers' portmanteaux. These Highland horse guides were characteristic and necessary products of the late 18th century in the Highlands. Not only could they act as guides and interpreters in an area of Britain in which the English language had not yet conquered, but they were men of extraordinary physical endurance and agility. They ran beside the heads of trotting horses, leading them over mountain tracks and showed no signs of exhaustion at the end of the day. Indeed one of them was said to be able to run and walk any Highland horse until it dropped. So much for the legend of the poor underfed Highlanders scratching a bare living from the soil! How many peasants from the rich farmlands of Southern England could have equalled such a physical feat?

My companion and I when we set forth on horseback in the Autumn of 1952 did not have the benefit of such runners nor a servant to attend us, but circumstances in other ways were more easy for us. Our routes were clearly marked, and we knew that we could get comfortable lodging and good stabling where we were going. We did set forth from

Inverness with one disadvantage which would have been unheard of in the 18th century: one of us had never ridden a horse before.

To explain this I must for a moment digress on the remarkable young man who had volunteered to accompany me from Inverness to Skye. There is, so it seems to me, nothing that he cannot do with his hands. He sails small boats all round Britain and helps to build them. He draws, paints, sketches and designs sceneries in theatres. He is an accomplished aviator who fought with bravery throughout the last war. He escaped from German prison camps twice. Yet (and how characteristic this is of our age) he had never put his leg across a horse until the day when we set forth from Inverness. Within three miles of the city he was trotting along beside me rising in his stirrups as to the manner born. By the end of our ride together, I, who have lived with horses since my childhood, was tempted to leave to him all the business of stabling, saddling, bridling, feeding and so on. But I did not. I had at least to keep level with him in the one physical accomplishment in which, when we set out from Inverness, I was superior to him.

It sometimes seems to me, recording my journey in the depths of a peculiarly savage winter, that I am over-inclined to dwell upon the sweetness and beauty of the autumn scene that I enjoyed throughout this tour. Nevertheless I must set down that I have never seen Loch Ness-side (from the north-east side which was the Boswellian and Johnsonian route) more beautiful. Everything was so calm and placid yet full of colour and slight motion that I recalled with pleasure one of the few commendatory remarks uttered by the travellers upon the actual scenery of the Highlands:

Boswell: It was a delightful day. Loch Ness and the road upon the side of it, between birch trees and with the hills above us pleased us much.
Johnson: On the right the limpid waters of Loch Ness were

beating their bank and waving their surface by a gentle
agitation. Beyond them were rocks sometimes covered
with verdure, and sometimes towering in horrid naked-
ness. Now and then we espied a little cornfield.

The truth was that these two highly percipient men
differing in character yet both essentially of the 18th
century were passing through one of the most beautiful
parts of the Highland scene on one of the loveliest of
autumn days. Yet with the voice of the 18th century they
pronounced upon it with such flaccid phrases as "pleased us
much" and the "limpid waters of Loch Ness were beating
against their bank and waving their surface". Note too the
use of that favourite Anglo-Saxon word horrid in Johnson's
qualification. It was a word used by soldiers, statesmen,
poets and even the most adventurous travellers to describe
anything in the Scottish scene that did not equal the rich
cultivation of the South.

We, however, allowed ourselves to enjoy the beauty
of this celebrated glen, now fortunately (and especially on
the unpopular north-east side) unfrequented by other
travellers. Soon we came to the place where once stood the
hut in which Boswell and Johnson had their first lengthy
encounter with the Gaelic language. The encounter is one
of the high spots of the tour. But let Boswell describe it
for himself:

A good way up the Loch, I perceived a little hut with an
oldish woman at the door of it. I knew it would be a scene for
Mr. Johnson. So I spoke of it. "Let's go in," said he. It was a
wretched little hovel, of earth only, I think; and for a window
had just a hole which was stopped with a piece of turf which could
be taken out to let in light. In the middle of the room (or space
which we entered) was a fire of peat, the smoke going out at a hole
in the roof. She had a pot upon it with goat's flesh boiling. She
had at one end, under the same roof but divided with a kind of
partition made of wands, a pen or fold in which we saw a good
many kids.

Mr. Johnson asked me where she slept. I asked one of the guides, who asked her in Erse. She spoke with a kind of high tone. He told us she was afraid we wanted to go to bed to her. This coquetry, or whatever it may be called, of so wretched a like being was truly ludicrous. Mr. Johnson and I afterwards made merry upon it. I said it was he who alarmed the poor woman's virtue. "No, sir," said he. "She'll say, 'There came a wicked young fellow, a wild young dog, who I believe would have ravished me had there not been with him a grave old gentleman who repressed him. But when he gets out of the sight of his tutor, I'll warrant you he'll spare no woman he meets, young or old.' " "No," said I. "She'll say, 'There was a terrible ruffian who would have forced me, had it not been for a gentle mild-looking youth, who, I take it, was an angel.' "

Mr. Johnson would not hurt her delicacy by insisting to "see her bedchamber", like Archer in *The Beaux' Stratagem*. But I was of a more ardent curiosity, so I lighted a piece of paper and went into the place where the bed was. There was a little partition of wicker, rather more neatly done than the one for the fold, and close by the wall was a kind of bedstead of wood with heath upon it for a bed; and at the foot of it I saw some sort of blankets or covering rolled up in a heap. . . .

She asked us to sit down and take a dram. I saw one chair. She said she was as happy as any woman in Scotland. She could hardly speak any English, just detached words. Mr. Johnson was pleased at seeing for the first time such a state of human life. She asked for snuff. It is her luxury. She uses a great deal. We had none, but gave her sixpence apiece. She then brought out her whisky bottle. I tasted it, and Joseph and our guides had some. So I gave her sixpence more. She sent us away with many prayers in Erse.

Mark here how, in this country as strange to himself as to Johnson, Boswell has begun to take the lead and moreover actually to venture to chaff his master on the subject of pretended rape. I cannot help thinking that the Highland air and the Highland scene were already beginning to have their effect on the volatile Lowlander.

I, however, could have told Boswell something about

the old lady in the hut which he did not know, and which might have tempered his and Johnson's mirth at the admittedly ridiculous prospect of either of them intending rape upon this ancient Highland woman.

In this same hut or croft or cottage twenty-eight years earlier there had occurred a scene which had left the memory of the horror of rape and murder committed by Anglo-Saxon invaders. It was a memory that might almost have soaked into the walls of the place. And absurd though the old woman's fears seemed to Boswell and Johnson, absurd though they may have appeared to many readers of the Journal since then, they were not without foundation.

In 1747 this Mrs. Fraser whom Johnson and Boswell interviewed had taken over the small property under the care of her chief, and from relatives who had been compelled to leave it in the preceding year. But she had not forgotten the circumstances in which they had gone.

In 1746, after the battle of Culloden, an officer of Cumberland's troops had entered this cottage and had found the men of the house away from home, and only a young girl and her grandmother in charge. He had ravished the girl with the assistance of some of his troops who held her arms and legs and then, in some on-rush of post-lustful fear, had strangled the grandmother in order to silence her.

His horrible crime, however, was detected and brought home to him, one hopes by the confession of one of his assistants. He was, so it is said, heavily punished, whatever that may mean, by Cumberland, who thought that this was going a bit too far even in the savage Highlands.

The Celtic people have long memories, and it may not have been only pathetic ageing female vanity that had made the old woman fearful of two English-speaking travellers who wanted to see her bedroom. It may have been deep, half-conscious memories of tales which had been told to her when she was younger that had arisen in her. It is pleasant to recall, however, that she parted from our two travellers on happy terms, without fears and "with many prayers in Erse".

After the travellers had left the hut, and as they went on by the loch side, it is significant to note that Johnson hints at the mysterious quality of Loch Ness. One longs to know what he would have said if he could have heard and investigated the modern stories of the Monster of Loch Ness. Legends about some creature in these depths had of course existed well before 1773, and Boswell and Johnson might indeed have heard them if they had wished to enquire. Johnson was proof against mere legend, but he might well have allowed his mind to speculate on the 20th-century versions of the tale if he could have looked into the future.

Johnson's strong sense of logic, his desire for the facts of evidence, were not so much in opposition as complementary to his desire to believe in the mysterious and the inexplicable. He sought out the inexplicable, the curious, the supernatural, even the mere oddities of life with a gusto which showed his strong inclination to want to believe in them, or at least to know about them. At the same time he would not allow his common sense to be outraged. He would have revelled in the evidence for and the dispute about the Loch Ness Monster that has obstinately continued to make news in the last twenty years. The whole story, with its fluctuations of good sense and its absurdities and its thoroughly convincing details, would have been just the kind of thing on which his mind liked to worry, on which he would have held forth from the safe distance of a Fleet Street tavern.

With such thoughts and with conversation of this kind we passed by the beauties of Loch Ness, never more mysterious than on this day of faintly cloud-flecked sunshine and mild breezes. Johnson's characteristic phrase about the waters "waving their surface" kept returning to my mind as we ambled along towards Foyers. I have often in the last twenty years looked for signs of the Monster, but never with greater eagerness than that day. But we were disappointed. The changing surface of the Loch, hinting as ever of mysteries hidden beneath it, yielded up no secret.

From Foyers next day we took the old road mainly across the hills and by heather to Fort Augustus. Once again I had proof of Johnson's fortitude in his old age. I was very glad to dismount and rest at Foyers, but the travellers of 1773 had kept on to Fort Augustus, a journey which we of course managed easily upon the second day.

The contrast between the agreeable hospitality we received at Fort Augustus and the agreeable night's rest which Boswell and Johnson enjoyed there provided a comment on the years that had passed between 1773 and the present time. Boswell and Johnson had been entertained by Governor Trapaud, a man according to Boswell of "the conversation of a soldier and somewhat of a Frenchman". The Fort as a military establishment in a savage and outlandish or rebellious district was nearing the end of its days of practical use. The Governor, in his somewhat decaying circumstances, must have been as pleased to meet travellers from the South as they were to enjoy the comfort of his Fort. Johnson many years later said that he could not remember a better night's sleep than that which he spent at Fort Augustus.

The Fort has long disappeared; but we slept within the walls of a building upon its foundations, and containing a few of the bricks and mortar of the old Hanoverian fortification. Hanoverianism as well as Jacobitism may be dead, but it would be difficult to find a stronger proof of this than the fact that the building which occupies the old Fort foundations is now a Benedictine monastery—an institution which would have been particularly repugnant to the Hanoverian regime in the Highlands. Yet we were quite beyond the last relics of the old controversy within the walls of Fort Augustus Abbey. Only the sound of Latin at prayers and a whiff of Gaelic round the corner remained to remind us that in the middle of the 18th century these two ancient languages were those most looked upon with suspicion by the Hanoverian authorities in these parts.

Latin words and a whiff of Gaelic. Yet all the 18th century was in the sound of these things in our ears. How would Johnson have looked upon a Romish monastery on the site of a Hanoverian fort? Johnson's sentiments might have been divided. Boswell, whose secret early religious history is now known to us, might have held more definite views: but he would have said nothing about them.

The next day, with a Latin benediction and a Gaelic farewell ringing in our ears, we set out for the hills and the true deep Highlands which Boswell and Johnson were to discover for the first time on the second day of their Highland journey.

IV

THE HIGHLAND WAY

THAT the travellers knew they were about to penetrate deeply into the Highlands upon leaving Fort Augustus is shown by their printed remarks, those made in Boswell's day-to-day Journal, the others from Johnson's recollection. Johnson says that "we were now to cross the Highlands to the western coast, and to content ourselves with such accommodation as a way so little frequented could afford". He later refers to the lonely mountain road which they were to set out upon as being "hewn to a level with labour which might have broken the perseverance of a Roman legion". Boswell contents himself by referring bleakly to the "eleven wild miles" which they were to cover before reaching the next house.

Gone were Johnson's "romantick" prospects of the limpid waters of Loch Ness "beating their bank and waving their surface with gentle agitation". Gone too with Governor Trapaud's Fort at the end of the loch was the last outpost of Anglo-Saxon, or at least Lowland, civilization. One suspects that Boswell, who was not yet enlivened by that characteristic fantasy and curiosity which had made Johnson undertake this tour, who as yet did not know of the island delights that were to await him, said good-bye with some regret to Fort Augustus with its claret, its brandy, its well-stocked table, its comfortable beds, and its French-mannered Governor. He was still slightly stunned with delight by the fact that he "had his venerable friend actually with him in Caledonia". He may indeed have been loosened from his Lowland inhibitions after leaving Inverness, but he may well have looked at the formidable hill over which General Wade's road was to lead him from Fort Augustus into the wilderness of the West with some trepidation.

The natural and, for the modern wheeled traveller, the only possible route from Fort Augustus to Glenmoriston through which the travellers of 1773 approached the West is a circuitous one. It goes up Loch Ness on the north-western side until Invermoriston and then all but turns back upon itself along the Glen. Wade would have no such turnings and twistings. He thrust his road directly west-wards and upwards from the Fort over the hill, and then downwards until it joins Glenmoriston about halfway through the glen. In Johnson's and Boswell's time this was the only road westwards. But for over a century it has been abandoned, and even the redoubtable Birkbeck Hill, in his reconstruction of Johnson's journey in Scotland over sixty years ago, had to take the circuitous Invermoriston route, rejoining Johnson, as it were, halfway in Glenmoriston. We, however, having tasted the mettle of our ponies, were determined to follow the exact path, and took to the hillside on an ill-defined track as soon as we had left the water at the foot of Loch Ness. We were rewarded, if somewhat uncomfortably, before we had demonstrated our fidelity to the full.

General Wade's road from Fort Augustus to Glenmoriston and the West is, for a large part of it, more than half forgotten. It begins roughly but quite distinctly from Loch Ness side, mounting up into the hills (having been recently put to some temporary use by the Forestry Commission), then, leaving the even rougher track down to Torgoyle, it climbs and plunges westwards amongst the mountains invisible to the eye of the land-traveller either on foot or on horse. It is marked with the faintest sug-gestion of ghostly dots upon the ordnance map and, having been unused for over a century, has for all practical purposes utterly disappeared. Yet, as with many historic landmarks

E

that have been lost and forgotten to those of us who crawl or ride about on the surface of the earth, it can still be seen from the air.

It was I who had traced out the dots on a pre-war map; it was my companion who had put the flesh of fact upon that string of dots by following the old route from an aircraft a week before our venture into the hills on our Highland ponies. Even before we reached the invisible part of the road this had struck me as an odd combination of modern and traditional methods of travel and map-reading. I was to find them even more peculiar when I reached the heights and was to rely solely on my friend's airborne vision of the road which Johnson and Boswell had climbed before us and in circumstances easier than we had done.

The first part of the ascent into the hills by the slightly reclaimed Forestry track presented no difficulties. Indeed it was exhilarating to feel the pull of our little beasts' muscles when they were faced with their natural instinct to climb and after their too-long exposure to the flat and easy roads by the Loch side. It was pleasant to look back upon the Great Glen opening beneath and behind us and to feel ourselves free of routes made hackneyed by a century of traffic. When, however, we reached the end and full height of the Forestry track that freedom became a trifle too boisterous for comfort. The equinoctial gale which we had sniffed at in the valley below now burst upon us in full force. By the time we had come to the place where all recognizable signs of roadway seemed to melt into the heather we had come to such a height, and I was so buffeted by the wind and the rain, that I was reduced to suggesting a compromise—that is to say to cut down direct to Torgoyle which I knew must lie directly North-West of us. It was impossible to hold a map in such a tempest, and out of the question to try and trace upon it the ghostly dots of the old road. But at least, if we kept straight on downwards and northwards I knew that we should find the shelter of Glenmoriston.

My companion, sniffing the storm happily like the sailor and the airman that he is, would, I am now happy to say, have none of this. Carrying his week-old aerial vision of the old road before him in his mind, he drove me onwards and upwards into the wind and rain.

Though I completely trusted my air-minded and prison-breaking companion I was extremely uncomfortable. I had torn a hole in my waterproof leggings the last time that I had mounted; and that hole was on the windward and rainward side of me. My left leg became waterlogged, my riding-gloves turned to pulp, and (gloomy thought for the future in these remote parts) my parcel of snuff which I had carried in a large so-called grease-proof packet got soaked through. Snuff that has been watered and then dried is useless; and snuff is to me what ordinary tobacco is to the smoker. The cold even at this period of the Autumn was intense, and we could not see more than a hundred yards in front of us. Through the rain a stag rose up in front, and after stamping contemptuously drove his hinds off. I did not quite like this; for though my companion was equal to any modern emergency I did not think that even he could cope with an angry male red deer in the middle of the rutting season; nor did I fancy myself in the role of a matador in so remote a spot.

The gale which so buffeted us seemed only to enliven our hill ponies. With energy which put us to shame they climbed up and down the gullies on our ascent and forded the now swollen hill burns as if they had been rivulets. It was interesting to note their footwork, so delicately feeling the way between swamps and rocks exactly confirming my companion's recollections of the road from his aircraft. Through their hooves they were able to perceive what his eyes and those of the eagles had seen already from far aloft.

When we reached what was obviously the summit of this ghost of a road I insisted upon dismounting and, sheltering behind the bulk of my pony, surveying what I

could of the scene. The desolation seemed absolute. There
was no sign of life, no red deer, no blackgame, no grouse
stirring in the tempest, only the rocks, the heather and the
tumbling streams. I felt or was aware of rather than saw
Ceann a' Mhaim with its two thousand three hundred feet
behind me. I knew that we were on the road on which the
two great travellers had preceded us in the 18th century;
but the road, as far as human eye could tell, from this the
highest point upon it, had utterly disappeared into the hillside again. I was looking upon a scene which was the same
as that which endured equinoctial gales for millennia before
the two travellers had passed here.

And yet (so incalculable are the things that stir the
imagination) with nothing visible to remind me of them,
with only the knowledge that I stood upon ground which
they had passed over, with which few had covered any
practical intentions for over a century, I felt closer to them
than at any other time upon my whole tour save upon the
all but desolate island of Coll and upon certain parts of
Skye.

I saw them with the eye of faith so clearly that it seemed
that I almost personally recollected them. I saw them far
more clearly than one does in those celebrated haunts with
which we have grown to associate them but which have,
decade by decade, been overlaid by the passing years and
by man's impatience for change. Certainly not in the
hideous confusion of 20th-century Fleet Street and the
Strand, not in modern Oxford, not in the High Street of
Edinburgh, not even in St. Andrews where one seemed
nearer to them than ever before, had I felt the fact of them
so clearly. Boswell and Johnson had passed over these
"eleven wild miles" in comparatively good weather and
with a comparatively clear road before them. But now in the
howling desolation of the wind and the rain and the driving
mist on this deserted summit I seemed to be aware of them,
ghostly, invisible to the fleshly eye, yet palpable, real as the

old road which I could not see yet which I knew lay hidden under the heather and the stones beneath my feet.

Such mountain gales and tempests and such moods as they provoke can blow themselves out with the same speed as that in which they arise. By the time that we had negotiated a deer fence by a method which took what remained of my breath away by its simplicity[1] and had come down into Glenmoriston the black and the grey clouds had scudded away from us overhead and were away up to trouble the head of the Great Glen. The sun, if in a slightly watery manner and apologetically, had come out again, and only the tumult of the swollen burns pouring into the River Moriston remained to remind us of the weather we had left behind. With the weather and the desolation went my mood.

The part of the Glen where we joined it looked particularly sylvan, green and almost well tended. The vision of the travellers whose footsteps we had recently been so laborious in pursuing faded from my mind as I saw running through the valley, rather than glen, the black strip of a modern motor road. There were, however, no motors on it. And as we kept by the grass to the side of it I was able to remind myself that it could not be far from here that Johnson in weather finer, and certainly drier than we had experienced, had rested and had conceived the idea of his book of *A Journey to the Western Islands*:

> I sat down on a bank, such as a writer of Romance might have delighted to feign. I had indeed no trees to whisper over my head, but a clear rivulet streamed at my feet. The day was calm, the air soft, and all was rudeness, silence and solitude. Before me, and on

[1] My companion took his pony along the fence to a gateway which had marked the ancient right of way, but which had been wired over by staples into the gate-post. Taking out a tin-opener he proceeded to work on these staples, his hands running with rain and blood until he had sufficient top wire down for us to amble our ponies across it. He then did up the staples again, and left the gate as we found it. This is surely the first recorded instance in Highland travel in which a deer fence has been dismantled and then remantled, and an 18th-century right of way re-established by so humble and utilitarian a thing as a tin-opener.

either side, were high hills, which by hindering the eye from ranging, forced the mind to find entertainment for itself. Whether I spent the hour well I know not; for here I first conceived the thought of this narration.

I was however anxious to press on to Anoch. I knew that nothing, not even the name, remained of this obscure hamlet with its now vanished inn which had provided so significant a point in the Boswell-Johnson itinerary. Nevertheless I was bent upon standing on the spot. Anoch ever since I first read of the 1773 journey had fascinated me. If one could in fact as well as in imagination roll back the years and spend a short period of time in one particular place with Boswell and Johnson in the Highland Hebridean and Western part of their journey, one would be hard put to it to make the choice: Raasay off Skye on the night of the impromptu ball; Coirechatachan on the evening of Boswell's drunkenness; the same place on the eve of the travellers' departure from Skye; the meeting with Flora Macdonald; the encounter with the deaf minister on Coll; the ruined chapel at Inchkenneth on the night when Boswell crept out in the darkness and alone so pitifully yet so passionately to invoke the Saint to pray for him for forgiveness for his sins; the ducal snubbing at Inveraray; the scene of the awful quarrel between Johnson and Lord Auchinleck, Boswell's father, and so on. But for me, high on the list would come Anoch and the day after Anoch when the travellers took the road Westwards under the guidance of MacQueen their landlord.

By the time that they had turned their horses' heads into MacQueen's inn at Anoch Boswell and Johnson had had experiences that were as new and strange to the comparatively much travelled young Lowland lawyer as they were to his revered English friend, who at sixty-four had been so completely habituated to the Southern Anglo-Saxon scene. They had travelled amongst hills more mountainous than any others in Britain, by scenes as remote, and to the polite 18th-century eyes as savage, as any in Europe, by waters deeper, more mysterious, more impetuous and untamed than any they had known before. They had heard the Gaelic language and had, through interpreters, talked with those who possessed that ancient European language and none other.

Today, despite the fact that it is possible to fly from Glasgow to the Outer Hebrides in one hour, despite two centuries of expropriation, of enforced emigration, of 19th-century sheep-farming and sporting encroachment, despite the years of "Balmorality", the curious and inquisitive modern traveller can experience all these things (even to the meeting with monoglot Gaels) that Boswell and Johnson experienced up to the point of their first night at Anoch. But he cannot join them there or thereafter; for at that place they were to enter a world and a way of living that has gone (in Scotland at least) forever.

When in 1746 the last armed rising in the Highlands was defeated many Highland and Celtic habits, institutions and customs died too. The hereditary jurisdiction of the chiefs was abolished. For thirty-six years the Highland dress of the kilt and the wearing of tartan was forbidden—and it is significant that this short period was sufficient to extinguish amongst the ordinary people of Celtic Scotland a garb to which they had been accustomed for over a thousand years. The Gaelic language was discouraged, frowned upon and given a socially discreditable as well as treasonable stigma; and finally the grim period of land expropriation and emigration, whether enforced or voluntary, began. Some of these changes would have happened even if there had been no Jacobite rising. (It is difficult for instance to think of the principle of hereditary jurisdiction surviving into the 19th century.) Some changes would have come more slowly or would have been modified, and some perhaps would not have happened at all.

It is possible that, unravaged by the sword and fire of

the conqueror, unexploited by the sheep-farmer and the plutocratic sportsman who was to follow him, the Highlands of Scotland might have kept something of their human past. They might have continued to shelter that proud, gay, valiant, often poverty-stricken, but often learned and always independent culture which had flourished in Gaeldom for so long. It was a way of life recalled in a hundred memoirs, songs, verses and evoked nostalgically sometimes sentimentally in the 19th-century romances and sometimes successfully as in R. L. Stevenson's novels.

This Highland life, though in the 18th century it was mingled with the fortunes and misfortunes of the House of Stuart, had its origins in something far older than Jacobitism. The utter collapse of the last Jacobite rising, however, with which in the popular mind of Britain it was associated, combined with the deliberate policy of "smoking the rats out", marked the beginning of the end of it. The ferocity of the policy of suppression and the whole weight of the changing years as the new Britain, now governed from London, advanced inexorably into the era of Anglo-Saxon rule and eventually of industrialism bred in the Highlanders that kind of despair to which this race, so splendid in attack, so self-sufficient when left alone, is temperamentally prone when abandoned.

That despair showed itself in a number of ways—flight into the New World, a rage of emigration which preceded the evictions, and in which the tacksmen (small gentry) participated as much as did the peasantry, an abandonment or concealment of tradition in defensive shyness and a sour puritanism bred of oppression and fear of the world. This was a puritanism which not only affected the Highlander's conduct but constricted his learning and the use of his ancient language within the boundaries of an arid theology. It dried up also his one-time celebrated *panache* once exhibited both in poverty and wealth.

A gloomy picture! Indeed the present writer feels not

only reluctance but a certain sense of self-reproach in putting it forward. How often does he not recall, even in these latter-day years, the enjoyment of the echoes of that *panache* in private conversation, in ceilidhs in the islands (ceilidhs that have not been organized but which have just happened), in whiffs of Gaelic speech, poetry, song, in moments of friendship in verbal contest, in anger and in the flush of passing pride! And perhaps most of all he recalls them in the easy laughter and talk by the kitchen fire when the whisky is going its way round and when the darkness of an Autumn night has fallen, and the morning is far away. No one who has reached middle life, and has travelled and talked and listened much in the Highlands and Islands of Scotland, can be without such memories, of private and intimate pleasure. But alas, the words private and intimate are the operative ones. The old Highland and Gaelic way of living and enjoyment has gone underground, and if it is an underground movement it is one not of resistance but of recollection.

When Boswell and Johnson were in the Highlands and Islands in 1773 this had not yet happened. The hereditary jurisdiction of the chiefs had been officially abolished and the Highland dress was still forbidden. But the authority of the chiefs who had been allowed to remain continued not in the half sentimental, half romantic manner of the modern Highland Games, but often as a real influence. The Highland dress again lingered in remote places and was worn by tacksmen out of a genuine conservative affection, and not as a country fancy dress. But, most important of all, the sour withdrawn puritanism had not set in. There were living men and women who could remember the free independent life of the Highlands before the catastrophe of 1746 and before the Highland spirit had gone underground.

Such a man was MacQueen, landlord of the inn at Anoch. He was a gentleman of the old Highland stamp, who, as Carruthers puts it, "considered himself a public benefactor by condescending to keep a change-house". This change-house or inn was much used by the cattle-drovers, and, even by 18th-century Scottish standards, was crude in its sleeping accommodation and possibly unclean. The living-rooms, partly built and furnished by MacQueen himself, were, on the old Highland principle of outward pride of display, neat and comfortable, containing a good library. MacQueen could read Latin and French and was a composer of Celtic verse. It would never have occurred to him that his own native tongue was in any way inferior to, or more private or more remote than, the more widely known languages. It was characteristic of his kind that he should have shown some slight offence when Johnson exclaimed in surprise at the presence of Prideaux's *Connection* upon his shelves.

He was a Highland gentleman who happened to keep an inn entertaining two travellers from the South. It was to him just as much an impertinence to comment upon his reading matter and his learning as it would have been to have done so on his breeding. He did not nurse his offence, however, for he obviously took to Johnson whose spirits expanded in these novel circumstances, and in after years (perhaps without knowing much of the fame of the old Englishman) used to refer to him as the *olla Sassenach*, the jolly Englishman. He had a pretty and well-bred daughter with a number of polite accomplishments learned in Inverness. The travellers, from their hints in their written remarks, were as surprised at the elegance of this young lady in such a place as they were at MacQueen's pride of lineage and learning. Fortunately enough they refrained from showing this surprise to her father.

The way in which the two travellers reacted to this first taste of Old Highland manners is interesting. Johnson comes off the better of the two. He was, says Boswell, "in excellent humour". The abundant and, in the circumstances, excellent food which he had in the neat forequarters of the inn (a broiled chicken, mutton collops, mutton sausages, five eggs to himself and lemonade made from fresh lemons— all prepared in the old style by the landlord's own hand) may have had something to do with this happy state of mind. It is likely however that Johnson was quicker than was Boswell in catching the true quality of his host, in relishing the fact that he was now deep into the kind of Celtic civilization which he had travelled so far to see. He was obviously taken with the charm and breeding of Mac-Queen's daughter and lent an attentive ear to the flow of MacQueen's Celtic oratory on the subject of emigration. And when the evening's talk was over he faced the discomfort of the crude, commonly shared and possibly verminous bedroom with greater fortitude than did his younger companion. Boswell was so surprised by this that he told the Doctor that (even at sixty-four) "he might serve a campaign".

Boswell then in a reported passage which I still find humorous, but which in the time and circumstances was hardly tactful, proceeded to twit the Doctor. He said that as he had now seen Johnson in rude conditions yet so happy in the land of oats, he would, on his return to London, compose an epistle in the style of Mrs. Gulliver to her husband Captain Lemuel Gulliver after he had come back from the land of the Houyhnhnms:

> At early morn I to the market haste,
> Studious in everything to please thy taste,
> A curious fowl and sparagrass I chose,
> For I remembered you were fond of those:
> Three shillings cost the first, the last seven groats;
> Sullen you turn from both and call for Oats.

So far so good; and the old man still in a good humour laughed. But when Boswell added that he would write the epistle in the name of Mrs. Thrale, Johnson was really angry, and Boswell had to substitute the name of the landlord of the Mitre Tavern before his companion was appeased.

This is a good example of how tactless Boswell, who prided himself on the subtlety of his address, could be. He knew that Johnson's affection for Mrs. Thrale at this time was something bordering on possessive love. He knew that people in London laughed at it, and he must have been aware that Johnson was sensitive to such laughter—guessing it from afar, even if he could not hear it. The truth was I suspect that Boswell felt a little out of it at Anoch. He could not follow the Doctor's generous appreciation of the scene, and upon finding that Johnson was prepared to put up with discomfort and fleas in the bedroom without complaint, he allowed himself this sally at the expense of his rival Mrs. Thrale, who was after all five hundred miles safely to the South of them.

Boswell's sensation of being not in keeping with the atmosphere at Anoch persisted till the next morning. For when he woke he confessed that all the talk of emigration on the previous evening accompanied by the thought that his landlord was soon about to leave the country threw him into an early morning panic, fearful lest he should be murdered and robbed by the departing MacQueen. This ingenuous admission shows how little the Lowland lawyer understood this strange, gently born, well-educated, proud yet (in Boswell's eyes) half savage innkeeper, who would have been mortally offended if he would have known of his guest's suspicions.

Boswell's volatility of temperament was, however, soon to lead him to a flux of sentiment in the opposite direction. MacQueen, who had obviously relished the company of these two visitors from the South after the usual cattle-drovers to whom he was accustomed at his inn, insisted on accompanying them for some miles on their journey to Glenshiel. On the way he told them, at first hand, stories of the rising of '45 in which he had taken part. While he listened to these stories Boswell "several times burst into tears"; though in his printed edition he modifies this into "I could not refrain from tears". Both in his original manuscript and in the book, however, he adds:

> There is a certain association of ideas in my mind upon that subject, by which I am strongly affected. The very Highland names, or the sound of a bagpipe will stir my blood and fill me with a mixture of melancholy and respect for courage . . . and, in short, with a crowd of sensations.

That Boswell was genuinely moved by MacQueen's eloquence is certain; and it is highly probable that he did actually shed tears—the plain statement in the original MSS. is convincing enough. Nor should anyone smile at him at this date for it. MacQueen, from what we know of him, was an eloquent and fiery man with poetic gifts. To have heard from his lips an eye-witness account of the dark day of Culloden and the terror that ensued, to have heard this riding westwards into the great mountains of Glenshiel, must have been a moving experience. Nor is the characteristic piece of half self-excusing self-analysis that follows Boswell's admission of tears quite as hollow as it looks at first glance.

Boswell's attitude towards Jacobitism, which I shall later discuss when we come to his meeting with Flora Macdonald, contained a strong dash of romantic and sentimental feeling—one recalls his anger in the London theatre, when the Highland soldiers were so ill-used by the Cockney mob—and he was quite prepared to give these sentiments full play in such remote circumstances as a West Highland glen, and in such company as he now found himself. Johnson was too genuine a Tory, and had his roots too deeply planted in a past which he could remember, to allow himself to be swayed by facile sentiment of this kind. Yet he too can scarcely have listened to MacQueen's

reminiscences unmoved. It is not so much significant, however, as characteristic of him that he makes no mention of
them.

As we left Anoch and followed the road on which the
travellers had passed and on which Boswell had wept his
genuine if slightly facile Jacobite tears, the dark weather
returned, and for the first time in Glenshiel I felt the
melancholy of these overwhelming mountains of which
both Johnson and Boswell complained. Usually my heart
rises with the hills and with the prospect of the Atlantic
which lies at the end of this great glen. On this occasion,
however, the colourless desolation of these ravaged deserted
and precipitous valleys oppressed me too. Nor was I enlivened by having to take our horses through an improvised
village of tin huts which since I had last been here had been
put up to accommodate the workers on the hydro-electric
scheme at Loch Cluanie. We were sufficiently soaked and
bedraggled and pathetic, our method of transport sufficiently out of date to bring the troglodytic inhabitants of
this industrial sore-spot set amidst the eternal hills out of
their huts to jeer at us and our horses. Mercifully the
encroaching darkness and the mist soon swallowed us up;
and mercifully too there soon shone through that mist and
darkness the candlelight of the Cluanie Inn where years
ago as a boy I had found rest and comfort on my first
journey alone through the Western Highlands. I found
them again.

A great cleansing wind, followed by an autumnal calm
early next morning, swept the glen clear of all the greyness,
darkness and wetness which had depressed us the night
before. We set forth at a good trot along the road and
towards the sea amidst a profusion of colours, as if the
mountains had been painted by Autumn especially to greet
us and had tumbled the colours down to meet us.

Soon we were at the place which in the tour was called
Auchnashiel where the travellers had been surrounded by

"the wild Macraes", none of whom could speak English and who had gazed upon their passing visitors as if they had been creatures from another planet. This scene, which is so admirably described by Boswell, had long remained in my fancy as one of the most evocative in all the mainland part of the journey. I insisted upon stopping and trying to locate the village from the few stumps of shielings visible, or all but visible, amongst the heather. I took out my battered copy of Boswell's account and read his description to my companion. This was all very well, and restored my friend's interest in the pair we were pursuing, particularly in Johnson, who stands out in a patriarchal light as he dispensed to the black-haired Gaelic-chattering crowd coppers, shillings, packets of wheaten bread and snuff.

This last word, however, was particularly unfortunate for me. It underlined a fact of which I needed little reminding. I had lost all my snuff in the storm in the hills on the day before and was feeling the lack of it sorely. Learned men who have studied the habits of those of us who have been foolish enough to become enslaved to the nicotine habit have said that a hardened snuff-taker is more difficult to wean from his vice than is a cigarette-, cigar- or even pipe-smoker, and suffers more when painfully deprived of it. I can well believe this. My nostrils had long been itching for a pinch of my own particular blend of coarse snuff, but when I read of Johnson's free-handed liberality with packets of what the Highlanders call "the dry dram" in this very spot a hundred and seventy-nine years earlier they began to twitch like those of a cocaine addict.

I calculated that, even with the aid of the nearest telegraph or telephone office miles ahead, it would take two days for a packet of snuff to reach me by express post from Inverness. I cursed the barren beautiful hills and the deserted village site crumbling into the heather, and for the thousandth time bewailed the fact of emigration. I reflected bitterly on the irony of the situation of finding myself in

the Highlands of Scotland without snuff—the Highlands
where once it had been in every man's pocket and where
there had been a hundred men to every little glen ready
to give it to any traveller.

In an effort to distract my mind from the hunger of my
nostrils I searched in pockets, also to see if I could find a
grain or two of snuff lurking there. I found none, but
unearthed a note I had made a few weeks before and had
consigned to the confusion of my laden pockets. It appears
(and this was on my note) that when an admiring crowd in
the West Highlands had been standing around Johnson
(no mention of Boswell by the way) an old man on the
fringe of the crowd had asked, "*Co an duine mor tha sud?*"
("Who is that great man?"). To which the reply was "*Sin am
fear a rinn a' Bheurla*" ("That is the man who made the
English language")—a reference to Johnson's dictionary.
The old man merely shook his head and made the comment,
"*Bha beagan aige ri dheanamh!*" ("Well, he hadn't much to
do!"). The coincidence of discovering this long-lost and snuff-
stained note at this very spot of Auchnashiel delighted me
and made up my mind for me that it was here that this
little-known incident had taken place. With the gratification of this discovery or conjecture my nostrils ceased to
twitch for snuff.

On we went down to the sea by Kintail and then
ascended the famous Mam Rattachan road. The wet
weather and the clouds came down from the Heavens to
meet our ascent; and the dark tunnel of the newly planted
firs made our journey appropriately lugubrious—appropriately because it was on Mam Rattachan that the most
serious and the most celebrated quarrel between Johnson
and Boswell took place. Indeed it was the only recorded real
quarrel that ever occurred between the two men. Johnson
was often brusque and contemptuous with his younger
disciple—sometimes brutal, and once indeed reducing him
to tears in public company. These storms, or more often

explosions, however, were quickly over. It is a tribute to Boswell's essentially good nature as well, as of course, to his pertinacity that he nearly always endured these Johnsonian buffets with no more than stunned silence or ineffectual and, it must be added, usually humble protest. The scene on Mam Rattachan, however, was more serious and, if we are to believe a remark of Johnson's uttered well after the event, nearly endangered the prospects of the whole tour by making him seriously consider returning to Edinburgh and never speaking to Boswell again.

The circumstances of Johnson's violent outburst are of course well known, but it is worth re-examining the scene for its causes. And, standing as I did at the height of this awkward pass looking down at the steep old road now avoided by the modern route, I tried to conjure up for my companion and myself what had happened!

Boswell had gone forward alone, according to him, to make preparations at the inn at Glenelg and to see if Sir Alexander Macdonald had sent the boat to take them across to Skye. It should be remembered that Skye was an important point in the journey, that Boswell had by letter made the arrangements with Sir Alexander and, being related to Lady Macdonald, that he had a kind of proprietorial interest in these arrangements. Boswell, however, cannot have got very far on his journey away from Johnson for he was called back by a "tremendous shout", and, upon returning, found the Doctor "really in a passion". "Do you know," said Johnson, "I should as soon have thought of picking a pocket as doing so" (riding on and leaving him alone). Boswell, alarmed, but stung and pricked into an extraordinarily tactless defensiveness, replied, "I am diverted with you." Thereafter, amidst the gloomy weather, upon this hanging strip of a road down the hillside and later in the wretched discomfort of the inn this quarrel continued in a state of Jove-like sullenness on Johnson's part and uneasy silence on Boswell's.

F

Boswell was so upset that he scarcely slept. Earlier in the evening he had a desire to reassure himself and reverted in another fit of tactlessness to an attempt to defend himself. Next day Johnson swept up the broken pieces of the quarrel and threw them away, but there had been the fearful and rearward threat that if Boswell had gone on he might have turned back and never have spoken to him again. That Johnson might have carried out this threat is possible. Having once turned back to Edinburgh neither his pride nor his convenience would have made it easy for him to suggest taking up the journey once more; and English literature might have been deprived of two of its greatest travel books. Indeed the rebuff to Boswell might have been so great that even his pertinacity might not with self-respect, and with the laughing eye of the world upon him, have survived it, and the relationship between the two men might have been permanently damaged with an even greater loss to letters.

We are so accustomed to praising Johnson's physical hardihood in undertaking this tour of the Highlands and Islands and in pressing forward with it to the end that we sometimes take too much for granted. We forget that the conditions at times, especially in this earlier part, may have been almost unbearable. Asthmatic, blind in one eye, corpulent, just on sixty-four years old, he had on this occasion had a huge day's ride followed by a tedious ascent of a wild hillside and was now descending the even wilder other side of it in the dusk. His weight was too great to be supported for long by one horse, and he was continually dismounting and mounting between two beasts. He was attended by guides whose use of English was defective, and now he saw the younger man, on whose knowledge of Scotland he was depending, disappearing into the night. On the top of all this (though Boswell gives us no hint of this) he may very well have been exacerbated by his companion's fussy and proprietorial airs in preparation for the much-looked-forward-to meeting with Sir Alexander Macdonald and the visit to their first island.

Our own journey up Mam Rattachan was, as I have said, dark, damp and gloomy, and when we reached the summit the low clouds were sweeping in the valley below us, making not only it, but the Sound of Sleat, invisible. Determined to keep to the Boswellian and Johnsonian route as far as was possible, I turned away from the new road and set my little horse at the old almost overgrown track that plunges much more directly down the other side of the mountain. After some time, however, I had to desist. The track became all but invisible and the trees crowded in, obscuring the way even more grimly. Stopping at what seemed to me a really impassable spot, I reined in and amidst the soughing of the trees, the drip from their branches and the insistent tumbling of a burn, gave myself up to thoughts of the past.

I could hear again the whistling and the twitter of the Gaelic servants as they tried to distract the huge and ungainly Englishman from his discomfort and distress by making the wild goats jump in his path. "Whu, whu, see such pretty goats." I heard the none-too-soothing comments of Boswell on this performance and his voice as he fussed about the preparations at Glenelg, and finally, as loud as the roars of the rutting stags which we had heard on our journey, there sounded in my ears the "tremendous shout" that recalled the too eager or erring disciple, the shout that nearly ended a famous friendship.

Turning my horse's head from this now unpassable spot, and turning my thoughts away from the 18th century, I climbed back to the summit to rejoin my companion who had found some kind of a shelter in which he was munching sandwiches and drinking hot coffee. "Look at that," he said, pointing downwards in the direction from which I had come. I drew in beside him and looked.

Once again, as upon the Castle Rock in Edinburgh, the capricious Northern weather had decided to illuminate the scene in the most theatrical manner and to lift my thoughts, leading them on to the further points in the classic journey of a hundred and seventy-nine years earlier. Though the clouds still rolled immediately below us hiding the length mainland between us and the sea, the Sound of Sleat was now clear; not only clear, but gleaming in the late afternoon Autumn sunshine. Beyond this narrow strip of the Atlantic, roseate in that same sunshine were the shores of Skye above Armadale. Behind them and to the North, dark blue as steel and sharp as steel knives themselves, were the peaks of the "flying island".

V

THE HEBRIDES

THIS was indeed a magical sight, and, apart from the beauty of it, was one to enliven and lead on any modern traveller following the story of Boswell and Johnson in Scotland. It was a magical sight for another reason, for from the moment the travellers left the mainland of Scotland and set sail for Skye and the islands a kind of enchantment comes over the tour as presented in Boswell's Journal. It is an enchantment that is not spoiled by the ridiculous and extraordinary encounter with Sir Alexander Macdonald on landing in Skye. Apart from acting as a kind of contrasting prologue to the joys of Skye that were to come, this absurd incident has a comical fascination of its own.

Nowhere on the tour did Johnson talk with greater fertility and to better purpose than on Skye—indeed some of the best talk ever recorded in all that Boswell wrote about Johnson took place on this island. Nowhere else was Boswell himself so ebullient, so much his real self. Nowhere is the old vanishing Highland scene recorded with greater gusto nor with greater underlying pathos by both men. For the traveller of today the overwhelming beauty of Skye—a beauty totally unperceived by the two travellers of 1773—provides in imagination a background of magic for what we know went on. And finally, it was on Skye that one of the most famous meetings in our literary history took place—that between Dr. Johnson and Flora Macdonald—the lady whom Sir Alexander Macdonald at the height of his quarrel with Boswell twelve years later was to refer to as "the Pretender's conductress". Even allowing for the 18th-century manner and for the Baronet's pompous way of expressing himself, the phrase has an odd ring in modern ears. It is as if the Prince had been some kind of bus or tram.

Also, one can be fairly sure that the travellers set foot on Skye, the true goal of their journey, with some excitement. Apart from the associations of the island's recent history, associations which held a fascination for them both, the place was as new to Boswell as to Johnson. It was the rebuff this excitement received from the manner of Sir Alexander's welcome that caused them to behave so peculiarly in that chieftain's house at Sleat.

I did not take my horses with me to Skye, partly because my companion had to return to his Air Force duties in England and partly because I was not sure about stabling facilities on the island. I was determined however to make my journey of mental refreshment in as leisurely a manner as possible. I therefore chose a central spot on the island and went on foot from it in all directions and to the places they had visited in 1773.

I went to Armadale, the first place where Boswell and Johnson touched Skye, but contented myself with a general view of the terrain; for there is little in the way of building and atmosphere that remains to remind one of the first Skye incident of the 1773 Hebridean tour. But in sober fact these few days at Armadale are not so much important as fascinating. The behaviour of all concerned is so extraordinary that it is impossible not to speculate about it and about the characters who played their part in these happenings.

To begin with there was Sir Alexander Macdonald, Baronet, 9th Chieftain of the Macdonalds, Lord of the Isles. He was the second son of Lady Margaret Macdonald, the Highland lady who had taken so much part in helping Flora Macdonald in her rescue of Prince Charles Stuart. She was adored by all the Skye islanders. Sir Alexander had succeeded to the chieftainship and the baronetcy upon the death of his elder brother, Sir James Macdonald, the mention of whose name ten years earlier had been responsible for the conversation that led to Johnson's and Boswell's Hebridean tour.

This Sir James had been a legendary figure even in his lifetime; and legend accumulated about him after his death. He had been described as the Scottish Marcellus, and an 18th-century Admirable Crichton. He was widely travelled, a remarkable linguist and was highly popular and admired not only in London but in other European Courts. Upon his early death at the age of twenty-four in Rome he was buried with a splendour "never accorded before to a Protestant in that city since the death of Sir Philip Sydney". From the point of view of his Skye tenantry as well as from ours he was remarkable in another way. He was no chieftain "tamed", in Johnson's memorable words, "into insignificance by an English education". He had sprung from an ancient line of Highland chieftains and felt it as well as knew it. He was a Skyeman, an islander and a Highlander to the core. He never forgot this proudest quality in himself; and this quality especially endeared him to his fellow islanders. Until the end of his short life he was active in schemes for their benefit which, if he had lived to carry them out, might have stemmed the tide of emigration in Skye, and perhaps by precept elsewhere in the Highlands. Up to the end, too, he spoke Gaelic to his private servants in Rome.

To be the second son of such a mother, and to succeed such a Celtic perfect knight as brother in the chieftainship of Lord of the Isles in Skye, would have been a difficult heritage for any youth. Nor was the time of Sir Alexander's accession in the year 1768 an easy one. The Jacobite rising had been crushed twenty-two years earlier; and the people of Skye were still uncertain of their fate. Old oppressive laws were beginning to relax, and the firm hand of a well-loved leader such as Sir James might have protected them in the new era which was beginning to dawn. Whatever one's views on the Sir Alexander who acted as Johnson's and Boswell's host in 1773, five years after his accession, it is impossible not to recognize his human difficulties and possibly to sympathize with him in being faced by them—even if one has no sympathy with the character of the man himself.

That character is not attractive. In the cool judgment of Professor Pottle in one of his many notes to the Isham collection of Boswell papers he was "not an ingratiating figure. Judging from his letters he was stiff, priggish, pedantic, everything that Boswell says he was. What can one do for a man who couches his abuse in original hexameters, and selects as one of his chief articles of grievance the fact that Boswell had not seen fit to print some Latin verses which his Lordship" (Alexander afterwards became Lord Macdonald of Slate) "had addressed to Johnson?" To this should be added the accusation of personal meanness which both Johnson and Boswell bring against him, an accusation which on the whole Professor Pottle accepts, and to which he adds here and there a point or two of his own discovery.

Finally a Scot of Highland descent might find Macdonald particularly antipathetic in that he was not only one of the earliest of those Highland chiefs who had been "tamed into insignificance by an English education" but one who had seemed particularly to relish such a process. He was inordinately proud of having been educated at Eton, not on any class-conscious grounds, but because Eton was an English seminary to which few Highland chieftains' sons went in his day. He was always airing his Eton Latin. And his English prose, even when angry, was flatulently pompous. He was willing to accept the privileges of being an hereditary Highland chieftain along with the romantic aura which by the end of the 18th century was recognized as a perquisite of that position—the painting of him in full Highland dress bears witness to this—but was not alive to the hereditary duties of being the leader and father of his clan. He gives the impression of being as proud of his baronetcy as of his chieftainship; and when, as a reward for raising fencibles for a Highland regiment, he was given a United Kingdom peerage (a supererogatory honour refused or evaded by at least one other Highland gentleman in his position) he took the territorial part of his title from a place in County Antrim in Ireland (Slate) presumably because it was pronounced like Sleat.

There were in the 19th century many amongst the Scottish and Highland aristocracy who like him had sold their birthright for a mess of British pottage. They preened themselves in the romantic glow of a long and celebrated Celtic lineage, but had no spark, let alone word, of Gaelic in them, regarding their tenantry as no more than rent-producing animals. In Ireland such landlords were of the imposed Saxon "ascendancy". It is Scotland's shame that we did not need to go to England for such. We bred our own out of the bluest of our blood. There are none of this kind today; though some still existed within living memory until the end of the last century. Alexander Macdonald, though he may not have been as bad as the worst of the 19th-century landlords, was one of the earliest of their kind.

It may be that with the memory of his Jacobite and, in Skye, much-loved mother, of his Celtic Marcellus of a brother behind him he felt unable to compete with those who had gone before him, or he may only have been another example of the reaction that sets in between generations. But, for whatever reason to which it owed its origins, his character was not of the kind to make an appeal to the Tory, the emigration-hating, the Jacobite-sympathizing Johnson, nor to the emotional, romantic and sometimes sentimental disciple Boswell.

But, having granted all this, here are points that (for

those of us who think we know our Boswell and our Johnson well) need some explaining or excusing. The pair who came to Skye on 2 September, 1733, may have done so with high expectations about the approach to the goal of their journey.

> It was curious to think that now at last Mr. Johnson and I had left the mainland of Scotland and were sailing to the Hebrides, one of which was close in our view, and I had besides a number of youthful ideas, that is to say ideas which I have had since my youth about the Isle of Skye. We were shown the land of Moidart where Prince Charles first landed. That stirred my mind.

But neither of them was a stranger to the host who was awaiting them; and, even if he did disappoint them, seen on his native heath, it is difficult to account for their conduct to him.

Boswell had known not only Sir James but Sir Alexander in London and had got on perfectly well with him there. He had also known his wife even better, Margaret Bosville, the daughter of a Yorkshire Squire of old lineage and a remote cousin of his own. Indeed in Boswell's erratic fancy she had once been considered as a wife for him and as the future "Lady of Auchinleck". There are some who put down Boswell's dislike of Sir Alexander and his highly critical remarks about his wife while on Skye to his jealousy at seeing them together in Scotland. But this won't do. Boswell had long since relinquished all thoughts of "my beauty of a cousin" and was at that time newly and happily married himself. Not only had Boswell known Sir Alexander and Lady Macdonald in London but so had Dr. Johnson. Yet mark what happens the moment the travellers arrived in Skye and at Armadale.

Boswell at once rearranges the sleeping accommodation set for him and Johnson by his host, he then descends to dinner which he finds "mean, and meanly served by the masters' helpings, as well as by the servants". He discovers also not enough to drink, and what there is is weak. Upon retiring to his chamber he is so disgusted that he proposes leaving the next day. He is only persuaded by Johnson to "stick it out till Monday" though Johnson himself was ill-pleased, saying that "he was just as one in a lodging-house in London".

Anyone may be disappointed by poor hospitality, but on the next day Boswell pushes matters further. He pumps his fellow guests and Skyemen for stories to his host's discredit, and after dinner, when Sir Alexander was out of the room, spoke of his brother the late Sir James. "The Highlanders fairly cried. We drank a bumper to his memory." Boswell's easily fluent tear duct came into play for "I cried too".

Later in the day he carried his resentment more honourably, or at least more openly, into the presence of his host. He met him by chance in Johnson's room where he was looking for pen and paper and this is what followed:

> I fell upon him with perhaps too great violence upon his behaviour to his people: upon the meanness of his appearance here [Carruthers sardonically suggests that Sir Alexander may have been retrenching in Skye; for a few months previously he had given a luxurious ball in Edinburgh], upon my lady's having no maid [she was with child] and being dressed no better than one. In short I gave him a volley. He was thrown into a violent passion; and said he could not bear it; called in my lady and complained to her, at the same time defending himself with great plausibility. Had he been a man of more mind, he and I must have quarrelled for life. But I knew he would soon come to himself.

This the unfortunate, or forgiving, or timid (as you will) Baronet did; for on the next day Sir Alexander came into Boswell's room while he was having his morning's butter-milk and "our quarrel was quite evanished". Boswell however did not let matters lie.

> I set Mr. Johnson upon him this morning, who said that in seven years he would make this an independent island; that he'd

roast oxen whole and hang out a flag as a signal to the Macdonalds to come and get beef and whisky. Poor Sir Alexander was
always starting difficulties. "Nay," said Mr. Johnson, "if you're
born to object, I have done with you." He would have a magazine
of arms. Sir Alexander said they would rust. Said Mr. Johnson,
"Let there be men to keep them clean. Your ancestors did not use
to let their arms rust."

It was in vain to try to inspirit him. Mr. Johnson said, "Sir,
we shall make nothing of him. He has no more ideas of a chief
than an attorney who has twenty houses in a street and considers
how much he can make of them. All is wrong. He has nothing to
say to the people when they come about him." My beauty of a
cousin too, did not escape. Indeed, I was quite disgusted with
her nothingness and insipidity. Mr. Johnson said, "This woman
would sink a ninety-gun ship. She is so dull—so heavy."

On Sunday Boswell, after a fluctuation between happier
spirits and the spleen, got so depressed by the atmosphere of
Armadale that he sought to relieve it "socially" by drinking
freely of punch and afterwards port. He got drunk (though
he does not mention this bout in the published version)
and again attacked Sir Alexander who was "again in a
passion". The two travellers left on the next day.

Thereafter in Skye and elsewhere on the tour Boswell
continually referred to Armadale, to the poor hospitality
there, contrasting it with the kindly abundance given in
many poorer homes, and to Sir Alexander whom he called
an "animal" and an "insect". Johnson, who was very far
from following Boswell in all his whims, indeed often oppos-
ing them out of no more than a spirit of contrariety, seems
positively to have encouraged his disciple in this matter.
Some time later he himself volunteered the statement that
his late host excelled the character of *L'Avare* in a farce and
that Foote the actor should take him off (Boswell years later
did introduce him to Foote, whether because he remembered this suggestion or by accident one cannot tell), and
that someone should set down the stories of his meanness in

a book before they were forgotten. Later still, and in reference to Sir Alexander's unpopularity amongst his own people, when he heard that he was frightened at sea he made the well-known comment that "Sir Alexander is frightened at sea but his tenants are frightened when he comes to land".

Nor did Boswell's beauty of a cousin Lady Macdonald escape the Doctor's ridicule. Apart from saying at Armadale that "this woman would sink a ninety-gun ship. She is so dull—so heavy", he imitated her behind her back at Coirechatachan in what must have been a ludicrous pantomime, providing a scene which is one of the most ridiculous in all Boswell's Johnsoniana.

> Mr. Johnson called me to his bed-side this morning, and to my astonishment he *took off* Lady Macdonald leaning forward with one hand on each cheek and her mouth open—quite insipidity on a monument grinning at sense and spirit. To see a beauty represented by Mr. Johnson was excessively high. I told him it was a masterpiece and that he must have studied it much. "Ay," said he.

All this is very strange. Apart from his forthrightness and brusqueness, Johnson was not a discourteous or malicious man, especially about ladies. If they offended his sense of decency he might rebuke them. If they were foolish or dull he might turn from them, but he was seldom downright rude about them. The only other instance I can recall is the celebrated lapse of Boswell's when he preserved Johnson's remark about poor Lady Diana Beauclark who had been divorced: "The woman's a whore, and there's an end on't"; nor do we know much about the conversation that provoked this possibly irritable explosion. The household at Armadale must indeed have left a powerful as well as disagreeable impression on both travellers, and it cannot be dismissed by merely saying that politically and personally Sir Alexander and Lady Macdonald were not the kind of people that Boswell and Johnson had come to see on Skye.

Stranger still is the subsequent history of Boswell's relationship with Sir Alexander. Despite all these scenes at Armadale they remained on good terms until 1785 when Boswell published his journal of the tour. This contained a watered down, but, reading between the lines, a fairly implicit account of Boswell's and Johnson's feelings while they were at Armadale and some references to Johnson's subsequent remarks, with names omitted, though no one in Skye and few in London could have been deceived by this. Macdonald, then Lord Macdonald, was understandably really angry. He wrote to Boswell a long and pompous letter in English, and in the inevitable Latin. He worked himself up as he wrote it, and near the end inserted what I can read only as an accusation of unnatural vice against Boswell. Poor Boswell had done much, and had been accused of nearly everything except this!

Boswell replied in a frightened and puzzled manner. In all his writings he never could see why people should be offended if he set down what he considered to be the truth about them. This was a genuinely ingenuous trait in his character which, though it made him many enemies, he preserved till the end of his life. There was further correspondence which led the two to the brink of a duel in Hyde Park. This was averted by Boswell voluntarily excising certain passages, but, unfortunately for himself, leaving the impression to the outside world that he had been compelled to do so by Lord Macdonald.

The nearest one can get to explaining these strange events and this odd conduct at Armadale is that both Johnson and Boswell were in a high state of expectation upon setting foot on their first Hebridean island, that that island was Skye, associated in both their minds with the events of twenty-eight years earlier, that their spirits were dashed by Sir Alexander's alleged meanness of hospitality and address, by Lady Macdonald's stupidity, that when they left Armadale and received such warm welcomes elsewhere, sometimes in humbler homes, sometimes amongst the gentry, they were continuously being reminded by contrast of their first douche of cold water from the Macdonalds. Boswell directed his animosity towards the Baronet rather than to his wife; Johnson distributed his disfavour equally between the two of them—remembering both of them with rearward taunts as late on his journey as when he was on Coll and Mull.

This does not excuse Boswell's rudeness at Armadale, nor account for the Baronet's apparently tame acceptance of it. It is possible that Macdonald was so overcome by having the illustrious Englishman under his roof that he dared not do more than make the usual weak man's temporary scenes and displays of passing, offended dignity, but that when Johnson was dead, and he himself a Lord, he could tackle Boswell alone.[1] If this is so it goes to prove his chicken-heartedness and is all the more to his discredit.

Unprepossessing, pedantic, priggish, "tamed into insignificance" he may have been, but one cannot, as one reads the evidence of the long-dead quarrel, refrain from a feeling of sympathy for him in his outraged feelings. Moreover if only because of one's affection for the characters of Boswell and Johnson one feels a touch of regret, even shame, for the blatancy of their rudeness towards someone who, with all his faults, was their host. Finally, one would give much to have heard the conversation between Sir Alexander and his lady after their guests had left Armadale and had continued their journey northward and deeper into a more hospitable, a more Jacobite part of Skye.

The next day the travellers reached Coirechatachan and

[1] That Macdonald was impressed by the dignity of having Johnson as his guest is shown by the Latin verses which he addressed to Johnson on the second day of the travellers' stay at Armadale. They are fairly feeble stuff containing no actual "howlers" and up to the ordinary 18th-century Eton standards, but certainly containing nothing in the way of scholarship or felicity of expression with which to ingratiate their author with Johnson.

there in humbler, but very much more congenial, circumstances, found solace and recompense for their stay at
Armadale. They stayed at this tacksman's house twice upon
their Skye journey, once after leaving Sleat, and once just
before they left the island on the momentous and stormy
voyage to Coll. Coirechatachan and its host and hostess,
Mr. and Mrs. Mackinnon, contribute so memorable a part
to the story of the journey, not only in Skye but in all the
Hebrides, that it would be a pity to treat it here, as did the
travellers, in two separate accounts. I, who kept my own
revisiting of the shattered shell which is all that remains of
"Corri" (as Boswell called Mr. Mackinnon, and as the farm
is now marked on the map) as a kind of *bonne bouche* for my
Skye perambulations, would prefer to leave it in my writing,
as I did in my journeyings, until the end of what I have to
say on Skye. After Armadale I went to Raasay which was the
travellers' next point of call after "Corri".

I took the boat from Skye to its satellite island of
Raasay glad that this was my first visit there. Often had I
seen Raasay both from the mainland of Scotland and from
Skye as well as from other islands. Often had I remarked
from many points of the compass its odd sugar-loaf-shaped
central mountain of Dun Cann with its top so flat that it
might have been cut off with the slice of a giant's knife.
Often, as I had looked at it from the sea or from land, had
my thoughts turned to the great days of Raasay House when
Macleod of Raasay had entertained the two visitors from
London and from Edinburgh. Often had I resolved to go
to the island and to see for myself the place, the island, the
house where had occurred those heart-warming scenes so
brilliantly, so heart-warmingly described by Boswell. Often
had I resolved to go to the place where he and Johnson encountered and enjoyed the old Hebridean innocent gaiety
of life at its very climax and just before it was to vanish—
in public at least, perhaps forever. Now I was glad that by
chance I had kept my first visit to Raasay until this time when

I was alone and when my mind was set wholly upon the events that had happened a hundred and seventy-nine years earlier.

A hundred and seventy-nine years earlier Boswell and Johnson after their two days at Coirechatachan, during which they had got the taste of Armadale almost out of their mouths, had set sail in "Raasay's Carriage", a Norwegian boat, and were rowed up the Sound to Macleod of Raasay's house on the island. From that moment and until they returned to the mainland of Skye Boswell's narrative gathers what one might describe as the quick pace of happiness and excitement which it is also positively exciting to read about and enjoy nearly two centuries later.

Accompanying the travellers on their voyage from the sea shore opposite Coirechatachan to Raasay were two men who stand out large and lifelike in Boswell's Journal, so that all who have followed the journey in his pages feel that they have almost made their personal acquaintance. The first was the Reverend Donald Macqueen, a minister of the Church of Scotland on Skye, who was to accompany the pair on nearly all their wanderings on that island and on Raasay. The second was the unforgettable Malcolm Macleod, cadet of the House of Raasay, whose reminiscences of the '45 were so eagerly seized upon and set down by Boswell as the first of his Jacobite jottings. His appearance moreover gave Boswell the opportunity for one of the most celebrated pieces of verbal portrait painting even he ever achieved:

> Along with him came, as our pilot, a gentleman whom I had a great desire to see—Malcolm Macleod, one of the Raasay family, celebrated in the year 1745 for his conducting the Prince with fidelity from Raasay to the Laird of Mackinnon's. He was now sixty-two years of age, quite the Highland gentleman; of a stout well-made person, well-proportioned; a manly countenance browned with the weather, but a ruddiness in his cheeks, a good

G

way up which his rough beard extended; a quick lively eye, not fierce in his look, but firm and good-humoured. He had a pair of brogues, tartan hose which came up only near to his knees and left them bare, a purple kilt, a black waistcoat, a short cloth green coat with gold cord, a large blue bonnet with a gold-thread button. I never saw a figure that was more perfectly a representative of a Highland gentleman. I wished much to have a picture of him just as he was. I found him frank and *polite*, in the true sense of the word.

This often-quoted description is, apart from its outstanding merits, worthy of remark on one or two other counts. It shows that Boswell at a comparatively early age as a writer was a conscious literary artist who could already achieve notable effects in his own medium quickly and easily. The passage presumably hastily written down in the day-to-day Journal of the tour that we now have in its original state is transferred unaltered to the published version of the *Tour to the Hebrides*. Secondly, Boswell's reference to Malcolm as a man whom he had had a great desire to see because of his connection with the '45 confirms one in the assumption that a large part of the traveller's desire to visit the Hebrides, and in particular Skye, sprang from Jacobite notions. And finally the fact that Malcolm wore the kilt, even though it was not of tartan, is interesting. It shows that the proscription of the wearing of Highland dress amongst those who had the tenacity to cling to old customs in remote parts of the Highlands and Islands was, though it had not been rescinded by 1773, beginning to wear fairly thin.

Within a few years emigration was going to remove most tacksmen and lesser gentry who could remember the Highland dress before proscription; and the kilt, save for military use in Pitt's regiments, was to drop out of use until the romantic revival of the early 19th century draped it round many an unsuitable pair of knees. Malcolm Macleod must have been one of the last of the pre-proscription

Highland gentlemen who were able to wear the kilt naturally and not as a piece of class-conscious fancy dress. I
exclude from this sweeping condemnation, of course, those
young people who since the war, whether in the Highlands
or in the towns, have given the old dress of Celtic Scotland a
new lease of natural life.

We are not allowed so detailed nor so brilliant a description of the other Skyemen who went with the travellers to
Raasay, the Reverend Donald Macqueen—"an elderly man
with his own black hair, courteous and rather slow of speech,
but candid, sensible and well informed, nay learned"; but
as the narrative of the Skye journey progresses his character
is slowly but surely built up from these small but well-
defined foundations. Mr. Macqueen was a Highland
minister of the old pre-puritan, pre-emigration times in the
best tradition of his kind. He was neither fanatical on the
one hand, nor given over to the easy acceptance of his
parochial rights as a kind of clerical country gentleman on
the other. He was of that school of Scottish Churchmen in
the 18th century known as "Moderates". These sought (after
the savage extremes to which Scottish theological controversy had gone in the previous century) to establish the
Kirk of Scotland on a foundation made not only of violent
anti-Episcopal and anti-Catholic fervour, but rather of
scholarship and true Christian practice. Despite their
occasional and inevitable differences of opinion on points
of doctrine, custom and historical reading, it is a proof of the
true quality and learning of the man that Johnson obviously
liked him, and indeed relished his company.

A Presbyterian in faith and a moderate Whig in politics
(moderate in that he could consort with and take pleasure
in the company of Jacobites and Episcopalians) he was also
a Celtic Highlandman to the very core of his being. If,
somewhat to Johnson's surprise, he could argue with him
against the validity of second sight this is understandable.
He had, amongst his widely scattered parishioners, to

contend with many beliefs that his Moderate Presbyterian philosophy made him regard as the remnants of paganism— and second sight may well have been one of these. On the other hand his Celtic heart, untrammelled by any doctrinal handicaps in such a matter, yearned to believe in the truth of Macpherson's Ossianic claims. And in this too he found himself at odds with the Doctor. But the sincere regard of the two men for each other survived these comparatively minor differences.

He was well liked throughout the length and breadth of Skye and was indeed loved by many for his kindly character, for his true Christian piety and for the fact that in difficult times he could act as a spokesman for the oppressed. There was in him not one touch of the bitter and withdrawn "killjoy" attitude which one has grown to associate with so many 19th-century and modern Highland ministers. He sat by and looked on with approval at the nightly dances at Raasay House, and, even more remarkable, Boswell tells us that he joined with the sailors on the voyage up the Sound in singing the Jacobite song *Tha tighinn fodham éiridh*. Incidentally Johnson's only recorded comment on this clerical and sailorly concert was the characteristic remark that "Naval music was very ancient".

Boswell's account of this voyage up the Sound is wholly delightful and is to be read and enjoyed at its best in the original croquet-box version. In this original journal we have all the conversation that took place on the voyage that Boswell can remember, including Malcolm Macleod's reminiscences of the '45 which Boswell in his publication saved up, along with his other Jacobite notes, for a complete and separate part of his book. Malcolm's recollections re-counted here, however, and, so it seems to the reader, almost audibly recounted and recalled amidst the sound of the waves, of the Highland sailors singing, of Dr. Johnson's deep voice pronouncing from high in the stern of the boat, of Boswell's excited chatter, give a much more lifelike quality to the tale of the Prince's wanderings and adventures than does Boswell's more formal account later published in a chapter to itself.

I would have wished to have made the same journey from the sea coast by Coirechatachan up the Sound of Raasay. I would have wished to pass as they did close by the Island of Scalpay, one of the many islands which Johnson proposed that Boswell should buy, on which he proposed also, and without a word of protest from Mr. Macqueen, to build an Episcopal Church, to found a school and set up a printing press for Malcolm Macleod "where we should print all the Erse that could be found". I would have liked to know that I had passed over the exact spot where Dr. Johnson's spurs, much to his temporary annoyance, were carried overboard owing to the carelessness of Boswell's servant ("there is something wild in a pair of spurs being carried into the sea out of a boat"). And I would in fancy have liked to think of them still there amidst the sea-wrack and the seaweed, only a little below me, and under the moving waters, awaiting their final regurgitation from the depths at the day of dissolution and of Judgment.

Finally I would have wished my boat to draw up at the little bay and harbour before Raasay House, "well defended by a rocky coast and a fine verdure about it, and beyond it hills, and mountains in a gradation of wildness". I would have liked to come into this landing place (almost unaltered over the centuries), come into it from the unchanging sea, and in the eye of fancy have seen stepping down across the smooth lawns the gay and hospitable company that met Samuel Johnson and James Boswell a hundred and seventy-nine years earlier. I would have liked to do all this, but alas, no boat procurable by me runs nowadays from the sea-coast by Coirechatachan to the bay by Raasay House. Instead I had to content myself with the ordinary transport from Portree to Raasay pier.

Content myself is a churlish phrase to use about a

short sea journey which, if it lacked the historical justification of an exact Boswellian and Johnsonian route, was full of West Highland and Hebridean autumnal beauty. The first snows had touched and were seeming not to blunt but rather to sharpen the knife-like edges of the Cuillin Hills. The pellucid waters of the Sound were as calm as they can be only on an early Autumn morning; and as I looked over the edge of the little boat by the pier before it started I could see deep down through twenty or thirty or more feet to the sea's floor. As we came out of Portree harbour and turned southwards, the length of Raasay stretched out before me. At the centre Dun Cann raised its oddly truncated height against the crystalline eastern sky, and below it and before it the autumnal colours of Raasay's fields, heaths and sea-coast lay in quiet but lovely profusion. It was a sight of great beauty; and as I passed by, and saw for the first time Raasay House with its lawns and its bay before it, on my way to the pier lying to the South of the island, I caught my breath in delight, not only because I was looking upon a building and a place which had long haunted my thoughts, but because the prospect was so beautiful.

From the pier I walked the mile or so up to Raasay House and asked permission to see over it. The House is now an hotel; but this was the off season, and no one was staying there. I was at liberty to wander through the rooms and the grounds as I pleased. I found for myself, though with the aid of directions given to me from the foot of the stairs, the room in which Dr. Johnson had slept, and was assured that the bedstead in it was the frame of the one on which the old man had lain a hundred and seventy-nine years earlier. As I was alone, and, as the bedding was stripped from it, I allowed myself the sentimental luxury of lying down on the bed and reflecting on the course of my journey and on where I now was. I thought, with a kind of smile in my mind, that Johnson had, in our modern parlance, got "something of a kick" out of sleeping on the bed which Prince Charles had occupied at Kingsburgh, a little later on his own Hebridean tour in Skye. In my present position I was, as it were, getting that same Jacobite "kick" but second-hand. But what a "second-hand" through which to receive it—the recumbent body of the great Samuel Johnson! The thought was sufficiently ludicrous as well as historically satisfying to make me laugh aloud—partly with pleasure and partly at the absurdity of my situation—and get off the bed.

I then went downstairs and for an hour or so wandered in the lower part of Raasay House and in the immediate policies. An early 19th-century front not without a kind of remote Edinburgh New Town or Regency grace has been added to the house, but it has, from the lawns and the seashore, hidden the old walls of what must have been a typical 18th-century Highland or Hebridean gentleman's house of the lesser kind. That is to say it must have been built fairly and squarely in the more modest and undecorated 18th-century but not Augustan fashion, able to accommodate in constricted circumstances some twenty or thirty people on high days and holidays—not a castle, but a laird's house of distinction. There has been, apart from the 19th-century front, some internal alteration of walls, but it did not take me long to get the feel of the old house within its new shell. I found, at least to my own satisfaction, the exact floor-space whereon was held the "little ball" which was held to welcome the travellers and which Boswell's pen has made deathless for as long as any shall continue to read his books.

How well Boswell begins to write at this part of his journal! How his talents effloresce to meet and deal with this memorable scene in Raasay House on the first night on which they came there! On Raasay Boswell enjoyed the happiest hours of all the tour. Maybe indeed he was never happier in all his life than during these four days on this, one of the most beautiful and fruitful of all the Hebridean islands.

Perhaps he was never happier than here, where the old innocent gaiety of life, still preserved untouched, as if it were from the Golden Age, had somehow lingered in a manner into the latter half of the 18th century, perhaps he was never happier than here, surrounded by hospitable Highland gentlefolk, young and old, who had passed through fires of endurance and high romance in the deathless story of the '45, yet who danced and sang and made merry as if no tragedy had ever touched them, danced and sang unaware of the fate that was so soon to befall their society and their kind. Perhaps he was never happier than here, where his revered and beloved mentor displayed contentment, nay a sense of delight, which must surely have lapped Boswell himself around in a delight that was truly joyous, and not, as was so often with him, febrile.

Those who have an affection for Boswell can find many places in his journals and his published writings which arouse pity in them. There are also times when he is wholly ludicrous. There are times too which we know of, as for instance the long period during which with patient and painful industry and in the face of discouragement of other people's envy and spite he was contending with the all but crushing disabilities which lay within his own temperament. These were the times when he was building stone by stone the greatest monument of biography in the language. Then one feels that admiration is scarcely a strong enough word due to him. There are the countless occasions when he is undergoing a fit of repentance, or as I would prefer to put it enjoying a resurgence of hope, and aspiration after goodness. When one reads of some of these occasions one may do no more than smile. There are other of these occasions which, if one has any heart, touch one to deeper feelings than laughter. They move one to admiration for his eternally sanguine temperament. There are times however when one feels that one can with relief just sit back and enjoy Boswell enjoying himself. The period of the four days that he spent

'Revising for the Second Edition.' A Rowlandson satirical print showing an imaginary scene of Lord Macdonald threatening Boswell, after the first publication of the Journal

(Courtesy of the British Museum)

The old house on Raasay as it was when Boswell and Johnson were
so memorably entertained there

(Courtesy of the British Museum)

on this lesser Hebridean island off Skye, in the company of
Dr. Johnson, the Reverend Donald Macqueen and the gay
Macleods of Raasay is one of these.

He danced every night, he drank enough to be sociable
and lively but never got so excited, as later on at "Corri",
as to get drunk. He renewed his youth by exercising himself
on the island like a schoolboy. He also exercised his ceaseless
curiosity and his powers of observation to their full and to
the eternal gratitude of anyone who feels within himself a
nostalgia for the old lost Highland life. And that curiosity
and observation bore fruit in some of the best writing in all
his Highland tour. Finally he seems to have displayed
easily, and without that ostentation which sometimes
marred it, his essential likability. If he was not so prominent
in gaiety as to be exactly "the life and soul of the party"
(there were others, notably Sandie Macleod, whose ebullience
of spirits was even greater than his) he obviously fitted in
happily to one of the happiest scenes that he and Johnson
ever enjoyed together. "I know not how we shall get away,"
said Johnson on the first evening they spent at Raasay, so
delighted was he by the entertainment they received there.
And in his own *Journey to the Western Islands* he ended his
chapter on this island with a passage full of the measured
dignity and customary dying fall of his melodious prose and
also full of sincere feeling:

> Such a seat of hospitality, amidst the winds and waters, fills
> the imagination with a delightful contrariety of images. Without
> is the rough ocean and the rocky land, the beating billows and
> the howling storm: within is plenty and elegance, beauty and
> gaiety, the song and the dance. In Raasay, if I could have found
> an Ulysses, I had fancied a Phoeacia.

Such was the scene on the island in which Boswell was
as truly happy as he had ever been and was ever likely to
be. When one turns the pages of his later memoirs and
follows him on his erratic career of folly and genius, of near

despair and flickering but persistent hope, it is a pleasant and comfortable thing to reflect on his four days in Raasay.

I have said that Boswell exercised himself on Raasay with the energy of a schoolboy: and indeed he did so—what with his exploration of the island and his dancing during the day as well as at night. I had the curiosity to try and follow as much of his footsteps as I could, and I admit that I was considerably impressed by his feat of September the 10th, when he walked round the whole island. He explored the caves, the sea-shores, the religious antiquities and curiosities of the place including a characteristic inspection, omitted in the published version of the Journal, of the cloacal arrangements in the Old Castle provoking from Johnson an equally characteristic sally when he pointed out his findings ("Mr. Johnson laughed heartily and said, 'you take very good care of one end of a man, but not of the other' "). He climbed to the top of Dun Cann, danced a reel with three other men on the top and finally returned having covered twenty-four miles of very rough going "not at all fatigued, and piqued ourselves at not being out-done at the nightly ball by our less active friends who had remained at home".

The paths which I followed were much smoother than the stony trackless routes which Boswell had had to take, nor did I go with him all the way. But I did go quite far enough to recapture in imagination what must have been the drive and spring of his expedition. Boswell was at the time past his first youth and for over ten years he had been undermining his admittedly remarkable constitution by hard drinking and other debauches which had regularly affected his health. My wanderings on the hillsides of Raasay increased my respect for the sheer ebullience of his physical as well as mental powers. When I got to the top of Dun Cann I found myself on the mountain-top in the open air and natural ballroom floor on which he and Malcolm and the "two other gentlemen" had out of pure exhilaration of spirits danced a reel. I was utterly alone beneath the wide autumnal skies. The heady colours of a West Highland Autumn day were spread out in rich profusion below me. There was nothing but the Cuillin Hills across the Sound to look down upon me. I had long wanted to dance a foursome on the top of Dun Cann, but on the whole I was just as happy that there was no one there to set to me. I reflected that if I had had more of Boswell's own temperament no self-consciousness would have prevented me from executing a few steps of a *pas seul* to mark the occasion. However, I did put a stone in my pocket from the ballroom floor to remember it by, and returned by the direct route to Raasay House.

When I got there I received news that the boat which was to take me back to Skye would be some hours late coming up the Sound. I was glad to have the opportunity to rest after my exertions and went at first to do so not in the fine new drawing-room at the front, but in the inner and darker and older part of the house where I told myself that I would be more at home with myself and with the past. But I did not find it so. Maybe I was tired, for I had got up early that day and had covered a fair amount of ground. Maybe it was the effect of the beauty and the loneliness of this island and the loneliness of this house in comparison with its happy and populous past which I had in fancy so often envisaged, maybe it was only the gathering dusk and the sense of winter just round the corner, but I found the old dark low-ceilinged rooms too melancholy for me. I returned to the modern plate-glass windows and watched the night fall blackening behind the even blacker hills of Skye as I waited for the steamer.

As I waited I let my thoughts run once again upon the scenes which had taken place upon the travellers' visit in those same dark low-ceilinged rooms behind me. Boswell's account of the four days is full of happy images well presented and memorable descriptions of pleasure. There was the "little ball" on the first night when they rolled back the carpet for the dance and when "Raasay danced with much spirit" and "Malcolm bounded like a roe".

There was the supper party to which thirty people sat down when "all was good humour and gaiety" and when the food was scarcely off the table before the singing of Gaelic songs began. There was the occasion when Lady Raasay showed Johnson "the operation of wauking cloth, that is thickening it as is done by a mill. Here it is performed by women who kneel upon the ground and rub it with both their hands singing an Erse song all the time. He was asking questions all the time . . . and amidst their loud and wild howl his voice was heard even in the room above." But perhaps the happiest occasion was the ball on the last evening of the travellers' stay. The fullest description of it is in the unpublished version, though in the published one Boswell allows himself a slightly warmer praise of Miss Flora whose beauty he says was celebrated all over the islands. In this unpublished version we have Boswell's jottings rather than the fruit of his reflections. But the effect he achieves brings the scene clearly before us.

We had a ball again tonight. Miss Flora is really an elegant woman (tall, genteel, a pretty face), sensible, polite, and good-humoured. I find it in vain to draw a portrait of a young lady. I cannot discriminate. She alone has been at Edinburgh. All the rest were never farther than Applecross, a gentleman's seat in Ross-shire on the opposite coast. Mr. Johnson said they were the best-bred children he ever saw; that he did not believe there was such another family between here and London; that he had never seen a family where there was such airiness and gaiety. Not one of the family ever had the toothache. They dance every night all the year round. There seemed to be no jealousy, no discontent among them. I asked Miss Flora, "Why, you have no idea then of the unhappiness of life that we hear so much of?"

"No," said she. "I have reason to be thankful." She had very good
sense without any aiming at smartness more than was natural
to her. The only fault Mr. Johnson could find with her was that
her head was too high dressed. Can there then be no misery
here? What says Mr. Johnson?—

> Yet hope not life from pain or danger free;
> Or think the doom of man revers'd for thee.

I must set him to inquire if evil has place in Raasay. They can
never have the sufferings of savages by being in want of food, for
they have plenty. And they have not the uneasiness which springs
from refined life. They work in every way proper for young ladies.
Miss —— plays on the guitar. What can disturb them? I can only
say that I was disturbed by thinking how poor a chance they had
to get husbands.[1] I mused on this, in the very heat of dancing.
It perhaps, though, does not occur either to them or to their
father.

The disappearance of the kind of life that had been led
in those rooms within the old part of the house on which I
had now turned my back has been apparently so complete
that it is with an effort that the modern visitor to the
Hebrides, unacquainted with the Highland story of the last
hundred and fifty years, can bring himself to believe that it
ever existed. He will have read Boswell's admirable and vivid
account of the gaiety and the wit and the liveliness and, to
all appearances, the all but flawless happiness enjoyed at
Raasay and will have had this account supported by the
more restrained, but nonetheless equally convincing,
observations of Johnson. He will have read too of the kind
of hospitality that the travellers enjoyed at other places on
their tour, at Coirechatachan, at Kingsburgh, Dunvegan,
Inchkenneth, and even on the occasion of their slightly
ridiculous but convivial stay at the Castle at Lochbuie.
With the exception of the humble tacksman's home at

---

[1] How like Boswell to indulge in such a reflection while dancing! But, as
Professor Pottle points out, he need not have worried: all ten daughters got
married.

"Corri" none of them quite equalled Raasay for sustained delight and high spirits. But in all of them he will feel communicated to him over the years a warmth, an uninhibited sense of welcome, courteous but gay, and utterly untouched by that puritanical restraint and tight-lipped, silent yet withal grave and sometimes dignified sense of disapproval which the modern world has grown to associate with the modern Highlands.

Today a visitor to the Highlands and Islands who passes through them as briefly as did the travellers of 1773 will enjoy scenery all but unchanged from a hundred and seventy-nine years ago. He will meet with courtesy and dignity from such descendants of the humbler of those who were there in 1773 who still remain in the "homes of the silent vanquished races", but of uninhibited gaiety and welcoming high spirits he will perceive nothing at all.

If like Boswell and Johnson he carries introductions to such Celtic lairds and lords as have still kept their estates or to those who have occupied the lands of the departed, he will enjoy civility and amiable hospitality, but it will be in no sense different from the civility and amiability that he might meet with in any comfortable country house in the South of England. If he does perceive any differences it will only be in the faint but well-bred air of fancy-dress and charade that is conveyed by the costumes of the male members of the party. He will note possibly a few antique domestic customs retained or revived, such as being "piped in to dinner", or, in extremely rare instances, being fortified for the day's exertions by what Boswell calls a "scalck", in Gaelic "sgailc", or early morning dram of whisky before setting out.

The visitor observes the natural scene which provided the background for over a thousand years of Scottish Celtic history and which, it is not too fanciful to suppose, contributed to the character and quality of the Scottish Highlander. He sees for himself the change which has come

over the human scene in the last century of this millennium
and he may well wonder how it all happened, and how it is
that so gay and friendly a society has apparently so completely vanished. "Why," he may ask, "is there no laird's
house on Raasay or anywhere else in the islands for that
matter where they 'dance every night all the year round'?
Why is Coirechatachan only a deserted shell, and the gay
hospitality of song and wit and sentiment and flowing all-
night conversation which the tacksman's family extended
to the casual visitor gone not only from 'Corri' but, so it
would seem, from all the Hebrides? Was what the travellers
of 1773 enjoyed no more than the departing flash of a
temporary Jacobite uprising of the spirit which has been
snuffed out or perhaps treacled down into neo-Bonnie-
Prince-Charleism or tricked out into the fun-fair atmosphere of the modern Highland Games?"

To such questions one prefers to return comment
rather than answer. I have already spoken my full in an
earlier chapter on the sad story of emigration and the em-
bittering effect it has had upon those Highlanders left behind.
I have said that it turned the eyes of their souls inward in a
melancholy form of spiritual introspection of a kind that can
be found at its most poignant in the Gael who feels that
all that he and his society had in this world is lost to him.[1]
The Celtic society of the Highlands was struck an all but
mortal blow by the disasters of the 18th century, and the
effect of that blow was spiritual—but the sad tale of it does
not need retelling here.

Rather I would speak of the island of Raasay, archetype
of so many other of the Hebrides. Before the disasters which
began two hundred years ago Raasay had a name for gaiety,

[1] There is a difference between this Gaelic spiritual withdrawal and the
manifestations of the extreme Protestant or Puritan or Seccessionist religious
minorities in England. The Highland Gael is a more imaginative man than the
Saxon in temperament, and even into the excesses of his religious discipline
and rule he seems to be able to infuse a kind of poetic melancholy which though
it is none the less depressing is somehow more dignified than anything to be
found amongst the extreme English nonconformist sects.

contentment, gallantry and romance which was known afar in the other islands and on the Gaelic-speaking mainland. From Raasay there came poetry and song and deeds of valour the origins of which lie far back in the mysterious depths of Gaelic oral tradition. Raasay long before 1773, long before the great days of 1745, had been a pearl amongst the Western isles; and the two travellers were fortunate enough to catch the gleams from it just before its lustre faded.

It is characteristic of so much that has happened in the Western Highlands and Islands that the Macleods of Raasay, one of the best and kindliest families of chieftains in all the Isles, should, though they struggled to the end, and into the 19th century, have failed and have been compelled to leave their centuries-old home. It is characteristic that upon their departure the curse of enforced emigration should have fallen upon this island with particular severity; and that, as a result, Raasay is now the home of the purest "secessionism" and apparently the purest spiritual pessimism.

The purest pessimism. . . . And yet, and yet there is another quality in Raasay which makes it typical of many of the other islands that have suffered its fate; but this quality is in Raasay strong, deep and not to be observed at once. It is this.

Wherever Gaelic is the predominant language in the islands or on the mainland there exists a deep but inextinguishable underground movement of poetry, romance and hidden gaiety. It is like a thread of gold ore running through the heart of a rock which flashes to the surface only when that rock is struck, or which gleams at some unexpected corner or side of it where the ceaseless flow of water has worn the rock thin. This underground movement, this thread of hidden gold in the character even in the demeanour of the most indrawn, withdrawn Highland Gael, is indestructible. As the mountain peaks of Skye, hidden for so much of the year in the mist and clouds, are themselves indestructible and are always there far above us when we cannot see them, so, deep below, there lies in any company of Gaelic-speaking Celts from the West and the Western Isles this underground movement of poetry and song and gaiety. And in the temperament of each of them there runs this thread of gold.

It is characteristic of Raasay that the people there, once so free and happy, of late so bitterly oppressed, and now so given over to the sad spiritual consequences of their oppression, should keep amongst them some of the purest ore of this hidden gold. Some of the oldest and best of the poetry of Gaelic oral tradition is still preserved on Raasay only to be spoken and passed on when no stranger is there and when no ministerial frown is to be seen, or no tight-lipped disapproval to be felt to check its flow. There are tales and even songs on Raasay full of the pride and poetry of the remote Celtic past. And as for gaiety! Well, it too is deep hidden, but it is still there, and they say that in all the Islands there is no one like a Raasay man at a wedding when the whisky is in him and when the old glory comes upon him again.

In men of this kind, few though they may be, the tradition of Raasay lingers on even though it may show itself only rarely. But the Macleods, once of Castle Raasay, and later of the house in which Boswell and Johnson were entertained, have been gone for over a hundred years.

In the first half of the 19th century the greater Highland chiefs and landowning families were able to survive either by turning over their lands to sheep-grazing, and subsequently by letting them for sporting property, or by investing their money in the rising tide of British commercial enterprise. The lesser chiefs (lesser only in the value and extent of their property) who stayed at home and endeavoured to meet the new world and new conditions by improving their estates in the more estimable way of planting, agricultural improvement and building were not so fortunate. They could not have chosen a worse period for putting such admirable intentions into practice than the forty or so years that followed Waterloo, and which in the Highlands culminated in the horror of the potato famine, with all the tragedy that this meant to their tenants. Such families were by 1850 often quietly snuffed out. The family of Macleods of Raasay was one of these.

James Macleod who in 1786 succeeded his father, the host to Boswell and Johnson, lived to 1824 and improved the estate by planting and by building which included the Regency front to the present Raasay House. These were the last achievements of the Macleods of Raasay on Raasay. His son, John, struggled against the adverse economic and social tide until 1846, when he was compelled to sell the estate and emigrate, as had so many humbler men of his name in the West Highlands before him.

The appearance of Raasay has an appealing quality, apart from any sentiments which may be aroused in one from anything one may have heard about its past, the family of its chiefs, and the poetic quality of its people. It is a douce island, softly coloured, with no very precipitate or rough hills. With its plentifully wooded plantations at the South end, its lawns, and its not very large chieftain's house, added to tastefully in the last years of the Augustan manner, it has a cultivatedly sylvan air about it. This contrasts pleasantly and far from inharmoniously with the wild grandeur of the hills on Skye and on the mainland, which stand beside it and over it.

For those who do know its past and who feel for it there is an element of pathos added to the patently appealing quality of the island. The woods which give so unusual a touch of quiet cultivation to this miniature Hebridean scene, and the "Edinburgh New Town" front to the house, proclaim the last efforts of the Macleods of Raasay for Raasay—efforts to come to terms with the new world of the 19th century in a gentlemanly way, but which, perhaps because they were attempted in a gentlemanly way, failed.

The woods still stand, and are never likely to be more beautiful than at the season at which I was fortunate enough to see them—the Autumn. The front of the house is as it was when James Macleod built it in the Southern and English manner to suit the English-speaking world into which himself, his family and his kind had through inevitable circumstances come to have their being. But behind that new front, deep and dark within the house, are the old rooms where Gaelic was the language, where Gaelic music was almost as frequent as Gaelic speech, where they danced every night of the year and where Boswell said to himself, "Can there be no misery here?"

When Boswell and Johnson were on the island Macleod had ten daughters, all of whom danced at the little ball on the last night of their stay there. All of them, as has already been recorded in a footnote, got married. One of them was by marriage a connection of the present writer's family. Through these ten daughters the blood of the Macleods of Raasay is to be found in their progeny all over Britain, Europe and the Commonwealth. But it is over a century since a Macleod of the Macleods of Raasay, who sheltered Prince Charles Stuart and later entertained Johnson and Boswell, has lived in Raasay House.

The Macleods of Raasay have their place in Gaelic history, and their name is unlikely to be forgotten even amongst a minority of a minority so long as men survive to tell stories of the Gaelic past in the Gaelic language. They made their brief but unforgettable appearance in English literature however because Boswell and Johnson visited their house in 1773 and set down in two classic English travel books their impressions of this house in the last days of its full happiness.

There was one Scottish writer who, though he wrote with the taste of Gaelic on his tongue, made his name in the English language. Neil Munro, that lovable teller of tales,

journalist and poet, writing amidst the smoke and the fog
and the clangour of modern industrial Glasgow, did not
forget the Macleods of Raasay. Indeed the fate of that
ancient house came to him as a symbol of Highland grief
when he heard the news of the death of his son in the first
World War, and he invoked the memory of his dead boy, a
Highland youth fallen upon the fields of France, in the name
of Raasay—"Lament for Macleod of Raasay".

> Oh Allan Ian Og! Oh Allan aluinn!
>   Sore is my heart remembering the past,
> And you of Raasay's ancient gentle children
>   The farthest-wandered, kindliest and last!
> It should have been the brave dead of the islands
>   That heard ring o'er their tombs your battle cry,
> To shake them from their sleep again, and quicken
>   Peaks of Torridon and Skye.

And then, as Gaels do when moved to their hearts' depths,
he reaches out to the past of the past and mourns the whole
vanished race of Raasay, gone long before he was born.

> Gone in the mist the brave Macleods of Raasay,
>   Far furth from fortune, sundered from their lands,
> And now the last grey stone of Castle Raasay
>   Lies desolate and levelled with the sands.
> But pluck the old isle from its roots deep-planted
>   Where tides cry coronach round the Hebrides,
> And it will bleed of the Macleods lamented
>   Their loves and memories!

VI

THE CAUTIOUS JACOBITE

I SAT in the tartan-decorated cocktail bar of an hotel on the mainland of Skye, and listened to a mixture of voices in Cockney, Glasgow Scots and Highland English. Now and again the faint sound of Gaelic might pass, or, by the ear of fancy, be imagined passing by the half-open window, or be heard ascending from the kitchen quarters not far from the high stools, the chromium furnishings and the tartan coverings of the bar chairs.

A friendly Cockney asked me what I was doing in Skye.

"Just enjoying myself," I replied.

"A bit late in the season?" he continued.

I looked out of the window on to the scene of tranquil autumnal beauty which, even as late as mid-November, was still holding its sway in these Western districts. "Oh, I don't know," I answered. "It's very lovely."

He too turned to look at the crystalline sea, so smooth that the coloured hills were, in reflection, inverted in it, and for a moment he seemed to be about to agree.

"Not bad," he admitted, "but it's hellish lonely in the winter. Fair hell it is. And you've come late too," he added reflectively, still apparently puzzled by my solitary, yet obviously transitory, presence in this bar amidst the advertisements for whisky, gin, "Prince Charlie's own liqueur", tartans, tweeds and other fancy goods. The cocktail bar did not quite descend to Scotch postcards with jokes about banging saxpences, hairy knees and kilted, crapulous, Scotch drunkenness, but I had caught a glimpse of them out of the tail of my eye in one of the village shops.

"And you, what are you doing here as late as this?" I asked, not only out of politeness; for though I am accustomed to some strange importations into the islands of the West, I couldn't quite place this modern Stratford-atte-Bowe voice with its flattened "abouts", "outs" and "rounds" in these surroundings.

"Me?" he replied. "Oh, I've a job of sorts that brings me up here a lot. Not all the time, thank you very much, but quite enough to know the place. They all know me here too," he added after a slight pause.

I supposed him to be some sort of well-established salesman or travelling contractor, for he seemed pleasantly at home, friendlily knowledgeable, and, as his next words and actions proved, not without authority or at least influence.

"Come on," he said, rising from his seat beside me in the window and advancing in a jocularly commanding manner towards the bar where a slight hubbub had begun. "Come on, enough of that. Keep it clean. Keep it clean."

An altercation between some Glasgow men, either the very faggest fag end of "the season", or some other travelling salesmen, had broken out, and the air was filled with the clucking sound of that adjectival present participle which remains one of the few unprintable words in the language and which, at the slightest provocation, pours forth in a cascade from the glottal-stopped sing-song of Glasgow speech. Order was restored, and my companion returned to my chromium-plated and glass-topped table.

"You'd think I worked here, wouldn't you?" he said to me with a jovial wink, as he rejoined me.

"Yes, I would," I agreed.

"Well, I don't. It's just that a lot of them know me. See?"

"Yes," I agreed again.

"Disgusting the way some of these fellows talk," he said, sitting down again. "And it isn't as if there was any sense in it."

"No," I agreed once more, "there isn't," and told him an anecdote to point out the confusion of meaning people can get into through using this particular participle. He laughed. Then, as the offending group of men left the bar to us alone, he was reminded of the coming winter, which he seemed to be convinced that I was going to endure. "My, but it can get lonely here," he said, shaking his head.

"But there's always next season to look forward to, isn't there?"

"Yes," he agreed, cheering up in his quick, amiable Cockney way at once, "and they've had *some* seasons too since the war, what with the Skye week, the bus tours and the steamer trips. They've had Americans and Canadians as well as half Glasgow and plenty of people from the South. Why! I've heard them singing 'The Road to the Isles' and 'Loch Lomond' out there on the front until you could hardly hear yourself ordering a drink in here."

"I suppose this bar does a pretty good trade then?"

"Yes," he said, "pretty good. But they're a very nice class of people. They come in here from the buses with their tartan tammies and their Skye souvenirs. One glass of Drambuie (that's Bonny Prince Charlie's liqueur, you know) and then they're off again. Very little drunkenness, except amongst the locals a bit, but they use the back bar, of course."

"Of course," I agreed.

"But they come in here in the winter," he went on, "when there's no one here. It's because the ministers won't see them. But they don't get drunk much here—just sit soaking and whispering away in their Gaelic. Funny lot!"

A funny lot, whispering in their Gaelic. The homes of the silent vanquished races. Gone in the mist the brave Macleods of Raasay. The phrases drifted across my mind together and got confused. I could not resist a slight shudder of mental distaste, but, having indulged in it, I hope not obviously, at once rebuked myself.

What right had I to object? The population of Skye

had dwindled and dwindled, yet the beauty of this most theatrically lovely of all the Hebrides had remained inviolate. Its carefully nurtured and well-boosted associations of "romantic glamour" had helped to spread its fame all over the world. What right had I to object if astute business men cashed in, as it were, on the vacuum with their tartan souvenirs, their Bonny Prince Charlie liqueurs, their bus trips in the footsteps of Flora Macdonald, and so on? What right (and I pushed myself even to this limit of charity) what right had I to object if even the lairds chose to work, up beanfeasts of loyalty from the plutocratic descendants of exiled Skyemen across the Atlantic?

After all, the same sort of racket was being worked, if anything on a larger scale, down at places like Stratford-on-Avon, with very little harm to anyone. Ye-olde-halfe-tymbered tea-rooms were proving just as lucrative for the English as were all these tartan gew-gaws for the mass-producing merchants of Glasgow. But as I reflected on the pleasant Warwickshire countryside in which Stratford-on-Avon was set, and on all the rich meadow-lands of Southern England, I perceived the difference. The English still did *live* there. The enclosures of the 18th century may have had their disastrous effect, and the Industrial Revolution (more terrible in certain parts of England than anywhere in Scotland) might have continued that evil, but the English poor, and even some of the English peasantry, were still at least allowed to live in England. Nowhere in that rich, alluring, frightening, fenced-in, infinitely attractive country, compounded half out of "dark Satanic mills" and half out of scenery as intimately lovely as any in Europe, could you find man-made deserts such as Knoydart just over there on the mainland, or near deserts such as those to be found on this very island of Skye.

No, the mischief, the bitter mischief, had been done here a century or more ago, when in tears and in the extravagance of Celtic sorrow, with curses in their hearts against their evictors, the real exiles had gone forth. All that was over and done with. What did it matter if a number of rich Americans, or inhabitants of the Dominions, or of England for that matter, chose at intervals to cover themselves in tailor-made fancy dress and, in these scenes of immemorial and inviolable beauty, go through the play-acting of clan loyalty?

Why! clan loyalty had died, not so much with the abolition of the hereditary powers of the chiefs (Celtic loyalty would have been stronger than any Act of Parliament passed at Westminster) but with the first emigrant ships containing the men, women and children driven forth from their homes. And except for one's dislike, purely on the score of taste, at seeing the ghost of something that was once honourable and of the very heart's blood of the Gael made the subject of pantomime for the benefit of the "glossy weeklies", one was bound to admit that these international clan beanfeasts in what remained of the inhabited Western Highlands and Islands did no one any harm.

Clan loyalty, in any practical sense, had been quickly dying nearly two hundred years ago. And, while I listened to my amiable little Cockney acquaintance prattling away, I reminded myself with a start that I had been reading only that day an account of one of the innumerable stages in its dissolution which had taken place in this very bay upon which I was now looking. On these waters, Boswell and Johnson had seen in 1773 one of the many emigrant ships about to set forth; and Boswell had heard of the wild grief of the exiles on their way.

The wanderings of the two travellers in Skye rightly make, for most readers, the most attractive, the most imaginative, the most highly readable portion of Boswell's account of the tour. Yet throughout Skye, where the two of them undoubtedly enjoyed themselves better and for a longer period than anywhere else in Scotland, there runs an undertone of melancholy which springs from the thoughts of emigration that were in the very air around them. It was present as the very faintest ghost of a suspicion even upon that little paradise of an island, Raasay, in 1773. It was most certainly overhanging Kingsburgh when Boswell and Johnson visited Flora Macdonald. Its odour was strong at Armadale in the presence of Sir Alexander Macdonald. And even at Dunvegan where Johnson found himself so comfortable and where Boswell's "Feudal" inclinations were obviously stimulated, both of them were conscious of the decay of the people's condition, the people on whom Macleod's feudal pride rested.

When my acquaintance in the tartan-decorated bar had finished telling me about the glories of the Skye season, I went out round the bay to see if I could locate in fancy the anchorage of the emigrant ship which Boswell had sardonically noted as making "a short settlement of the differences between a chief and his clan". I imagined, from the short hints that Boswell drops, that it must have been lying well out, preparatory for sailing, and that the poor people had said their last farewells. The waters of the bay were quite empty, and my melancholy fancy was allowed full reign. But, despite my charitable resolutions, I was not to be too depressed about the present; on the whole, pleased that there was no pleasure steamer coming round the point. When I got back to my lodgings I found some letters for me —the first since I had left the Lowlands. This, by a small coincidence, set me thinking of the two travellers of 1773 once again.

When Boswell and Johnson arrived on the mainland of Skye from Raasay, they rested and dined at Portree, and they too received, for the first time since they had entered the Highlands, letters from the South. My letters had contained nothing but business, but Boswell had received a communication from his wife which he records with a note of obviously sincere affection in his private, but not published, Journal. It is obviously sincere, not only because he set it down for his own eye alone, but because it does not carry the additional exclamations of painful self-examination and self-reproach which letters from "my esteemed spouse" were wont to arouse in Boswell in later years. He had not long been married, and had not yet begun his career of trivial marital infidelity and generally trivial bad behaviour which, in his moments alone with himself and alone with his later private jottings, distressed him as much as they distressed his wife. Yet, even to the end, with all the distractions of London, both reputable and disreputable, to allure his attention from her, he never lost his feeling for her. Is it too much to say that, in spite of himself, and in spite of all he did to hurt her and himself, he loved her until her death, and beyond?

I do not think it is. Love is one of the most misused words in our language, and, even when it is not defamed by petty or gross application, its meaning and shades of meaning are shifting and elusive. Passion, devotion, affection, even pity, all these emotions can be contained and can mingle in the feeling expressed in this one monosyllable. That Boswell at first loved his wife with the normal passion and devotion of the man who marries for love rather than for *convenance* cannot be doubted. Few, I think, save Boswell's most implacable enemies, would deny that when, in its normal course, that passion faded, its place was taken in his heart by enduring affection pitifully shot through, and perhaps made all the more poignant, by pity—pity on account of the wounds which his own behaviour inflicted on the object of his affection. I would go further: I would say that that affection was sufficiently enduring, despite all the offences which Boswell committed against it, to be called devotion. Boswell loved Johnson as his dear friend and great and revered master—the touching scene near the end of Johnson's life when Boswell put before the Doctor his friends' plan for the Italian holiday, the repeated and spontaneous exclamations of affection that passed between the two men can leave no doubt on that score—and in the eyes of the world Johnson was unquestionably the most important human being in Boswell's life. I do not agree. I think that Margaret Boswell was nearer to his heart than anyone else, and that when at Auchinleck he saw and wept over the cold body of his "dear, dear Peggie", he suffered a more agonizing though less stunning blow than when Johnson died.

"I have been faithful to thee, Cynara! in my fashion," sang Ernest Dowson about an attractive Soho waitress who would not listen to his love-making nearly a hundred years after Boswell's death. "I cried," he declares, not unlike Bozzy, "for madder music and for stronger wine"; and in the lines "But when the feast is finished and the lamps expire, then falls thy shadow Cynara! the night is thine" there is an authentic Boswellian echo—save for the fact that with Boswell the shadow, the genuine and distressful shadow of his wife's image, however far away he was from her, was more likely to fall during the morning hangover than at night. But with this the affinity between Dowson's eighteen-ninety-ish mood, which inspired his curiously memorable verses, and Boswell's marital relations ends. Boswell was admittedly an incurable attitudinizer, and saw himself in innumerable rôles, heroic, distinguished, and "romantick", but he would never have attitudinized to the extent of composing melancholy and melodious verses (even if he had had the poetic gift of being able to write them— which he had not) on the theme of his marital infidelities and on the fact that the memory of his wife haunted him. He hated the distress that his follies had caused her too much for that; he was too fond of her, too devoted to her, or, more simply and as I would prefer to put it, he loved her too much and was too ashamed of the wrongs he inflicted on that love.

However, in Skye in 1773, he had no need to torment himself with such thoughts. Margaret Boswell may well have

shown herself none too pleased with the idea of the "Highland jaunt" when she had first heard about it from her
husband. We know that her husband's devotion to Johnson
rather more than puzzled her. She resented it without being
able to name the cause of her resentment, as she so well
could with many of the other distractions which led her
James away from his domestic hearth. We know that she
had expressed her uneasiness at being left alone when the
two travellers had parted from her in Edinburgh; and the
thought of her uneasiness at home obviously touched
Boswell in the better part of his kindly nature. But of the
bitterness of self-reproach he must have suffered only the
faintest (and perhaps prophetic) twinge when he received
her first letter at Portree.

Perhaps he did wonder for a passing moment whether it
was not as much his fault as hers that she was unable to enter
into his "Johnsonian enthusiasm", perhaps he wished that he
could have shared with her some of the happiness he had
enjoyed on Raasay, and perhaps he would have liked her to
know how innocent that happiness had been.[1] And finally,
and with some justification, he may have had some com-
punction at leaving her at such a time when she was once
more with child. But if such thoughts did pass through his
kindly but quickly moving fancy, they must equally probably soon have passed. There was the memory of Raasay
just behind him. Here he was upon the much-looked-
forward-to Island of Skye with Dr. Johnson. And, upon this
very day, the two of them were to set forth for Kingsburgh,
where they were to meet and stay under the roof of the
"celebrated Miss Flora Macdonald". Throughout his
association with Johnson, Boswell particularly relished
being the agent by which the Doctor was introduced to
unusual or remarkable people. The prospect of bringing
Johnson and Flora Macdonald together must, upon leaving

[1] In his unpublished journal Boswell toys with the idea of bringing his wife
and daughter at some future date to Raasay to "pass an Autumn there".

Portree on Skye, have driven all other thoughts, including any ephemeral twinges of conscience, out of his eager mind.

The journey to Kingsburgh, however, was a depressing one. It rained hard, and Johnson appeared to be out of humour, talking of his longing to be in "civilized life again" and throwing out hints, much to Boswell's alarm, about cutting the tour short. Boswell does not tell us much of his own conversation upon leaving Portree and on the way. It may well have been that his fussy and anticipatory chatter had provoked a reaction in Johnson, who up till now had discovered a really lion-hearted capacity for enjoying the Hebrides and showing that he too could display the Highland spirit, whether in confuting Sir Alexander Macdonald or joining in the hospitality of Raasay.

It rained too when I set out for Kingsburgh from Portree. And when my Cockney friend, who happened to be going North, offered me a lift for part of the way, I accepted without hesitation. There did not seem to be much point in trudging along a metalled surface in a Hebridean autumnal rainstorm just because Boswell and Johnson had gone vaguely in the same direction. I knew, moreover, that we should strike the old tracks across the moors before we got within a mile or so of Kingsburgh. It would be time enough when we reached them to take to walking again. The rain too might have lessened by then, and there was plenty of argument for approaching the ill-defined old pathways, which I had puzzled out for myself on the maps, in as fresh a condition as possible. Not that these tracks offered the slightest prospect of arduous exercise. It was merely that I wished to have leisure to study for myself what remained of the old approaches to so classic a spot as Kingsburgh.

It was at Kingsburgh that Prince Charles Edward Stuart had been given shelter and had rested on his first night in Skye after his rescue from the "Long Island" by Flora Macdonald. It was at Kingsburgh that there occurred some of the most evocative and best-attested scenes and detailed

incidents in all the Prince's wanderings. It was gallant old
Macdonald of Kingsburgh, who was his host and protector,
Kingsburgh, whose character, whose very appearance and
tone of voice seem to live for us over the centuries—so
vividly, if briefly, does he appear in history. He shares also
with Flora the distinction of being amongst the few people
about whom, in the somewhat over-written and certainly
over-disputed story of the '45, there is no room for controversy. And finally, it was old Kingsburgh's son Allan
whom Flora had married and who had but recently succeeded to the small estate. So it was to Kingsburgh's house
that Johnson and Boswell went when they paid their visit
to her in her Skye home in 1773.

My companion who had so kindly given me a lift for part
of the way to Kingsburgh was, as one well acquainted with
the show business of Skye, not ignorant of Kingsburgh's past.

"You won't find much left there now," he said as we
approached the place where I wanted to be put off on the
old track. "They pulled down Bonnie Prince Charlie's house
about a hundred years ago."

"Yes, I know."

"Pity," he went on. "They could have made quite a
nice little place out of it if they'd kept it. Not exactly an
hotel. I don't suppose it would have been big enough for
that, but a kind of guest house, if you take my meaning."

"Yes."

"Teas in the front hall. Bonnie Prince Charlie relics and
pictures on the walls and on the stairs. Sixpence extra to see
his bedroom, and another sixpence to see Flora Macdonald's
if you've got that kind of mind. And Bob's your uncle, eh!
Pity," he continued after a pause, "but that's your Highlanders and Skye people all over. No drive about them at
all. They'll always let a thing like that slip through their
fingers. And a hundred years ago, when they pulled down
the house, I don't suppose there was anyone there to tell
them all about it."

"No, I don't suppose there was."

Perhaps he detected a slight lack of enthusiasm in my replies. "No," he repeated. "No, you won't find much about. Bonnie Prince Charlie and Flora Mac there now."

"Well, it isn't exactly that sort of thing I'm after," I admitted.

"No?"

"I wanted to have a look at some of the old roads round about Kingsburgh."

"Oh," he asked, with a touch of interest, "a surveying job?"

"Not exactly," I laughed. "I'm interested in some people that came to Kingsburgh some time after Prince Charlie and by the track that must be over there."

"Really," he said. "And who might they be?"

"Dr. Johnson and Boswell."

"Dr. Johnson!" my companion exclaimed. "You're right there. He *was* in these parts so they say. Funny thing that. Him always going on against the Scotch, yet coming all the way up here to Skye. And it must have been some journey in those times."

"It certainly was."

"I suppose he wanted to have a kind of look-see at the Scotch for himself. Still it was a funny thing him coming all the way up here. I've never been able to figure it out properly."

"It is rather puzzling," I agreed, and then as I was at that moment getting out of the car to cross the moor towards the track where the old man had struggled so uncomfortably through the rain to keep his celebrated rendezvous at Kingsburgh house over the hill there, I felt I really must correct myself. "No," I added, "I don't think it was so much puzzling as interesting."

"Really," my friend said as he waved to me through the car window. "Well, you must tell me all about it some time over a drink back home."

"I will," I promised.

I found the old approach to Kingsburgh easily, and as the rain had slackened down to the merest pretence at a Scotch mist, I had a fairly comfortable and leisurely time reconstructing for myself the way the travellers had come. I did not bother to do more than inspect the site of the old house; for there is little nowadays in the human aspect of Kingsburgh to evoke 18th-century memories. Raasay House, as I had come upon it, had stood, as it were, preserved under the glass case of a quiet West Highland autumnal day, its early 19th-century front merely protecting it, its lawns, stretching down to the old harbour, inviolate from the day when the travellers had landed, and the company had stepped down from the house to greet them. There is nothing of this at Kingsburgh where the old farm has long been obliterated and the policies around it altered. Only the moors without, the soft, gentle surrounding hills, and the old tracks, here and there all but swallowed up in the heather, remain from the days of the Macdonalds of Kingsburgh, of Prince Charles, and later of the two travellers from the South who had come to pay their respects to the "Conductress of the Pretender".

There are some scattered crofts near to Kingsburgh; and, coming from one of these, I met an old man. He was the nearest approach to a monoglot Gael that I have encountered away from the Outer Isles; at least his English was lame enough to make communication in that language difficult. Eventually we settled down to a compromise communication composed of short sentences on either side in a mixture of both languages. He told me about the present state of the land round Kingsburgh and, when I showed interest in the general geography of the surroundings, he pointed out some of the other earlier tracks to the farm. While doing so he referred to the "Prince's well" or drinking place by the pathside where Charles had stopped to refresh himself. This is, of course, quite an acknowledged minor

I

point in the carefully worked out itinerary of his wanderings on Skye, but it gave it, for me, a faint touch of added authenticity to hear it referred to thus casually, and in Gaelic.

I wanted to follow this now-obliterated track as far as the well and beyond. So, summoning up enough resources in Gaelic to say a polite good-bye, I bade farewell to the old man and went off across the moor. I left him, I am sorry to say and through no intention on my part, with the impression that I had been deceiving him, that I knew more Gaelic than I pretended, but that I had grown ashamed of the tongue. At least that was what he declared, and to give it added point, in English, as I left him.

Having approached Kingsburgh from the direction that Boswell and Johnson had come, I now attempted to do the same from the Prince's viewpoint. I located the possible neighbourhood of the well, but got only the vaguest idea of the track. At the end, however, I was able to get some general impression of the layout of the land in all directions, which must have altered very little in the last two centuries. To appreciate this better I climbed one of the small hills in the neighbourhood and looked out over Kingsburgh, what remains of its policies, the moor and the nearby sea-shore. The weather had now more or less cleared up and I was able at leisure and in comparative comfort to look my fill. It was a suitable place, indeed about the most apposite spot on the surface of the Earth for anyone interested in so remote a subject to reflect on the debated question of the degree of Jacobite feelings shared by Johnson and Boswell.

Over that moor below me there had come in 1773 the two travellers riding through the rain and intent upon an encounter which has aroused as much interest and speculation as any recorded in all Boswell's voluminous and detailed writings. That this meeting had been well planned in advance there can be no doubt. Apart from what we know of the character and cast of mind of the two men and of

'The Dance on Dun-Can' on Raasay. From the set of Rowlandson
satirical prints

(*Courtesy of the British Museum*)

Portree on the Isle of Skye as it must have appeared to Boswell and
Johnson

(Courtesy of the British Museum)

their many reasons for making this extraordinary Hebridean tour, there are other indications of their intentions well before they reached Kingsburgh. Before they got to Skye, Boswell had spoken of the strong feelings aroused in him by the mere thought of coming to that island associated with the immediate Jacobite past. And Flora Macdonald can have been the only person with Jacobite associations from that part whom they could have had any expectations of meeting. Boswell had included in his journal at Raasay a note which clearly covers some unrecorded conversations and arrangements: "We had resolved to visit Kingsburgh and see the celebrated Miss Flora Macdonald." And, as already mentioned, Sir Alexander Macdonald ten years later was to complain that Boswell had told him that his "only errand in Skye was to visit the Pretender's conductress". He further added that Boswell had "deemed every moment as lost which was not spent in her company".

It is all the more tantalizing then that we have no record of the conversations that must have occurred between Boswell and Johnson on this subject in advance. They must have talked about Flora possibly in London when the idea of the tour was at last taking shape and becoming a definite possibility, and certainly as the tour itself progressed and as they drew nearer to Skye. And while it is unlikely that they would have committed to paper, in the form of letters, their hopes and plans for seeing the Jacobite heroine, they, or at least Boswell, must surely have sent messages to the household at Kingsburgh about their coming. Of all this we hear nothing save that Flora said, upon their meeting, that a fortnight before, when she was returning to Skye from the mainland, she had heard that Mr. Boswell was coming to Skye, and one Mr. Johnson, "a young English buck", was coming with him.

I believe that this lack of information about their plans to visit Flora Macdonald, which is all of a piece with the paucity of knowledge which we have about the long, slow projection of the whole tour in advance, was part of a deliberate silence on Boswell's part. I believe also that this silence sprang from the awkwardness, to put it at its mildest, that he would have found in admitting publicly that he and Johnson were, in his own words (which he was careful to keep out of his published version of the tour), "visibly of the 'old interest' [to use the Oxford expression], kindly affectioned at least, and perhaps too openly so".

Just how "kindly affectioned" and how "openly so" can be deduced from various remarks made by Boswell throughout the tour and addressed half to the reader and half to himself. We can also gain some light by comparing the notes which he made in his original journal at the time of the meeting with Flora Macdonald with the excisions and revisions which he felt obliged to make before publishing his book over ten years later.

Johnson's position, which we know about not only from Boswell but from other sources as well, is clear. As a young man he was politically a high Tory with all that was meant by those words in the first half of the 18th century. There can be no doubt that, whatever reservations he made later on, he did then believe in, if not actively support, the claims of the House of Stuart to the throne. In his youth he certainly detested the early Hanoverians. On one occasion the mere mention of the name of George II threw him into such a passion, such a physical fury of shaking limbs and stammered words, that the company of his friends was astounded. When it came to the rising of 1745 little is known about his activities. Boswell in his *Life*, explaining his inability to trace his thoughts and movements at this time, says "That he had a tenderness for the unfortunate House" (of Stuart) "is well known; and some may fancifully imagine that a sympathetick anxiety impeded the executions of his intellectual powers" in these years. One well-known writer of recent years did "fancifully imagine" an excellent tale on this theme. John Buchan in his novel *Midwinter* supposes Johnson to have been actively, if secretly, concerned in the affairs of 1745.

In his later years his Toryism, while it became more pronounced as a philosophy, an attitude of mind, weakened in practice, certainly in Jacobite politics. He accepted the Hanoverian *fait accompli*; and as George II was succeeded by the less disagreeable George III, he developed for the King "born a Briton" a respect and even an affection which it is unfair to ascribe in any large degree to the fact that he drew his pension from Royal sources. By the time that Boswell met him he rather more than tolerated the Hanoverian regime, and would have viewed with horror any civil war that had attempted to upset it. Nevertheless, and despite the remarks which Boswell is careful to quote about his "later thoughts" on Jacobitism, old loyalties kept rising in him. Late in his life when he found himself at Derby, whence the Highland army had retreated in the affair of 1745–46, he said of the rising "It was a noble attempt". He also said that if a popular poll could be taken the Ruling House would be sent packing and the Stuarts, presumably, restored.

This half-silenced ghost of old affections, this lingering tenderness for the House of Stuart, to use Boswell's words, may well have been one of the motives behind the astonishing yet characteristically sudden proposal made by him in the early days of his friendship with Boswell to visit the Scottish islands. Even in 18th-century London, so remote from the 18th-century Hebrides, he must have known that in these islands there remained the last living, and last hopefully believing, Jacobites in the United Kingdom.

With all this Johnson's sentiment for Jacobitism was not sentimental. He had once been in the fullest sense a Tory, and that had meant being a supporter of the House of Stuart. He remained a Tory to the end of his days, but when Jacobitism became impracticable he abandoned its support but did not forget that he had once thought differently.

When I say, on the other hand, that Boswell's attitude was sentimental I do not wish to sound too contemptuous. He had been born and brought up in the strictest Whiggish and anti-Jacobite circumstances. If when he grew to manhood he moved away from the influence of these circumstances it was not due to any reasonable change in his political views, but because he found those circumstances uncongenial. His association with Johnson had much to do with this movement, and he began to model many of his sentiments, if not his opinions, on those of Johnson's. He had heard the ghost of Johnson's old loyalties speaking now and again casually through Johnson's lips; and if he could not share those loyalties (he had none in his own past to share) he could imagine that he shared in the sentiments they produced: in a word, he could sentimentalize over them. But he could do a trifle more. If he had no personal loyalties to hark back to he had family pride to take their place. He was more "feudally" born than was Johnson, and could in his attitude towards Jacobitism afford the luxury of a feudal point of view on the whole, fairly recent, and vexed question. Hence Boswell's silly injection of snobbery, a purely personal snobbery, into his sentimentally acquired Jacobitism. He, James Boswell, the descendant of "a long line of Scottish Barons", could take an entirely family and almost personal point of view on the Jacobite question which had originated in the Scottish feudal past.

But apart from the influence of Johnson's sentiments upon his own capacity for sentimentality, Boswell, one must remember, came into his own young manhood at a time when it was safe to indulge in sentiments about the '45. By the 1760s and 1770s the last Jacobite adventure was beginning to acquire the first faint embarrassing blushes of a "romantic story". Now that the attempt was over and had safely failed, it was safe to wrap the memory of it up in lavender-scented cloths, put it away in a drawer, and take it out again, when one felt inclined to indulge in the bitter-sweet scent of its fading romance. Young ladies all over the United Kingdom, as well as elderly Episcopal clergymen in Edinburgh, Oxford and London, could without danger drink toasts over the water; and, particularly in Scotland, feminine talents could lend themselves to the composition of tuneful melodies and nostalgic words on the theme of "Will ye no' come back again?" Boswell was quite emotional enough, and quite enough in the fashion of his age to have been affected by all this.

At the same time it is only fair to the age as well as to Boswell himself to point out that this later 18th-century "tenderness" for the Jacobite story cannot be compared with the meretricious nonsense which the modern writers of fiction, of songs, and even the producers of Technicolor films have produced on the theme of Jacobitism. Despite the truly shocking travesties and variations that have been made upon it, the poignant simplicity of "Will ye no' come back again?" can still speak to us from well over a hundred and fifty years. And there are other songs and scraps of verse from the twilight of Jacobite feeling at the end of the 18th century which can, even today, touch one with their nostalgic effect just because they were the product of true feeling and not of false sentiment.

The modern neo-Jacobite fiction, the mush of Bonnie Prince Charlieism, which sprang from late Victorian senti-mentality, but which still survives, has attempted to make out of the story of the '45 a "drawing-room fairy-tale for greensick girls". With many readers it nearly succeeded; and indeed did so to the extent of provoking an almost equally unpleasant reaction from modern Whig essayists and writers who have seemed to take a pleasure in exuding the bile of their denigration on the great story, and who cry down, as far as their acidulous temperaments allow them, every noble incident in it. Between these two extremes of false sentiment and acidulous debunking, there is very little sense uttered on Jacobitism today. But there was very little, if anything, of this sort of thing in the late 18th-century of Lady Nairne on the one side and the Whig Lords of the Court of Session on the other. Boswell's romantic fancies, whatever else they were, were very far removed from the Bonnie Prince Charlieism of today.

Yet, even as he indulged himself in these romantic fancies, even as he sentimentalized on the theme of Johnson's older loyalties, while justifying that sentiment on the score of his own "feudal inclinations", he must have been very well aware of the disastrous impression such feelings would make if they were generally to be known in circles highly important to his wellbeing. There could have been nothing in all the London and Johnsonian influences on the erratic James Boswell that would have caused him more embarrassment in his relations with his purse-string-holding father, with his family circle and with much of his important Edinburgh background than any suspicion of a taint of Jacobitism in him—that would indeed have been the last straw.

Lord Auchinleck, to take the very peak of the opposition, would, if he had heard of such a thing, have been not so much appalled as finally convinced of his son's utter irresponsibility, verging upon madness. Jamie might drink more than was good for him, but so did many better men in 18th-century Scotland, though most of them had better heads and had the sense to do it in Edinburgh rather than London. Jamie might run after the lassies and make a fool of himself in doing so; but again, so did many better men of his Lordship's acquaintance. Indeed, Dr. Boswell, Lord Auchinleck's own brother, admittedly a crank, but a crank who moved in respectable circles, had elevated wide, or as he called it, patriarchal fornication to the position of a virtue in his peculiar creed that derived in part from the Old Testament and in part from an odd form of Puritanism.

Jamie might be taking an irritatingly, indeed a dangerously, long time about settling down, about getting out of his erratic head dreams of a distinguished military, literary or political career—aye, trying a "toot on a new horn" as his Lordship characteristically expressed it. He might earn his grim old father's contempt by his love for London, for the finery of southern and foreign society, for all that "Signor Fiddle-dee-dee" way of life which Auchinleck so despised. He might do all these things, but there remained the hope that now that he was married, settled down in Edinburgh, and now that he was practising at the Scottish bar, good and ordered behaviour might be forced upon the heir to the Auchinleck estates. But Jacobitism, no! That would be the irremediable folly, the last infirmity of a mind now proved to be ignoble.

To a man of Lord Auchinleck's background, position and cast of mind, Jacobitism was, in any of its forms, about the worst thing imaginable—the worst because it was an evil of home manufacture. In Lord Auchinleck's own adult life-time it had, from his own home country of Scotland, struck at the very existence of that Whig society and way of life which was the essence of what Auchinleck considered was the true, the real, the only Scotland, the Scotland he represented. Not only did Jacobitism spell Toryism, Episcopacy, Popery, foreign manners and other detestable importations, some of them new, some revivals from an age which he and his kind had believed that they had, in Scotland at least, spurned behind them forever, but it had another and to them shameful element. It had re-arisen in Scotland, at their very doorsteps, and in so dangerous and revealing a form that for years after 1745 the very name of a Scot was over a large part of Britain synonymous with "a rebel". This was, for a respectable Lowland Whiggish Scotch Judge, a disgraceful and shameful thing. And, even as late as 1773 (though the danger was crushed and safely past), to sentimentalize over this shameful and disgraceful thing would in Lord Auchinleck's eyes have been, quite logically, as bad as, if not worse than, actively supporting it.

Later on in the tour, at Auchinleck, Boswell was to be present at the tremendous row between his father and Johnson, provoked by a dispute on Toryism and Whiggery. His unusual, but in this instance comprehensible, reticence in refraining from reporting a word of this famous, but now forever lost, battle of the giants, has been regretted by generations of his readers, including, one may add, many who have condemned Boswell for his lack of taste or excessive candour on other occasions.

James Boswell had quite enough of trouble in his relationships with his father, and one would not wish him to have had any more. Nevertheless, just as one regrets the loss of a verbatim report (as only Boswell could have done it) of the Auchinleck-Johnson scene, so there are moments when one almost wishes one could have heard Lord Auchinleck's comments if he could have looked over his son's shoulder and read his admissions of sentimental Jacobitism. Nor would those comments have been softened if he could have seen the passage which Boswell put in his private and unpublished journal a page after (and perhaps arising out of) his admission of "too openly so"—a passage possibly written down as a kind of memorandum to himself to play for safety:

I, again, have all that Mr. Johnson has, and something more, for my high notions of male succession make me mount up to distant times; and when I find how the Stuart family's right has been formed, it appears to me as but very casual and artificial. I find not the firm feudal hold for which I wish and which my imagination figures. I might fix my eye at the point of James IV, from whom my ancestor Thomas Boswell got the estate of Auchinleck, and look no further, had I a line of males from that Prince. But Queen Mary comes in the way; and I see the sons of Lennox on the throne. Besides, I consider that even supposing Prince Charles to have the right, it may be very generous for one to support another's right at every risk, but it is not wise, and I would not do it. Mr. Johnson's argument of right being formed by possession and acknowledgment of the people, settles my mind, and I have now no uneasiness. With all this, he and I have a kind of *liking* for Jacobitism, something that it is not easy to define. I should guard against it; for from what I have now put down, it is certain that my calm reasoning stops short at action, so that doing anything violent in support of the cause would only be following a sort of passion or warm whim. And talking much in favour of it may even in this secure and more liberal reign hurt a man in his rising in life.

This is Boswell at his most ingenuously ineffective. Judged by the standards of honest Whig, sound Tory, or even of a sentimental Jacobite, trying for "safety first", it is very feeble stuff. Had Lord Auchinleck had the opportunity of commenting on this composition of snobbery, pedantry, timidity, false sentiment and ineffective caution, blended with "dangerous thinking", one feels that one would have agreed with some of the devastating remarks he would certainly have made. But he never did have that opportunity. Nor indeed did anyone else (save Johnson who read the journal as it went along, and possibly Malone who assisted Boswell in preparing his manuscript for the press) until in the 1930s the Malahide croquet-box yielded up its secrets. For when it came to publication, Boswell did not so much revise this passage as excise it and insert one much more innocuous from many points of view.

Boswell wrote this, the original and excised passage, in his journal after he had met Flora Macdonald and just after he had heard from her her account of her part in the rescue of 1746. He had also heard Johnson say "all this should be written down". By this time he had picked up during his journey with Johnson on the mainland, at Raasay, and on Skye some three separate accounts of first-hand experience of the '45. It may well have been then at this juncture that Flora's narrative combined with Johnson's exhortation that made him decide to combine all the accounts into one story which he would present himself. This he did in his published journal of the tour, and at this point, just after visiting Kingsburgh.

One can understand his decision, but also regret it. There is a freshness in his notes of Malcolm Macleod's account which he heard during the sail from Skye to Raasay, to the accompaniment of the sound of oars, of the sea and of the sailors singing in "Erse" as they rowed, a freshness which is lacking in Boswell's composite presentation. One would have liked also to have some of Flora's own words in the description of the part she played in the affair. Boswell could have given us this so well; and the loss is, for his admirers as well as for lovers of Highland history, an appreciable one. Moreover, I cannot help thinking it significant that in the manuscript of the original journal there were only bare and brief notes on Flora Macdonald's story which were, of course, extended into the accepted and well-known version in Boswell's publication. It looks as if Boswell either relied upon his memory ten years later or merely based what he could remember on the accepted facts about Flora's rescue of the Prince.

Having made this small complaint let me pause to exculpate myself of the possible charge of niggling criticism or of a larger ingratitude. On the contrary, it is at this point that I feel most strongly conscious of Boswell's achievement and of his great legacy to us who come after him. One does not need to be a Jacobite or to be knowledgeable in Highland affairs, or an ardent Johnsonian, to feel at this point a large gratitude towards Boswell. One needs surely to have no more than an interest in human nature, in the drama of human events, and the most ordinary historical sense to appreciate the remarkable fact that Dr. Samuel Johnson actually met Flora Macdonald, talked with her at length, heard from her of her rescue of Prince Charles, and all within the classic but now crumbled walls of Kingsburgh. This fact was entirely due to Boswell's assiduity.

This meeting might well be described as the culminating

point in Boswell's effort in making the ten-year-old dream of the tour to the Hebrides come true. But his achievement does not end there. If Boswell had not been Boswell and had not retained and given to the world, more than ten years later on, his own observations, how little we should know about it all, how little not only about the meeting with Flora Macdonald but about what went before and came after! Even the most fervent admirer of Johnson's capacity for dignified reticence would, I think, have been disappointed if all we had had as an account of the affair had been these few lines which Johnson gives it:

> We were entertained with the usual hospitality by Mr. Macdonald and his lady, Flora Macdonald, a name that will be mentioned in history, and if courage and fidelity be virtues, mentioned with honour. She is a woman of middle stature, soft features, gentle manners and elegant presence.

If Boswell had not been Boswell, this is all that we should have had. But Boswell was, on this memorable occasion, not only Boswell, but Boswell at his best. His reporting is at its happiest—faithful, detailed and evocative, and he himself is at his most likable. He is friendly, warm-hearted, appreciative to the point of enthusiasm, yet without foolishness. And he and Johnson between them, as I shall hope shortly to show, capture the impression that the essential Flora Macdonald made when one first met her. As for his host, Allan Macdonald, Boswell discovers once again in his description of him written on the spot, and only very slightly altered for publication, his powers as a portrait painter of a Highlander of the period:

> It was fine to see Mr. Johnson light from his horse at Kingsburgh's, who received us most courteously, and after shaking hands supported Mr. Johnson into the house. He was quite the figure of a gallant Highlander—"the graceful mien and manly looks". He had his tartan plaid thrown about him, a large blue bonnet with a knot of black ribbon like a cockade, a brown short coat of a

kind of duffle, a tartan vest with gold buttons and gold button-
holes, a bluish filibeg, and tartan hose. He had jet-black hair tied
behind and with screwed ringlets on each side, and was a large
stately man, with a steady sensible countenance.

Boswell obviously enjoyed himself and made himself
pleasant at the supper over which this "figure of a gallant
Highlander" presided:

> We had as genteel a supper as one could wish to see, in particu-
> lar an excellent roast turkey, porter to drink at table, and after
> supper claret and punch. But what I admired was the perfect
> ease with which everything went on.

And if he adds, but only in his original notes, "My
facility of manners" (carefully underlined) "as Adam Smith
said of me, had fine play" the small boast came surely from
nothing more than a friendly heart in a happy mood.

There was, however, a shadow lurking at the back of
this agreeable scene and excellent supper. Allan Macdonald
was, as were many other Highland gentlemen of small estate
at this period, hardly pressed. His farm, to which he had but
recently succeeded, was failing, and he and his family were
on the verge of emigration. Boswell was aware of this:

> My heart was sore to recollect that Kingsburgh had fallen
> sorely back in his affairs, was under a load of debt, and intended to
> go to America. However, nothing but what was good was present,
> and I pleased myself by thinking that so fine a fellow would be well
> everywhere.

And if, after his "governor", as "honest Mr. Macqueen", the
minister, who was also present, called Johnson, had gone to
bed, if Boswell wound up this evening of sociability slightly
tinged with melancholy by getting mildly drunk, it was only
what was expected of him—or indeed of anyone who sat up
over the glasses with Macdonald of Kingsburgh late at night,
late in the year 1773 in the island of Skye.

It is understandable, but a pity, that we have no record

of the latter part of the conversation on that late evening. I admit that I would like to have known whether, as the punch sank lower in the last bowl, Kingsburgh talked of the future, and of his emigration, whether he blamed conditions for its necessity or admitted (as one must in honesty agree was so) that his own fecklessness had contributed its share. And, above all, I would like to have known whether he paid any tribute to his wife's undoubted cheerfulness and fortitude in facing the distressful departure. Probably nothing of the kind was spoken of. Kingsburgh was a Highlander and a gentleman. But one cannot help wondering. There were three bowls of punch, and plenty of wine had gone before them.

Boswell presumably did not disturb Dr. Johnson when he went late to bed in the room which he was sharing with the great man; for on the next morning when he emerged from his slight hangover (which we learn about only from his original notes) he found his companion in a beneficent mood. Johnson had been sleeping surrounded by tartan curtains, and in the bed on which Prince Charles had lain in 1746.

To see Mr. Samuel Johnson lying in Prince Charles's bed in the Isle of Skye in the house of Miss Flora Macdonald struck me with such a group of ideas as it is not easy to describe as the mind perceives them.[1]

[1] It is at this point in his published version that Boswell decides most obviously to protect himself from the imputation of Jacobite feelings. In his publication he precedes this passage by saying "Dr. Johnson's bed was the very bed in which the grandson of the unfortunate James the Second lay on one of the nights after the failure of his rash attempt in 1745–46". He then adds below a well-known and characteristic footnote in which he lays before us the mental processes he went through in trying to find a suitable way of describing Prince Charles without offending anyone. He proudly drags in the fact that he had referred the matter to George III himself who, according to Boswell, approved of his decision to call Prince Charles Prince on account of his Royal Sobieski blood. What had really happened was that Boswell had accosted the King at his levee in 1785 and had put before him his difficulties. The King apparently in order to get rid of Boswell had concluded the interview by saying that he really thought it of no consequence what title was used. This satisfied Boswell who retired delighted but not before (as Professor Pottle points out) he had informed the King that he, Boswell, was seventh cousin to Prince Charles, and that this implied cousinship to King George III himself.

In this room, which was much decorated with maps and prints, there hung "Hogarth's print of Wilkes grinning with the cap of liberty beside him". One pauses to wonder how on earth it got there. It is possible that Hogarth who had painted Flora when she was in London had given her this print as a memento of their meeting.

The presence of Wilkes's unprepossessing image, at any time distasteful to Johnson, did not, however, seem to disturb him. While Boswell was being sociable below on the previous evening, the old man had obviously sat reflecting and pondering by himself in this historic room, for he had written on a scrap of paper which he had left lying about *"Quantum cedat virtutibus aurum"* ("With virtue weighed what worthless trash is gold!"). When Boswell discovered this scrap of paper on the next morning he could not at first see the significance of it. But before the second edition of his book was out an "ingenious friend" of his had informed him. Johnson was obviously referring to the reward of £30,000 which the Government in 1746 had offered for the apprehension of Prince Charles, but by which no Highlander could be induced to betray his presence.

Boswell's discovery of this tell-tale piece of paper, coupled with Johnson's air of smiling and withdrawn contentment, which is implied in Boswell's account of him, has prompted some readers of the tour to speculate as to whether there was some element of conspiracy during his stay at Kingsburgh. Johnson had withdrawn early from the supper-room and before the glasses had begun to circulate. So too had his hostess who, in all probability, had shown him to his room (the travellers had gone straight in to the hall and stayed there to supper immediately after their nightfall arrival from Portree). Is it not possible then that he had taken this opportunity to talk with Flora and indeed to discover to her of some of his own thoughts? There have been some ingenious reconstructions of the "imaginary conversation" type on this theme.

It is just possible; and there is no reason why the more romantically minded Johnsonians (for there are such) should not weave their fancies about the idea. It is, however, I am afraid unlikely. It is not that Johnson was incapable of, or would have been averse to, such a conversation if he had thought it proper. He had an emotional curiosity which Boswell knew about, but which he did not always display to the younger man. It is more likely, however, that the cold which Johnson had caught on the rainy journey to Kingsburgh was the reason for his quiescence and for his early retiring. His hostess probably did show him to his room and did inform him of its history; Boswell's discovery of the scrap of paper on the following morning points in that direction. So also does a scrap of conversation recorded at breakfast on the next day:

> He said he would have given a good deal rather than not have lain in that bed. I said he was the lucky man; and to be sure it had been contrived between Mrs. Macdonald and him. She said, "you know young *bucks* are always favourites of the ladies."

But what points against the idea of anything like a private conversation having occurred between him and Flora is that after these few remarks he deliberately set out, and with an old man's courtesy, to draw from his hostess her account of her part in the affairs of 1746:

> He spoke of the Prince being here, and said to Mrs. Macdonald, "*Who* was with him? We were told in England there was one Miss Flora Macdonald with him." Said she, "They were very right."

It is extremely unlikely that Johnson would, for any reason, have gone to this length to deceive Boswell if he had talked the matter out with Flora the night before, and even more unlikely that she would have abetted him.

It was after this that she gave them a full account of the

K

rescue of 1746. Johnson listened to her with placid attention
and said, "all this should be written down". And with this
we hear the last of Flora Macdonald from Boswell in his
account of the tour.

To return to his first words in description of her, "a
little woman of mild and genteel appearance, mighty soft
and well-bred". There are those who are disappointed that
Boswell did not let himself go in more detail, and in what
is known as "colourful description" when he saw Flora
coming modestly in to the supper at which, for the first
time, she showed herself to her husband's guests. It seems
to them that in speaking of her in these apparently quiet
terms he was taking a leaf out of Johnson's book of restraint.
They are wrong; for Boswell's words in the original version
quoted above (incidentally a slight improvement on the
version for publication) were written immediately after his
meeting with Flora and long before he saw Johnson's description. They are wrong too, I believe, in wishing Boswell
to have decorated with any more unnecessary words his first
impression of her.

It is just possible, though he says nothing about it, that,
in his "romantick" notions in advance about what a Highland
heroine ought to look like, Boswell may have been a trifle
disappointed himself by the unassuming appearance of the
little married woman, mother of seven children and just
over fifty years of age, as she was when the travellers met
her. Or it is equally possible that disappointment may have
been read into his description of her by some of his
later readers filled with notions, not so much romantic as
sentimental and false, inspired by the gew-gaw tartan
romances of the neo-Jacobite school of fiction.

However, whether Boswell and even Johnson were disappointed at their first sight of the little woman (which is
doubtful) they were obviously soon impressed by her
voice, demeanour and manner—by the patent distinction
of her quality. "A little woman, of mild and genteel

appearance, mighty soft and well-bred"—"soft features, gentle manners and elegant presence." There are in the Highlands today ladies in all walks of life to whom such descriptions would apply; and I, for one, am quite content with the epithets and phrases which Johnson and Boswell used to present Flora Macdonald's appearance and to convey the impression that her quality made upon their first meeting with her.

There is a French word which for centuries has had a long lodging in Scotland, and has for us acquired new colourings. In the Scots tongue, douce does not only mean sweet and well-mannered, it implies a gentle and quiet charm compellingly exercised. To this quality of douceness Flora Macdonald added the distinction of Highland breeding and more than a touch of Highland fortitude. Johnson and Boswell, of course, both paid tribute to the way in which, on one celebrated occasion, she publicly showed this fortitude. We who come after them know how she also displayed fortitude in the more arduous because more long-drawn-out, wearisome and less obviously heroic circumstances of her private life. For it is indeed a mistake to think of Flora as the heroine only of the '45.

After her captivity, after her pardon and also after the considerable fêting which she received in Edinburgh and London, she returned eventually to the islands untouched either by the long period of anxiety which she must have endured or the fuss that had been made of her. When at home again she married Allan Macdonald it was not because he was the son of the gallant old Kingsburgh who had been concerned with her in the Prince's affairs, but because he was a suitable young man drawn from her own background. That was the background of the gentler classes in the old Hebridean and Gaelic life from which fate had so peremptorily, if briefly, called her, but in which she must now have supposed she would peaceably continue the rest of her existence.

This, however, was denied to her. The first twenty-five years of her married life were passed in the gradual realization of the fact that her class and kind in the Gaelic life of Scotland were doomed. By the time that Johnson and Boswell visited her she had known that this doom had reached her and her own household. In 1773 the family of Kingsburgh were already preparing to uproot themselves from all the circumstances which they held dear and to emigrate.

This they did in 1774 and to North Carolina. No sooner were the Macdonalds settled there, however, than the American War of Independence engulfed them. Flora's husband and son were captured and held captive, while fighting on the Royalist side. She returned to the Hebrides and eventually to Skye. On the way her ship was attacked by a French privateer and in the action, in which she assisted the sailors, her arm was broken. She died in 1790 and is buried in a spot set apart for the graves of the Kingsburgh family.

It is usual to point out that through her bravery Flora Macdonald imperilled her life and fortune for the House of Stuart in 1746 and for the House of Hanover in the American War and at sea. Less spectacular, but no less remarkable, is the bravery which sustained her throughout the sad and slow decline in condition and circumstance of her family and kind. All contemporary evidence bears witness to the courage and cheerfulness which she showed to the end. The calm, characteristic and wholly feminine fortitude which she displayed in the rescue of 1746 was not inspired by a sudden flash of transitory and youthful heroism, it was a quality she was to sustain throughout her sixty-eight years of life.

Such was the little woman of "soft features, gentle manners and elegant presence" whom Johnson and Boswell met in 1773 in her home in Skye which she was shortly to leave, as she then believed, forever.

inspired by the Jacobite past of Scotland at which no nonsense had been spoken.

At most of such assemblies, whether in Scotland or
England, the sensitive observer can feel little but embarrassment; and the last thing that he could wish for would
be the presence of the shades of Johnson and Boswell, or
indeed of any men of good sense from the 18th century. But
here on South Uist in 1953 it was different. There was no
pretence and much of quiet reality. We were here to honour
the memory of the girl from South Uist, and amongst the
children of the children of those who had known her when
she was a girl. The travellers of 1773 would, I am sure, have
been interested and glad to have mingled and talked with
the people of South Uist of 1953, the posterity of those
whom they did not get quite far enough to have visited a
hundred and eighty years earlier. Johnson would have been
glad to have seen his prophecy about Flora Macdonald
being fulfilled, and I cannot help feeling that he would have
been touched to have heard the words of his prophecy
being spoken on such a spot at such a time.

And as for Boswell, my friend Boswell, I can see him
after the short ceremony had ended, eager and voluble,
threading his way through the Gaelic-chattering crowd,
anxious to shake the hand of and to speak with the great-
great-grandson of the little woman whom he had met on
Skye so long ago.

VII

THE RIGHT END OF THE ISLAND

SKYE can beat all one's defences down. All attempts one may have made to look coolly, clearly, objectively on this somewhat over-publicized, over-romanticized island are, upon one's return to it, after long absence, doomed to failure: one surrenders, usually after the third day, and without a struggle, to Skye's overpowering appeal to the senses.

For it is overpowering. It is an appeal which conquers all that man can do to kill the atmosphere of the island by so pitiably reducing its population, by sentimentalizing its history by false romanticism and by vulgarizing its beauty by exploitation. The very stones, grasses, seas and air of Skye are triumphant over all such things.

Railway and steamboat posters and even films in inglorious Technicolor on Skye may insult one's recollections of the Western hills and seas. Dance bands may ooze out syncopated versions of what are known as "Skye and Hebridean melodies". Or that unfortunate phrase may bring to mind another sound made with more serious intent but with equally lamentable results—the thin high wailing of a ladies' clarsach—accompanied choir in the back quarters of some Edinburgh or Glasgow tea-room hired for the purposes of a "cultural ceilidh" or in the more gilded surroundings of the drawing-room of some London hostess who has fallen under the influence of Celtic Twilight Sleep. The ear of fancy can still remotely catch the sound of that wailing and the eye can in recollection summon up the image of the choir plucking timidly at the strings of their little Highland harps, looking like nothing so much as a group of tartan hens pathetically trying to struggle through a wire fence. One may recall all these things, but the fact of Skye remains.

It not only remains, but proclaims itself serenely and to none with greater or more poignant effect than to the traveller who has not been made aware of it for some time. To him, at the first sight of the fantastic airborne peaks of the Cuillins cutting the clear skies above him, or of the antlers of them tossing away the spume of the mist and the rain out into the Atlantic, it will seem that all such petti-nesses, such vulgarities, such pathetic follies, are themselves tossed away into the realm of laughter or the limbo of forgotten things.

As I journeyed to the North-west of the island, to the ultimate points of their tour reached by Johnson and Boswell, I enjoyed as never before this overpowering appeal of the fact of Skye. Overpowering it may have been, but I found it more exhilarating, even intoxicating, than over-whelming.

The long spell of quiet, drawn-out Autumn weather was beginning to break; but it did not break with one sudden crack. One morning would dawn as tranquil as those which I had hitherto enjoyed since I had set out from Edinburgh, only to be followed on the next day by storm and wind and rain. That storm and wind and rain would at short intervals not so much cease as occasionally retreat round the corners in order to spring upon the huge landscape and seascape at dusk, and with all the greater force. During these intervals the physical fact of Skye emerged not battered or subdued, but sombre, angry and yet still triumphant. On the next day again we would be back to tranquillity; and to look at them you would think that these mountains and seas had never been touched by anything more forceful than pale Northern sunshine and cool Autumnal zephyrs. As November retreated, and as I leisurely went further northwards and westwards, I got the impression of having the island more and more to myself. The last tourist had long gone away. The true winter routine of the real inhabitants had not yet quite begun. Life seemed, and for my special purpose, inspection and pleasure, to be standing still.

I rebuked myself for not having returned to Skye earlier. Travelling amongst the seven hundred and eighty-seven islands of Scotland from Unst at the North of Shetland to the most south-westerly dracaena-fringed rock sheltering in the warm seas by the coasts of Kintyre, Ireland and Ayrshire, has always been one of my primary pleasures. And never have I had greater delight in this pleasure than since the war, when I have had more leisure to indulge in it. Though I had known Skye as a child and a young man, I had not come back there for years. Perhaps (and I now admitted this to myself) I had yielded to a touch of unconscious snobbery in avoiding what had seemed to me to be the obvious. Or, more charitably, it may have been that with the pleasure of finding new islands and enjoying all over again certain small intimate ones which I had considered as my own, I had simply not had the time to include this the largest and most famous of the Hebrides. Well, for whatever reason I had neglected it, here I was again and enjoying in a kind of physical way I had never done before the "obviousness" of Skye. If this was obviousness, I reflected, looking round on the splendid panorama of the North West on a day after storm, I could well afford to give subtlety in my insular wanderings something of a rest.

The gusto of my pleasure in Skye at this season and at this my long-postponed revisitation of it was increased by the reason which had brought me here. There was a purpose in my wandering alone from Raasay to Portree, and then northwards to the ghost of Kingsburgh and finally further northwards and westwards to the ultimate points of the tour of 1773. And that purpose which had given me an added zest in Skye was in itself much helped by the quality of what I saw and felt around me. Upon the abandoned road through the mountain pass from Fort Augustus to Glenmoriston, I had, through the very wildness and desolation of the storm-swept path which we beheld, become so keenly alive to the fact of the travellers' presence a hundred and seventy-nine years earlier. So here too, in this lovely scenery that was lying lonely upon the lip of winter and, so it seemed at this season, upon the edge of the world, I felt once again as close as I had ever been to the two travellers.

And indeed, though they do not say so, to the travellers themselves it must have seemed something like the edge of the world when they came to the North West of Skye in the Autumn of 1773. This was, they knew, as far as they could reach in the Northern and Western direction, and, if they looked at the map, they cannot surely have failed to be a little impressed by their arrival in such a place. In Gaelic, Skye, because of its shape, is known as the "flying island". To me, as I have looked at it on the large-scale elevation maps with the island attractively coloured as it often is to mark the levels of the various heights in green, gold, brown and black, and set in a sea of conventionally perpetually summer blue, to me it has often appeared rather as the leaping island. It leaps in an extravagant upthrust sprawling gesture from out of the heart of the mainland mountains into the northern wastes of the Atlantic far away. In the remoter circumstances of Johnson's and Boswell's day it must have seemed to be leaping and sprawling even more remotely.

Such feelings, if they had them, may have been softened by the amenities of Dunvegan Castle, but they cannot but have been continually aware of the high point of detachment upon which the old castle on the rock stood. And when, even though it was on their way South, they came by Talisker, more wildly situated than Dunvegan, they must have felt, even if they did not appreciate, the overwhelming presence of the Western mountains and the Western seas.

Boswell does indeed hint at the wildness of the seas and the rocks by Ulinish and Talisker as if their presence had made him, despite the domestic comfort he enjoyed within doors, slightly uncomfortable. And there is the scene when Boswell argues with Lady Macleod about the necessity of her keeping to the rock of Dunvegan at all costs and despite all inconveniences, and when, to his gratification, Johnson "with a strong voice and most determined manner" supports him. "Madam, rather than quit the old rock Boswell would live in a pit. He'd make his bedchamber in the dungeon. . . . Madam, were it in Asia I would not quit the rock."

Apart from this passing whim of "romantick" or "feudal" argument, however, and apart from a few other indications that the mountains were large, the seas sometimes rough, the rain often severe, and the weather occasionally fine, neither here nor anywhere else in Skye does the physical fact, the truly extraordinary appearance, of Skye seem to have made any impression on the travellers except in its effect on their comfort. No one who has any feeling for the 18th-century world of Johnson and Boswell or any knowledge of the way their minds worked expects them to have been so untrue to type or to themselves as to have been moved to awe or touched in their sense of beauty by Skye. At the same time no one from this age of today who has seen, and as I did, who has walked alone through the North West of the island in the full pride of the dying Autumn season, can fail to wonder, if only in passing, at their complete and obviously un-affected imperviousness to all they saw around them out of doors. Skye, and particularly the parts they saw of it, is so unusual that it impresses everyone today. It is no mere romantic corner of Great Britain (a land not given to remarkable extremes) but a place that can strike silence and wonder into visitors from all over the world. You would have thought that Boswell and Johnson would have noted the effect of its appearance, if only to say how much it impressed them and how much they disliked it. But no; they said nothing, save perhaps this:

"Boswell, we came in at the wrong end of this island," said Johnson when they reached the comfort of Dunvegan. "Sir," replied his disciple, "it was best to keep this for the last," to which Johnson, looking round at Lady Macleod's drawing-room, said, "I'd have it both first and last."

Johnson's glee when he found himself in the agreeable circumstances of Dunvegan (Boswell says he became quite joyous, and laughed) is understandable. He had had, up to this date upon their tour, one of the worst and most trying journeys from Kingsburgh. After he and Boswell had left Allan Macdonald's boat, which took them across an arm of the sea, they had to cover very rough and wet ground, which necessitated Johnson dismounting and trudging through the bog. Later on, at a very narrow pass overhanging a "steep declivity" he fell off his horse flat on his back, fortunately on the safe side. At times the travellers felt so remote and lost that they were grateful for occasional sights of the sea— "that universal connection". At the end of all this the large rooms, the warmth, the fine family pictures, the "admirable tea", the kindliness of Lady Macleod, the laird's mother, and the pleasant civilities of his young sisters who had been "bred in England", must have come upon Johnson's spirit, as well as upon his physical state of being, like a balm—and all the more agreeable for being unexpected.

Johnson had most certainly enjoyed the innocent and gay hospitality of Raasay. Its vivacity, however, its full-bloodedness, may have somewhat exhausted the old man. The constricted circumstances of Raasay's house full to over-flowing with people of all ages who were not only ready to burst into song on any occasion, but, according to Boswell, danced every night of the year, may have tired him. Indeed he rather pathetically said to Boswell, who had remarked how happy the Raasay folk had been to have him there, "Yet we have not been able to entertain them very much." At the farm at Coirechatachan he had enjoyed himself and was, as we shall see, to enjoy himself even more later on. But here too the ceaseless flow of pre-puritan Celtic gaiety, expressed often in song and conversation in a language he could not understand, tired him.

At Kingsburgh the travellers had been more comfortable than at any place since they had entered the Highlands, and though there is no question that Johnson was moved to find himself in such a place and in such company he may very well have thought of Kingsburgh as being the climax of the Skye part of the journey. He may have wondered whether there was much point in pressing on their travels to the far North West. He had, it is true, met the young laird of Macleod who was staying at Raasay when he was there and had taken a great fancy to him, but was it really worth all this intensely uncomfortable exertion to see him in his own house? After all had he not already seen what the upper classes of Skye could offer at Macdonald's at Armadale? And he had not been much impressed by that. But the first half-hour of rest and refreshment and easy society at the truly feudal yet civilized seat of the Macleods of Dunvegan must have convinced him that all this effort to reach the ultimate point of Skye had been really worth while. "Boswell" (not "sir", mark you, but Boswell), "we came in at the wrong end of the island" is one of the most spontaneously heartfelt of his recorded remarks.

And if I did not go quite so far as to echo that memorable exclamation of content rumbling down to me from the past, by saying when I reached Dunvegan "I have arrived at the right end of the island", I did admit to myself that I had come to one of the most unexpectedly pleasant spots on it in an unexpectedly pleasant way. By the time I reached Dunvegan I had, since Kingsburgh, abandoned anything like the exact route of 1773, and had been wandering through alternate sunshine and storm vaguely in the Western and Northern parts of Skye. I had, of course, been to the places Boswell and Johnson had visited and written about, but not in due order and without much plan beyond enjoying myself and gathering general impressions. Now, when I reached Dunvegan, the first point the travellers had made in their Western trip in Skye, and which I had made the last, I decided that this was the spot to rest and re-collect myself and my thoughts.

Circumstances seemed to agree with me and to point in this direction. I found Dunvegan Castle empty, but Mrs. Macleod of Macleod had most kindly left instructions that I was to be allowed to wander as I willed throughout the castle and its policies. This I did, reflecting how oddly solitary my perambulations and equitations, as Johnson would have called them, had been—that is if I discounted the presence of my companion on the hill pony in Inverness-shire. But then he had been ideally silent, and had by his strong, sensible, and yet occasionally monosyllabic presence by my side only served as a kind of emphasis to our joint solitary state. No, by solitary I meant not pushed around by other people, not prevented by other people or other circumstances from wandering and observing and thinking as I pleased. Above all I had leisure and freedom to do that wandering and thinking alone—alone save for the sometimes shadowy and sometimes pertinaciously real presence in my imagination of the two who had been before me in 1773.

And so it was at Dunvegan. Alone I wandered about the castle looking at the noble pictures, the deep, comfortable and in their antique way noble, yet not grandly spacious, rooms and stairways. I had childish memories of Dunvegan, and had carried over the years impressions of something vast. Those impressions had been fortified in the intervening time by Boswell's feudally magnificent descriptions and by the prints of pictures in old editions. Now, as happens to so many places which have been carried about only in the retina of the childish eye and which are come upon again in later life, the place seemed not so much to have shrunk as to have become more compact. In some ways this made it more impressive. Compact, thick-walled, placed upon a sea-washed rock, here was a true castle, not a "romantick" dream, but a true castle fortified in time and against time.

This was the castle in which Johnson and Boswell had spent nine of the most contented days of their journey and in which Johnson talked as nobly as ever he talked and was recorded as he had never been recorded before. And in it I wandered alone and without being told what to do. Even any sense of purpose, any recollection of what I was here for was quiescent. I looked at nothing simply because I ought to look at it, inspected nothing simply because it had to be seen. I merely laid myself open to impression and to my own thoughts. I even came by chance, and by no more than chance, upon Johnson's well-known letter sent to Macleod thanking him before leaving Skye for his hospitality. It was there framed upon the wall; and as I passed down that wall I took it in my stride, or rather in my stroll, scarcely bothering to read all of it that was exposed; for I knew it well already. Still, it was interesting seeing it there. Interesting! Perhaps a little more than that. Perhaps the faintest *frisson* passed through me as I paused opposite it.

Dear Sir
    We are now on the margin of the sea, waiting for boat and wind. Boswel[1] [sic] grows impatient; but the kind treatment which I find everywhere I go makes me leave with some heaviness of heart an Island which I am not likely to see again. . . .

"An Island which I am not likely to see again." With the slight melancholy of those words in the well-known handwriting and in the fading ink sounding in my mind, I wandered out in the Castle policies and on this the last

[1] Birkbeck Hill says that Johnson often left out the final consonant in Boswell's name in his handwriting.

day of this remarkable Autumn weather that was to be allowed to me, I pondered autumnally upon Dunvegan and the West of Skye and the travellers who had been here.

No wonder that Johnson had put the characteristically nostalgic touch of "an Island which I am unlikely to see again" in his letter of thanks and farewell. He had been uninterruptedly content, even happy, at Dunvegan, and that contentment lasted for days after he had left the castle and until he and Boswell got to Coirechatachan. There that contentment had not so much faded; it was merely that the old circumstances of movement, excitement and curiosity, not unmixed with romance, that had held sway at Raasay and elsewhere had come upon him again. And that is very different from contentment.

At Dunvegan and in the West, however, Johnson had luxuriated in a sense of civilized enjoyment. The result was that his power of talk, which may well have been dammed up for the past week or so, was released, and the torrent of conversation that flowed forth from him showed him, for the first time in all Boswell's writings about him, at his most characteristic and at his best. Excellent and fascinating though they may be, the previous extracts of recorded conversation in the tour do not come up to what we are given in this part of Skye. They are a foretaste of, indeed they are as good as, what we are to get years later on in Boswell's greater work *The Life*. It is here at Dunvegan, Ulinish and Talisker that the Doctor stalks on to the stage (followed it is true at a respectful distance by his hosts and other Highland friends and acquaintances) and commands that stage and everyone who looks at it. It is this that is the important, the significant thing about Dunvegan in the tour as recorded by Boswell. And it is a tribute to Boswell's powers and perception as a biographer that he seems to have recognized this significance. If Johnson stalks on to the stage at Dunvegan, Boswell quietly retreats to the wings, notebook in hand. It was not only Johnson who

L

gave us of his best at Dunvegan. In his *rôle* as a biographer Boswell seldom surpassed what he achieved at Dunvegan, Ulinish and Talisker.

And what talk he has preserved for us here, and on what a characteristically Johnsonian range of subjects!—Making women do penance in church for fornication, from which it was but a step to discussing the various degrees of guilt in adultery (a subject started by Macleod on the first evening in the Castle, and apparently without offence to anyone); Dr. Cadogan's book on the gout, and the merits of practising what you preach either as a physician or a moralist; natural goodness; Burke's oratory; the habit of strong drink (with some carelessly produced references to Johnson's own past in this habit); the merits of cloth made from vegetable as compared with that made from animal substances; the clothes Johnson would insist on his ladies wearing were he to keep a seraglio (with a famous and humiliating drubbing delivered to Boswell who ventured to "laugh immoderately" at the idea); polygamy; cunning; idleness; antiquarianism; second sight; Macpherson and Ossian; the assiduity of the Scotch clergy as compared with the English; duelling; the duties of a Highland landlord; the commercial age; an account of "the whole process of tanning"; the operation of coining; the nature of milk; the science of butchery; fame in London; the speed of horses (with references to Johnson's own fox-hunting past); the abilities of the wicked; the comparative discomfort of prisons and ships; poetry; religious feeling; and, of course, some passing references to death.

These are but some of the topics touched upon by Johnson during this memorable period. And not only did he touch upon them; always he seemed to be in command of them and of the company who heard him. Seldom, in all the records of his conversation, has his talk been so luminous and so exultant. He was happy; and he made those round him happy as only he could by giving them (and for once this *cliché* is justified) "a feast of reason and a flow of soul".

Small wonder that when the laird one night was surrounded by a number of his clan and when Johnson sat with him in the midst of them, Boswell records that they "listened with wonder and pleasure while he harangued"; and that when Mr. Macqueen heard him on the subject of coins he thought Johnson "had been bred at the mint"; and that later when the sage was discoursing on beer that "he had been bred a brewer". Small wonder too that Boswell was enjoying himself. Listening here remotely to his mentor on the top of his form, Boswell compares himself to a dog

> who has got hold of a large piece of meat, and runs away with it to a corner, where he may devour it in peace, without any fear of others taking it from him. In London, Reynolds, Beauclerk, and all of them are contending who shall have Mr. Johnson. We are feasting upon him undisturbed at Dunvegan.

One can sympathize with Boswell in his only complaint during this period, which was that Johnson gave him so much to remember and record when in company that he had to spend all his spare and private time writing up his journal, and could scarcely ever see Johnson alone.

And so it happens that the recorder of Boswell's movements upon this tour must too leave him alone at his private, exhausting but absorbing task of recording the golden hours of the great man's talk. He must leave him alone for the simple reason that there is nothing that we know about Boswell in his long solitary hours of writing during this period of comparative rest and refreshment. And, even when he was not alone, but was one of the company whom Johnson so delighted, he is much more out of the picture than at any other time since the two travellers reached the Highlands.

There are, it is true, one or two glimpses that we catch

of him. There was the partly ludicrous and slightly pathetic incident when Colonel Macleod made an unwitting reference to Boswell's "forwardness" in manners (being sure that, if the King of Sweden would not speak to Johnson and Boswell, Boswell would certainly speak to the King) followed by Boswell's characteristically surprised and half-wounded defence of the quality of forwardness in himself —a defence which he offers to his readers only. There was Boswell's topographical attempts to explain the appearance of the alleged temple of Anaitis, fully displayed only in the unpublished version. There is the aside which Boswell permits himself, apparently to himself alone (for it too appears only in the unpublished version) when he expresses his lively fear of the itch, bugs and other parasites. This, as Professor Pottle claims, is another indication that the prevalence of vermin in the 18th century has been much exaggerated. "This passage shows that Boswell at the age of thirty-three had never had scabies and was familiar neither with the habits or appearance of bugs."

And finally, as already referred to, there is the ridiculous figure he was compelled to cut when he laughed at the idea of Johnson keeping a seraglio, and when Johnson, to pay him out, expatiated on Boswell's duties were he to be admitted to this establishment of Johnson's: "Yes, if he were properly prepared; and he'd make a very good eunuch. He'd be a fine gay [fat] animal. He'd do his part very well." Even in the unpublished version from which this last sentence is taken, Boswell cannot bring himself to tell us in detail how Johnson continued. He merely says that

> He returned to my office as eunuch and expatiated upon it with such fluency that it really hurt me. He made me quite contemptible for the moment. Luckily the company did not take it so clearly as I did.

Then with characteristic good humour, and with an equally characteristic pat on the back for himself, he adds:

Perhaps too I imagined him to be more serious in this extra-ordinary raillery than he really was. But I am of firmer metal than Langton, and can stand the rub better.

It is, however, only in these and a few other incidents that Boswell appears at all distinctly in the light in this corner of Skye. For the rest of the time he is borne happily un-resisting and equally happily noting and recording the large flow of Johnson's talk.

As I sat in the policies of Dunvegan on this the very last day of Autumn (for I had now quite made up my mind that this was the final drop of 1952 sunshine that I could extract from the year, and that the true winter, not the transitory gales, would sweep everything away on the next day), as I sat there and looked out over the blood-red of some miraculously surviving fuchsia blooms on to the grey of the castle and the green and the blue of the sea beyond, I wondered what there was left for me to say. Dunvegan of 1773 with its huge river of happy talk, its small incidents, amusing, informative or pathetic, has been caught and held for us in Boswell's narrative. He captured it for posterity as surely as for a few hours this Autumn day was capturing and holding motionless for me this magical autumnal scene with the same old castle still set in the middle of it. It is all there for the readers of today as crystal clear as for the readers of 1785 when Boswell's book first came out. This, the first really lengthy great essay in setting the essence of Johnson's genius down, is as enjoyable today as ever it was; and further comment on it would be superfluous.

Comment would have been superfluous; but I did allow myself reflection on two of the other members of the cast who had, as it were, followed Johnson about on the stage at Dunvegan and the North West.

Norman Macleod of Macleod, twentieth chief and host to Boswell and Johnson at this castle, was a romantic and likable figure. Boswell does not give us one of his excellent pen-pictures of him, but by inference leaves a very agreeable impression of this high-spirited and generous youth. He tells us how popular he was with his people, how he loved to have his clan around him and to visit them and to enjoy himself with them in their homes.

> "Government," said he, "has deprived us of our ancient power; but it cannot deprive us of our domestic affections. I would rather drink punch in one of their houses (meaning the houses of his people) than be enabled by their hardships to have claret in my own."

Johnson took a strong fancy to Macleod, and when he heard that he had been left with debts of £40,000 and annuities to the amount of £1,300 a year, he said:

> "Sir if he gets the better of all this he'll be a hero; and I hope he shall. He's a fine fellow Macleod. I've not met with a young man who had more desire to learn, or who has learnt more. I've seen nobody that I wish more to do a kindness than Macleod."

It is characteristic of Macleod that he should have offered Johnson the gift of the Island of Isay, which was in one of the sea lochs in his estate, provided Johnson occupied it for three months of the year. Johnson was highly delighted with the notion and received with satisfaction the toasts which the company gave to him when they drank his health in the territorial manner—"Island Isay your health!" Boswell does not record, possibly because he did not know it, that they could hardly give him the territorial title of "Isay" direct without the word "Island". Isay is a variant of the Gaelic for Jesus. But I think Johnson would have been all the more delighted if someone had told him what Isay meant in Gaelic. It would have been something to have taken his title with him into England and into the English language, and have been toasted in a Fleet Street tavern as "Island Jesus your health!"

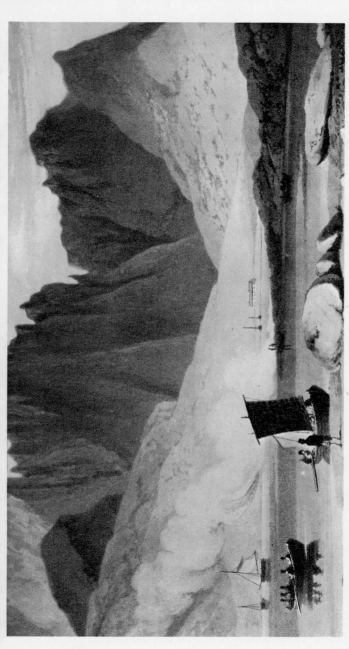

'The Black Coast of Skye.' An early romantick view of part of the
Cuillin hills

(Courtesy of the British Museum)

Dunvegan Castle

(Courtesy of the British Museum)

Macleod's history in the years after the travellers had left is well known, but it is perhaps worth recalling here. It was unfortunate for his tenantry that this generous landlord should have turned his dashing temperament towards the army and a distinguished military career, which led him away from Skye. He managed to amass in India, where he soldiered brilliantly, a sufficient fortune to pay off his debts, but like many another man of spirit he could acquire money but could not keep it. He left the estate in 1801 more heavily in debt than when it came to him.

During his career his warm heart earned him many eulogies, including one the reason for which would certainly not have pleased Johnson. Burns referred to him as:

> . . . a chieftain worth gowd
> Though bred amang mountains o' snaw.

Not exactly Burns at his best! (Not even accurate: there is probably more snowfall in Burns's native Ayrshire than in Skye.) But the lines were at least a tribute to what must have been a generous, and when one thinks of Macleod, a characteristic, impulse on his part. They were a tribute to the fact that at the time of the French Revolution Macleod had become in Scotland one of the "Friends of the People". It is amusing to think of the comments of his neighbour, Lord Macdonald of Slate, when he heard the news.

I see Macleod as a true Celtic chieftain, one of the last of his kind, but living into a new age to which he adapted himself more successfully than did his namesakes at Raasay. He was probably amongst the last of his kind to speak a certain amount of Gaelic naturally; for it is difficult to see how he could have moved as freely and as friendlily as he did amongst his tenantry without doing so. Yet one cannot but regret the very success of his career in the army and elsewhere away from Skye. He can be described, despite the debts he left, as being, from the point of view of British glory, a success in the new age, but in the end it was the new age that was successful in overcoming him; and it was Skye that suffered.

It is pleasant to record that he transmitted to his grandson that quality of generosity towards and feeling for his tenantry and clan which he showed in his own youth. It is melancholy to have to add however that that same grandson ruined himself nobly in the exercise of this quality. He succeeded in 1835 to an estate even further encumbered with debt. He struggled as manfully as he could to maintain his position: he did more. During the truly appalling potato famine or starvation of the 1840s which struck the Gaelic world not only in Ireland but in the Western Highlands and Islands, he did everything in his power to relieve and support his tenantry. But his power was limited. A little over a hundred years ago he left his house and home, a man ruined in his efforts to support not only his ancient and honourable family, but his people of Skye. He became a clerk in a Government office in London where his scholarly knowledge of languages was of use. How Johnson would have loved the man, how nobly he would have spoken of him! And how glad Johnson would be to hear that for a long time now the Macleods have been back at Dunvegan!

The other figure which I see distinctly at Dunvegan and in the Western part of the tour of Skye is that of the Reverend Donald Macqueen. I have always had a fondness for this amiable minister, and though Boswell presents him to us in quiet colours he has been none the less very much alive for me. He lived for me even more clearly in my imagination as I pondered at Dunvegan and looked down at the castle and the countryside in which those disputes (perhaps a little timid on his side, perhaps a little overbearing on his antagonist's) took place between him and Johnson.

Macqueen's appearance and manner, slow-spoken, decent, elderly and dressed in sober black, has been sketched for us in a few words by Boswell on the occasion of his first meeting with him on the sail to Raasay, and I have already spoken of his "moderate" theological and political position in his church, and of the esteem in which he was held in Skye. If he had left the travellers at Raasay and had not gone on to Dunvegan and the West with them we would have been left only with the impression of him as a courteous, reserved Highland minister with the quiet good breeding of his kind untinged with fanaticism. At Dunvegan, however, and thereafter, he comes out more into the open. And though he never for a moment lost the carriage of his manners and breeding, and never showed a touch of the religious fanaticism which later travellers discovered, or claimed to have discovered, in Skye, we find him as a man of opinions, and prepared to stand up for these opinions, even against Johnson, and even if rather ineffectually.

Macqueen was a gentleman, well read and religious. At the back of all this, however, he was a Skyeman, and an islander, and a Celt to the core. He was prepared to listen respectfully to Johnson on almost any subject, including morals and church matters, but when it came to the world of Celtic belief and of Celtic tradition and literature he had to say his say, even if he didn't always say it very well. His opinion on some of these subjects, on which he was really qualified to speak, was damaged by the fact that he also fancied himself as an antiquarian in matters outside the Celtic world; and in arguing about these he put himself so obviously in the wrong that his other views were suspect— and have remained suspect to generations of readers of Boswell and Johnson.

At his first meeting with Johnson he spoke against second sight. This almost certainly surprised Johnson a little, but he could not bring any arguments to bear against Macqueen on this matter even if he had wished to. Johnson had heard of second sight as a strange peculiarity possessed by the Highlanders and Hebrideans alone in Great Britain. Johnson had never before been to the Highlands, and was, amongst other things, quite frankly anxious to collect information on Highland peculiarities about which he did not know but had only heard of. But here the Skye minister, who had spent his life on the island and who was a son of Skye, was on his own ground. He spoke of his own experience and from his own experience expressed his disbelief; and when he coupled second sight with the superstitious belief in witchcraft and told of a challenge on this subject which he had offered from his own pulpit, there was nothing which Johnson could say.

When it came later on at Dunvegan to Macqueen's dabbling in remote antiquarianism, archaeology and the like, Johnson and he had common ground on which they could argue. And Johnson good-humouredly demolished poor Macqueen's nonsense about the ruins near Dunvegan being the remains of a temple of the Goddess Anaitis. With somewhat less good humour, both Johnson and Boswell took up Macqueen on the literary subject of Ossian. And here neither side would give way. Boswell irritably and not very perceptively says "Mr. Macqueen is the most obstinate man I ever found. He has not firmness of mind sufficient to break. He is like a supple willow. No sooner is he pressed down than he rises again just where he was." Neither the Ossian claims nor Mr. Macqueen, as I believe, can be dismissed quite so easily as that.

To take up these three points of discussion—second sight was one of the many subjects on which Johnson found it alluring to speculate. He had an intensely curious mind on such things, and, one suspects, may have been disappointed at meeting so blank, and, in the circumstances, so authoritative a denial from the Highland minister. As for Macqueen's views, there is no reason to suppose that so decent, honourable and truthful a man was not sincere in his refutation to Johnson of second sight *from his own experience*. With all that, one should remember too that he had two good reasons to make him wish to express his

disbelief to the great English doctor, moralist and churchman whom he had just met.

The first was the straightforward one that he would
find such a belief offensive to his faith, and particularly so
on the Skye of the 18th century where part of a Christian
minister's task was to contend with hidden pagan beliefs
that were then much stronger than now. The second was
that Macqueen, especially in the first hour or so of his
acquaintance with Johnson, would naturally wish to defend
the reputation of his island and his own Celtic people from
the suspicion of superstition.

Even at this day and time, remote from the 18th century
and away from Skye, one can sympathize with Macqueen.
His people, as he very well knew, were not savages, and he
would be chary of admitting so easily before this great
man to what might appear to be a crude and savage belief.
One does not need to be a Highland minister but only a
Scotsman of Highland blood living in Scotland to know the
defensive feeling that makes one deny the ready-made
rumours of the Celtic "other world" with which some of
the best intentioned visitors come so well supplied to
Scotland, and about which they are so full of curiosity. It
is not that one disbelieves, it is merely that something like
a sense of decency, coupled with national pride, makes one
withdraw at the first eager question and seek refuge in
denial.

Then there is another important point that should be
remembered. Second sight, even if one only admits its
possibility, is a most uncomfortable thing. It must obviously be uncomfortable for those who believe that they
possess the power of seeing tragic or even lesser events in
the future. It is uncomfortable also for any thinking man
to entertain the notion that such a belief may be a true
one. The thing smells of Determinism; and one naturally
recoils from it.

Most people of Highland blood who have moved amongst

Highlanders and Hebrideans, in so far as they allow themselves to think about second sight at all, hope that it is not true, yet are assailed by doubts that it may be. Moreover anyone who has lived amongst the Celtic Highlanders knows that this is one of the most difficult subjects to get a true Highlander to discuss. And it is next door to impossible to get any Highlander to admit that he has the faculty of second sight or has ever even transitorily suffered from possessing it. Any reader of these pages who, upon a Highland tour or jaunt of his own, encounters a Highlander who claims easily to have had second sight is herewith assured that he is talking to an impostor.

Poor Macqueen's essay into learned archaeology with the "temple of Anaitis" is worth no more than an indulgent smile from the learned, and a slightly more sympathetic one from myself who knows how easy it is for someone living as remotely as Macqueen was to let his fancy run riot. There is no need here to retell the well-known story of how Johnson defeated Macqueen's theory that certain ruins near Dunvegan had once been a temple to the Goddess Anaitis of Asia Minor referred to by Pausanias and the elder Pliny. This, however, can be added, which Macqueen did not discover and which Johnson had no means of knowing. The ruins were ecclesiastical and their Gaelic name (spelt by Boswell) Annuit really derived from Annait or Annaid, the oldest ecclesiastical term in the islands indicating here the mother church or original monastic foundations.

With the dispute between Macqueen on the one hand and Johnson (with Boswell in the background) on the other on the authenticity of Ossian, the remote and shadowy Highland poet, one comes upon a subject which could take up the remainder of this book and then leave volumes of (to me) fascinating speculation untouched. Avoiding, however, the temptation to lengthen even this one chapter unduly, I embark upon a recollection of, a setting forth of, this dispute only in so far as it affects the men who were disputing, the Johnsonian and Boswellian tour itself, and the Scotland of their time.

Johnson's violent and celebrated quarrel with James Macpherson over the authenticity of Macpherson's Ossian and his translations from the Gaelic of what he, Macpherson, claimed to be ancient and complete epics from Scotland's remote past had taken place well before the tour to the Hebrides. There were those who said that Johnson had come to Scotland to gather evidence on Macpherson's own ground with which to refute him. This is much of an exaggeration. Johnson may have had the passing notion of hearing a little more to Macpherson's discredit while he was in Scotland, but he would never have made such a journey merely to refute someone whom he considered he had already abolished.

Johnson's case against Macpherson was twofold. First he claimed that Macpherson had fathered an impudent fraud upon the world, that his claim to have discovered a manuscript containing an ancient Celtic epic was a lie, that Macpherson may have picked up vague oral traditions in the Highlands and a few scribblings from these traditions, but that he himself had forged the rest, and had out of his own invention blown up this huge piece of cheating to the size in which he presented it. Second, he dismissed the works themselves as worthless. When Dr. Blair asked him whether any man of a modern age could have written such poems, Johnson replied, "Yes, sir, many men, many women and many children." He later said that anyone could write such stuff if he could "abandon himself to it".

Johnson's polemics against Macpherson, and in particular his letter to him ("I hope I shall never be deterred from detecting what I think a cheat by the menaces of a ruffian"), are famous, and make good reading. And perhaps because of this and because of the, to them, shadowy nature of the whole dispute, most English readers of Boswell and Johnson accept without question the belief that Johnson demolished Macpherson's claims and the merits of Ossian itself. This is, to put it mildly, an exaggeration.

We now know that there did indeed exist in the Highlands and Islands considerable fragments of long traditional Gaelic narrative and descriptive poems, that some of this poetry was committed to paper, that Macpherson genuinely, if not in a very scholarly way, did collect these fragments, did see a number of manuscripts, and that the most famous, most complete and authentic of these manuscripts (that of the Dean of Lismore) was the one which Macpherson deposited with his London bookseller, but which no one bothered to inspect. Macpherson's belief in the third-century origin of Ossian was a delusion, though a sincerely held one. His claim to have discovered a complete epic in manuscript began as an exaggeration, and as he was opposed and derided, grew by his own defensive and offensive tactics into a falsehood. But Johnson's sweeping dismissal of Macpherson as a cheat and a fraud are themselves absurdly and characteristically exaggerated.

As to the merits of the poems; leaving aside the remarkable influence they had on all the English-speaking people of the time, on the romantic movement in Europe, on such men as Goethe, Schiller and Napoleon (who carried an Italian translation in his pocket throughout his campaigns), there is this to be said. Embedded in Gaelic tradition and unknown until Macpherson drew attention to it, there had been a remarkable body of purely native and ancient poetry, some of it containing beauties which were then new to literature and thought, some of it original in other ways, and most of it the product of something to be found only in the ancient Gaelic civilization.

Everyone nowadays accepts the Border Ballads as a part of the literature, not only of the United Kingdom, but of Europe; and everyone recognizes Walter Scott's part in preserving these ballads for posterity. The Gaelic traditional narrative and descriptive poetry is no less remarkable, and in some ways even more so, than the Border Ballads. Though Macpherson was a lesser man than Scott, and though his temperament led him into preposterous claims, in helping to preserve this Gaelic poetry, he made a contribution to literature of the kind that Scott had made when he preserved the Ballads.

The practice of reciting Gaelic narrative poetry exists in the Highlands even today. Mr. Derek S. Thomson, the well-known Gaelic scholar, has described how as late as 1949 he heard in Benbecula an old seanchaidh chanting an Ossianic lay by his fireside.

Poor Mr. Macqueen was incapable of tackling Johnson on the factual side of the Macpherson controversy; nor could he really dispute with the great Englishman on the merits of Macpherson's English translations. Macqueen had, however, ever since he could remember, heard Ossianic poetry from the lips of the traditional story-tellers in Skye, and could himself repeat much of it. He knew that this poetry was genuinely old, and had been genuinely passed from one generation to the next. He knew enough of the tenacity and faithfulness of his own Celtic people's memory to know also that these poems had almost certainly been handed down faithfully with little alteration. And finally, deep in his own Celtic heart he recognized much of this Gaelic poetry as true poetry, even if only he and his fellow Gaels could appreciate its full beauty. But how could he convince Johnson (Macpherson or no Macpherson) on this point? How could he even begin to argue with him when Johnson not only did not know a word of Gaelic but ignorantly dismissed the language as "barbarous"?

For an admirer of Johnson this makes disagreeable reading. It is disagreeable also to read of Johnson's fulminations against the Scottish clergy in Macqueen's presence when he referred to one of his brother ministers, Mr. Kenneth Macaulay of Cawdor, as "the most ignorant booby and the grossest bastard". But it does no good to dwell on such things. Let it merely be admitted that this, one of the greatest of Englishmen, could discover in himself great English faults.

Rather let us say good-bye to the Reverend Donald Macqueen remembering Johnson's farewell words to him, spoken at different times. "I shall ever retain a great regard for you", and later, "Dear Sir, do not forget me". If Macqueen was shaky in his arguments and persistent in his minor points of pedantry, let us remember that he had long been isolated from learned discussion, and until the memorable three weeks he spent in Johnson's company he had had no one on whom to sharpen his faculties. "Sir," said Johnson, "he is so much at the head of things here that he has never been accustomed to being closely examined; and so he goes on quite smoothly." And if Johnson was somewhat overbearing to him, let us remember that if there was one subject in the world about which Johnson would be unlikely either by temperament or inclination to know anything, it was Gaelic poetry.

Lady Macleod at Dunvegan (one recalls Johnson's "Is not this a fine lady"), Sheriff Macleod of Ulinish, "a plain honest man in brown, much like an English Justice", Colonel Macleod of Talisker, Maclean the laird of Muck, who did not like being addressed territorially as "Muck" but preferred "Isle of Muck", these and other figures come in the wake of Johnson on to the stage at Dunvegan and elsewhere on this part of Skye. In the few sentences that Boswell devotes to them they come to life and then fade away again in a manner in which other personalities on this tour do not. This, one feels sure, was not due to any lack of character in themselves. It was simply that, at Dunvegan, Johnson's huge contentment filled the stage, and left little room for anything, or indeed anyone, else.

In a short time the travellers were to return to Coirechatachan, where the old vivid Highland life of the kind that they enjoyed at Raasay was to resume its sway, and where

even Johnson was to be swept along only as a part of the
general gaiety and happiness. These were circumstances too
in which Boswell was come once more to the fore and was
to distinguish himself in some unforgettable scenes.

It was then with a sense of something like excitement that
I too set out to revisit Coirechatachan and travelled southwards through Skye and through the gathering storms of
winter.

M

VIII

COIRECHATACHAN

IT was about eleven o'clock at night when Boswell and
Johnson returned to Coirechatachan on their journey
South from Dunvegan and on their way out of Skye. I
visualize it as having been a calm autumnal evening of the
kind that blesses the Hebridean scene between storms, for
Boswell says that one star was enough to give them light
on their way up the glen that leads down to the sea-shore,
and at the top of which lay the hospitable farmhouse of
Coirechatachan, forever famous in Boswellian and Johnsonian annals.

It was eleven o'clock in the morning when I returned to
"Corri", as it is now marked on the map; and so violent and
stormy was the day that I felt that even Boswell's single star,
if it could somehow have miraculously shown itself through
the grey daylight, and the racing, mountain-beating and rain-
vomiting clouds would have tempered the ferocity of, even
if it could not have illuminated, the scene. It was one of the
days of most savage weather that I can ever remember in
the Western Highlands: indeed, having spent all my post-
war winters in the South of Scotland, I had forgotten that
such days could exist. Half-blinded by the rain, I moved
into the wind slowly and at an angle, rocking on my straddled
legs as I did so. My oilskin jacket and trousers were pressed
hard against the form of my body by the strength of the
tempest, and were so gleaming with water that I must have
presented something of the appearance of a primeval man
fighting his way through chaos. But I kept on, for I was
determined not to seek shelter except under the ruined
walls of Coirechatachan.

At such times, when every muscle of the body is occupied in struggling with the elements, one does not have
much leisure for reflection: the very thoughts seem to be
beaten out of one's mind and carried away by the wind as
would be one's words if one were so foolish as to attempt to
speak. Nevertheless, I can recall some ideas that did not so
much pass through my mind as whip about my head as I
battled into the storm towards Coirechatachan.

It was, I remember thinking, peculiarly inapposite that
I should be approaching Coirechatachan, of all places,
on this Boswellian and Johnsonian journey on such a day.
Coirechatachan, as I shall hope to recall to the reader when
the effort of setting down my own recollections of this walk
through a Hebridean gale are over, was the place above all
others where Boswell and Johnson met the warmest-hearted
and most naturally hospitable of greetings throughout all
their Highland tour. Not even Raasay (which with all its
delights was a laird's house) could compete with what Mr.
and Mrs. Mackinnon, the farmer and his wife at Corri,
could offer to the travellers in the way of the sheer animal
spirits of hospitality. It was indeed a laughable mischance
that so eager a Boswellian as myself should be approaching
the ruins of Corri through conditions that made me feel as
if I were walking over the edge of the world into howling
desolation.

And yet was it not a salutary reminder to me? Here
had I been dawdling about the Highlands in one of the
loveliest and certainly most placid Autumns within memory,
but might I not have been tempted to take too soft, I will
not say too roseate, a view of the Highland jaunt of 1773?

The weather in the Autumn of that year had been
abominable. Some days must have been as bad as the one
which I was now enduring; and throughout the general
level of wind and rain had been far worse than anything I
had had consistently to put up with. The discomfort must
have been, even to 18th-century travellers, out of the

ordinary—long rides over rough tracks on inadequate ponies, filthy bed-linen, uncertain food, periods of enforced idleness within doors, and at least one long-drawn-out episode (the journey from Skye to Coll) of real danger. And finally, it was all very well for me to dwell with pleasure upon those times when Johnson showed real understanding of and sympathy with the Highlanders of his day, but had there not been another side to this as well? Had he not often brutally and ignorantly, as well as sometimes reasonably, attacked my compatriots in a manner which had justly earned their anger and his own reputation as the first of all Scot-baiters?

I laughed, in so far as the wind would allow me the luxury of such a sound, as I recalled my last conversation with my little Cockney friend, whom I had met once again on my way South from Dunvegan. My admission that I had been going to Kingsburgh out of Boswellian and Johnsonian interest had aroused his curiosity, and after having made a few enquiries as to how I had got on, he gave me his own views on Johnson and the Scots, somewhat strengthened by a number of whiskies and the fact that we were alone in the bar.

"Yes," he said, "old Johnson fairly made himself unpopular in these parts. You can take my word for it."

"Did he?" I asked, mildly curious to find that any 18th-century reputation had lived long enough for such an assertion to have been made so flatly, even personally, in such popular circumstances as a modern tartan-decorated cocktail-bar in the Isle of Skye.

"Did he not! Why, his name fairly stinks here."

"Oh come," I protested. "I don't suppose one in a hundred people in Skye has ever heard of him."

"Maybe not," he replied, with the relentless illogicality of the half-drunk, "but his name stinks all the same. Mind you, I'm not saying that a good deal of what he said wasn't true . . ."

"Have you read what he did say?"

"No, but I've heard a good deal about it in my travels up and down these parts."

I was interested enough to wonder whether in the course of his wanderings over the years my casual, but loquacious, acquaintance had not come across some genuine traditions, some real if weak and remote ripples made by the stone cast so many years ago into the pool of Highland life by Johnson's visit, and I pressed him for details.

"Yes," he went on, "they don't have much use for old Johnson up in these parts. Why, I'll tell you something" (here he dropped his voice and bent confidentially towards me, as if, even in the deserted bar, he was fearful of being overheard). "Why, d'you know, they even painted pictures of him with his name and all written underneath it on the bottom of chamber-pots, so that when they—well, you take my meaning—when they did it, they could do it right on the top of old Johnson."

He leant back and looked at me triumphantly as if he had now dealt his ace card, and had settled the last point of curiosity that could trouble me.

"Have you seen any of these chamber-pots?" I asked, for I had heard similar tales about many famous and infamous men since Johnson's day.

"No, I haven't actually seen one of them," he admitted, "but I've heard about them."

He then proceeded to meander on about his travels and what he had heard on nearly every subject that he could think of, soon leaving both Johnson and Boswell, whom he had mentioned in passing, far behind. It was obvious that at some time, somewhere, he had read something derogatory about Johnson in some Scottish journal or book, or had, at the most, heard some Highlander (possibly a minister or journalist) speak contemptuously of the great Englishman, and the incident had stuck in his acquisitive and inquisitive Cockney mind.

As I pressed on through the storm, I recalled this

conversation with sardonic amusement, and wondered what sort of a madman my Cockney friend would take me for if he could see me now, enduring all this to get to a ruined farmhouse where Boswell and Johnson had once enjoyed themselves. A fresh buffet of rain-drenched wind, taking me from an unexpected quarter, reminded me also (since I was in this determinately unsentimental mood) to ask myself what some of my own compatriot Highlanders, contemporary with Boswell and Johnson, would have thought of me. What would they have thought of me, one of their remote successors, if they could have foreseen me engaged upon such a journey, undertaken at least at the beginning with the pious intentions of enjoying for myself what I could recall from actual experience of what Johnson and Boswell had enjoyed in the Highlands of 1773? I thought I could supply the answer. I could recall at least some of the lines and images from one of the Gaelic satires which had been unleashed after the publication of Johnson's own book. The most violent had been launched as early as 1775, and was by James McIntyre of Glencoe. I determined to look it up again when I got back to Edinburgh and, if only as a corrective to my roseate views on the Highland jaunt, to set some of it down in a literal translation:

ON SAMUEL JOHNSON, WHO WROTE AGAINST SCOTLAND

Indeed I do not believe that the monster's ancestral root
Is of the Clan MacIan (Johnson):
Rather he was begotten to his mother
By a stranger with the nature of Venus.

A clown without manners full of spite,
A slave who is disrespectful to himself;
The best meat when it spoils
Will double its smell of corruption.

You are a slimy, yellow-bellied frog,
You are a toad crawling along the ditches,
You are a lizard of the waste,
Crawling and creeping like a reptile.

You are a filthy caterpillar of the stool;
You are an ugly, soft, sluggish snail;
You are a tick (such as) it is not easy to draw from
What you grip in your claws.

You are the weedings of the garden,
You are the straw and the chaff of the winnowing,
What time productive seed is sown;
You are a dun-coloured heap of tobacco.

You are the malingerer from battle,
You are the kite of the bird world.
You are now the secret butt of the bards.
Among fish you are the cub of the dogfish,

Or that sullen beast the devil fish;
You are the chicken in the midst of corruption,
The badger with its nose in his buttocks three quarters
    of a year,
A sheep-tick that is called the leech.

Foul is the wealth that you share,
And if it were not that I do not like
The name of satirist,
I myself would earnestly desire to abuse you.

There were some words and lines of this that came back to me in the storm: but it was not until I got back to Edinburgh that I was able to copy the whole transliteration. While looking up this shriek of Celtic exultant rage by McIntyre of Glencoe (which, by the way, the English-speaking reader is assured is not quite so ridiculous in Gaelic, possessing as it does in its native state a kind of verbal swing and verve) I came across some other Gaelic verses against Johnson, launched in the late 18th century. McIntyre's outburst was spontaneous and was composed almost immediately after the appearance of Johnson's book. When, however, the Reverend Donald MacNicol of Lismore in 1779 published, in English, his *Remarks on Dr. Samuel Johnson's Journey to the Hebrides*, there was a further outcrop of Gaelic "satires" praising MacNicol and abusing Johnson.

MacNicol's work is now rare and is known only to keen students of Johnson's life. Its eagerness in attack, its sweeping inability to see any virtue in Johnson's observations on Scotland, and the glee with which it fastens on every mistake or exaggeration which Johnson made, renders it, to modern readers, both tiresome and ridiculous. Its national perfervidness, never a characteristic much appreciated in Saxon eyes, must have irritated even its contemporary English readers, accustomed though they were to verbal vigour in controversy; but Johnson himself is said to have been more amused than angered by it.

Despite all this, MacNicol's *Remarks* is something more than a curious collector's piece of Johnsoniana. MacNicol was not "a low man" or a "blockhead", but a minister of repute and learning. As a linguist, a scholar, a fluent writer in English, and above all, as a really learned native Gaelic speaker, and a true and industrious collector of Ossianic ballads *and* writings, he was one of the few men alive at the same time as Johnson who could take the Doctor on and beat him from superior knowledge on one point. He could tackle Johnson when he committed himself to such statements as that Gaelic or, as he mistakenly persists in calling it, Erse (much to MacNicol's annoyance, not only on scholarly grounds but "because Erse has a filthy sound"), is "the rude speech of a barbarous people who had few thoughts to express, and were content, as they conceived grossly, to be grossly misunderstood". Johnson was capable of similar sweeping and characteristically chauvinistic judgments, for instance, about contemporary French literature. But most of these judgments, however preposterous, however much dictated solely by a desire to be contrary, however much designed to knock his opponents down by sheer assertion, were not based on pure ignorance, as were his foolish, and in the circumstances ill-chosen, statements about Gaelic. MacNicol therefore had little difficulty in dealing with this sort of thing. The trouble with him began when he allowed Johnson's undoubtedly tactless taunts on more general matters to provoke even worse manners in himself.

Johnson had declared that before the Union of Parliaments, "Scottish tables were as coarse as the feasts of Eskimoes, and their houses as filthy as the cottages [sic] of Hottentots." This, it should be remembered, was not thrown off in conversation, but published in a book. MacNicol characteristically and perfervidly descends at once to personalities. "Any one who has ever seen the Doctor in the act of feeding or beheld the inside of his cell in Fleet Street would consider the feasts of Eskimoes and the cottages of Hottentots injured by comparison." Even at this date, and with Boswell's own celebrated descriptions of Johnson's gross eating habits, and the slovenliness of the interior of his house before one, this retort of MacNicol's can raise a faint, if affectionately wry, smile, and may well have provoked a snigger or two amongst Johnson's enemies at the time. It was not, however, the kind of way in which to refute Johnson's book.

MacNicol's *Remarks* at once let loose a flood of Gaelic "satires" on Johnson from minor bards who, however fluent in their own tongue, were incapable of writing a sustained work in English in refutation of the great man. MacNicol became overnight their champion; and the satires are almost as full of extravagant praise of the Minister of Lismore as they are of abuse of the author of a *Journey to the Western*

Islands. Only three of these are now extant, and this sort of thing is an example of what MacNicol's book could produce from his fellow Gaels. The translation again is literal:

You will see with your own eyes
That the Gaelic is full of sap,
Not wanting in readiness for imparting instruction,
Strong and steady and fluent,
Though you revile it as a fable.

The Gaelic is as fluent and copious
As are the streams, and very prolific,
Very smooth, stable and certain;
It was bold of you to condemn it,
Seeing that never will you understand its idiom.

It was the book of the Reverend Mr. Donald
That warned me of your romancing;
Had I got it when I was younger
I would not have pardoned your boasting
Without contesting against you for the right.

It was MacNicol of Glenorchy
Who sized you up with accuracy,
Who knocked the bottom out of your history
Like the melting of snow in the torrent
With his precision and without wavering.

Repent without hypocrisy,
With ceaseless watching for the good of your soul.
And acknowledge with trembling
That you deserve damnation
Before it becomes too late.

Put your repentance down in writing
And do not keep it secret;
Every day keep telling
That you were not a truthful journalist,
And we shall yet make peace with you.

No avowal or confession
To a priest or a churchman
Will blunt our sword
Or weaken our fight,
But a confession to the world.

Let us talk with one another
To see who is the sharpest,
In the shindy the satirist raised!
And let us not part with our reason
Vain talk will not avail us.

This is a war marching song that will be dear
To every Gaelic literary hero.
This is my constant prayer for you—
That you demonstrate your valour
To the carrion who contemned us.

Apart from their remote interest to those who have so fallen under the spell of Boswell and Johnson that they are curious about any repercussions the tour made in the Highlands, these outbursts of Gaelic rage and sensitivity have a claim to attention from anyone interested in late Highland and Celtic tradition.

It is an odd thing that Johnson was responsible for the final flare-up of a Gaelic literary tradition which, by the end of the 18th century, was almost dead. For nearly a thousand years, the ability to throw off a *rann* or a set of violently abusive verses in correct literary form (though apparently composed without meditated effort and with no more driving force than rage) had been one of the functions of a true bard. In the days of clan warfare, such shrieks of anger, always contained within the form of strict literary convention, and sometimes even achieving certain poetic standards, had been useful partly to let off steam, partly to enrage the enemy, and partly to intoxicate the warriors on one's own side.

After the break-up of the clan system in 1746, however,

the *rann*, which had been a product of purely internal Celtic warfare, fell out of use, and its place was taken by verses of melancholy, verses mourning the whole state of Gaeldom—a subject too large and looming to be made the subject of even the most angry satire. Johnson's tactless and certainly ignorant remarks about the Gaelic language, however, without going deep enough, did get just sufficiently under the Celtic skin to provoke an outburst from such bards as could remember the old tradition.

After this outburst the *rann* survived only as a private means of abuse and certainly never circulated in the country in the way that these verses on Johnson did. Thus it happens that the great Tory and lover of tradition was, by accident, the cause of the last exercise of an old tradition in an ancient language. I like to think that Johnson himself would have smiled indulgently if any of his Highland friends (and he had a number) had dared to tell him this. I confess though that I would not have liked to have told any of the angry old bards that the great Sassenach had only smiled.

Then through the rain and wind, I saw the shape of the Coirechatachan ruins coming up and taking shape in what was visible in the glen before me. I had last seen the ruined farmhouse of Coirechatachan some twenty-five years earlier when, as a young man, I had been walking in Skye. I had not then become so absorbed in the Boswell and Johnson tour in the Highlands and Islands as I am now. Nevertheless, Boswell's account of Corri had, combined with his celebrated admission of having got drunk there, made sufficient impression on me to lure me away from the main road between Broadford and Sligachan to look at the place. Coming upon it now through the wind and the rain upon a savage autumnal day in the early 1950s I could, by a freak of memory, very distinctly recall its early appearance upon some fine day in nineteen twenty something. It had a roof upon it then, but had, of course, been utterly abandoned for many years.

Now in the 1950s some storm, even more violent than
the one I had been encountering, had stripped the roof off,
and the walls were crumbling. When I had last seen the
house it was a corpse, now it was a ghost. The last stones
would soon crumble and fall away from each other, and
the immemorial heather from the immemorial purple hillside would have its way. The ruin, however, was sufficiently
unlike a ghost or a dream. Moreover, as it came out of the
mist and the rain and the wind at me, it was welcome as
bringing me. to a much-needed halt. It even promised
shelter if not exactly comfort. So horizontal indeed was the
path of the storm-projected rain that I was able to find a
spot beneath one of the eastward walls of Corri that was
almost dry. I sat down upon it, and taking out my sandwiches and whisky, mused, almost in comfort, on the theme
of where I now was.

The cessation in the struggle, the mere feeling of, if not
the fact of, dryness, the warmth of the good food and the
spirit inside me and above all the knowledge of what were
the stones against which I was sitting, and which stuck so
uncomfortably into my back, produced a glow of reaction
from my uncomfortable and cynically questioning mood. I
threw away the last that I could remember of McIntyre's
scurrilous lines into the wind, and forgot them. MacNicol's
piece of pompous and perfervid pedantry followed them, at
least as far as my own thoughts were concerned, and I
settled down to more agreeable reflections. Who could be
sour and pedantic and critical and ungenerous seated upon
the turf of Coirechatachan, and with the walls of all that
remain of the old farmhouse sticking into the small of
his back?

Boswell and Johnson came to Coirechatachan on their
first visit direct from Armadale on 6 September. They
were at once welcomed into what even then must have been
a small and slightly overcrowded farmhouse by their host
"Mr. Mackinnon, a big jolly man". There then ensues from

Boswell's pen what Professor Pottle describes as a "lyric paragraph" of description of the delights of Coirechatachan hospitality inspired, no doubt, by comparison with the austerity regime at Armadale. Possibly out of a desire not to appear too engrossed with his smaller creature comforts, he omits this description from his published tour:

> The house was of two storeys. We were carried into a low parlour, with a carpet on the floor, which we had not seen at Armadale. We had tea in good order, a *trea* (tray), silver tea-pot, silver sugar-dish and tongs, silver tea-spoons enough. Our land-lord's father had found a treasure of old silver coins, and of these he had made his plate. Mr. Johnson was quite well here. Mrs. Mackinnon was a decent well-behaved old gentlewoman in a black silk gown. At night we had of company Coirechatachan and his wife; Mrs. Mackinnon, daughter to his wife and widow of his son; Mr. Macpherson, minister of Sleat, and his wife, daughter of Coirechatachan; a niece of Coirechatachan's, Miss Mackinnon; Miss Macpherson, sister to the minister; and Dr. Macdonald, a physician; as also young Mr. Mackinnon, son to Coirechatachan. We had for supper a large dish of minced beef collops, a large dish of fricassee of fowl, I believe a dish called fried chicken or some-thing like it, a dish of ham or tongue, some excellent haddocks, some herrings, a large bowl of rich milk, frothed, as good a bread-pudding as I ever tasted, full of raisin and lemon or orange peel, and sillabubs made with port wine and in sillabub glasses. There was a good table-cloth with napkins; china, silver spoons, porter if we chose it, and a large bowl of very good punch. It was really an agreeable meeting.

After a short interval, in which Boswell says that Coirechatachan (Mr. Mackinnon) "had hospitality in his whole bearing" which interval of reflection, as it were, he includes in his publication, Boswell goes on to a further paragraph, subsequently cut out from the version intended for the public eye:

> How superior was our reception here to that at Sir Alexander's! Mr. Johnson got a good bedroom to himself. When I went up-

stairs, Mrs. Mackinnon received me in an opposite bedroom with three beds in it, and with an air of hearty cordiality said, "Come away and see if you can sleep among a heap of folks"; then kissed me on each side of the face, and bid me good-night. I had a good clean bed with red and white check curtains to myself. In a bed with blue worsted stuff curtains lay Donald MacLeod and Dr. Macdonald; in a red one of the same kind, the minister and young Mackinnon.

I paced out the foundations of the old farmhouse at Coirechatachan, and by what I believe was fairly accurate guesswork, was able to get some idea of its old height when the full building was standing. There can be no doubt about it, it must have been a pretty small and compact building, designed not for show or for the entertainment of guests, but as no more than an honest shelter for an honest farmer and his family half way up the glen. Yet there is equally no doubt that the ebullient and kindly and, in the best sense of the word, gentle spirits of its 18th-century Highland master and mistress made this small house fill and glow with a traditional hearty yet gentle Highland hospitality which many a larger nobleman's seat lacked.

The overcrowding of this farmhouse when guests were being entertained would, of course, by modern standards, be extremely uncomfortable. The reason for Johnson getting a bedroom to himself was probably partly out of respect for him, and partly on account of his age. Boswell, though a comparatively young man, was not unknown in Scotland at the time, and the good folk at Coirechatachan would certainly have heard about his father, the Judge, but on both visits he had to sleep in something amounting to a dormitory. While there was nothing slapdash, slovenly or downright unclean in the furnishings and hospitality extended to the gentler guests at Corri, there was a good deal of the rough and ready. One of Boswell's room-mates, a minister, had the little Gaelic serving-maid to valet him (or rather to help him to fold up his clothes) when he went to bed. There is no indication that he was not perfectly sober when, so unconscious was he of her presence, he urinated in the chamber stool while she was in the room, merely turning his back upon her while doing so. Boswell calls this "a remarkable instance of the simplicity of the people of Skye".

The living-rooms, the main and frequently used hall, which opened directly on to the moor, were constantly filled with changing and shifting crowds talking, and frequently singing, in two languages—English and Gaelic. These crowds were composed not only of the resident or transitory guests, but of farm-hands, near-neighbours (that is anyone who lived less than three miles away) and casual travellers.

It is characteristic of the Highlands and Hebrides of the time that such a seat of genial if crowded hospitality, neither aristocratic on the one hand nor of the peasant class on the other, should not have lacked cultivated literature, which would have surprised most visitors from England and which delighted both Boswell and Johnson. They found there Hector Boethius in Latin, Cave's *Lives of the Fathers*, Baker's *Chronicle*, Jeremy Collier's *Church History*, Johnson's own small Dictionary and "several more books".

Boswell's talent as a truthful chronicler, the man with an eye for detail, combined with the capacity to convey atmosphere, is most evident at Coirechatachan. On the travellers' first visit there he clearly rose to the occasion in his customary ebullient fashion. It was not only that he felt the relief of escaping from Armadale, but that his keen nose scented enjoyment and sociability from the moment that he was welcomed by the "jolly big man" who had "hospitality in his whole behaviour".

Having followed that scent into the crowded farmhouse with his ready enthusiasm, I see him after a little as a trifle stunned by the clamour of the chase. If he had been chilled and irritated by the chieftain's reception at Armadale he may, as the cicerone of the greatest Englishman alive, have on another score felt a little bit out of it after the first tumult of welcome was over. Here were laughing, shifting, changing, uninhibited crowds of Highland folk, going about their business as well as enjoying themselves and making other people enjoy themselves without restraint and with characteristic lack of formality. Much of the conversation, and nearly all the singing which spontaneously punctuated that conversation, was in a language he could not understand.

It is perhaps not surprising that at the end of the second day he was, in reaction, to suffer from one of those bouts of incalculable melancholy which alternated with his high spirits, and from which, on the whole, he was fairly free on the tour. With the knowledge of how much he was in later years to be the victim of this deep malady, and how constant were his struggles against it, his note in his private Journal, with his hopes for the future, makes pathetic reading:

> I had a slight return of that spleen or hypochondria or whatever it should be called, which formerly made me so miserable, and which operates not only as to the present, but throws a gloom upon everything, whether past or future. The blackness of the imagination blackens every object that it takes in. How much reason have I to thank God that I have now hardly any remains of so direful a malady! The cheerfulness and constant good sense of my valuable spouse have had the happiest influence upon my mind.

Boswell's freedom from this constitutional melancholy during the most part of the tour was due probably to a number of causes. He was, in his achievement of a long-planned venture, happy without being over-excited. He had the stimulating yet refreshing fact that Johnson was always with him. He was physically healthy. His twin obsessions of wenching and drinking were almost banished into the background. His eager curiosity was continually being stimulated and satisfied. He had a full-time job in arranging the tour as it went along, and in avidly, and as it proved, capably, gathering the fruits of it, not only in this essay in Johnsonian biography, but in noting everything he

N

saw around him. This was a task that brought out the best in him. It kept him mentally active and sufficiently to the fore on nearly all occasions without exciting in him that pathetic and ridiculous vanity which, when it retreated from him, so often left him sad and frightened. At Raasay, at Dunvegan, at Coll, on the journey at Inveraray, and even at Armadale, he was always occupied in a multitude of ways doing that which he was supremely qualified to do—entering happily into the stream of social life and noting down for posterity the details of its perpetual flow.

At Coirechatachan and on the second day with Johnson possibly upstairs, happily engaged with books in his own room, with the full-blooded Gaelic gaiety all around him in the parlour and hall, he may have found that the stream of life overwhelmed him and left him alone. If so, the ensuing melancholy was fortunately short and transitory. It did not deprive him of his keen powers of observation, even when the fit was on him, and above all, though it returned to him again as a result of excess, it did not affect his unforgettable account of the second visit to Corri when he and Johnson came there again on their way South from Dunvegan on 25 September.

It was late indeed when by the light of one lone star the travellers knocked on the door of the farmhouse on their second visit. They cannot have been expected, for Mr. and Mrs. Mackinnon were preparing to go to bed. It is hardly necessary to say that despite this the travellers were at once and most hospitably received. A good fire was laid on and a midnight supper put on the table. Johnson, who was less overwhelmed by the tireless vigour of Coirechatachan hospitality, who was more in control of himself than was Boswell, and who consequently, one suspects, enjoyed the two visits there the better of the pair, went off to bed soon after supper. Boswell remained, and there then ensued the famous drunken bout which was the only one of the few occasions of intemperance which Boswell indulged in during his tour, which he recorded in his published version. His enemies, both in his lifetime and throughout the 19th century, have loved to remember and ridicule this celebrated lapse, so casually confessed. This is what happened:

Dr. Johnson went to bed soon. When one bowl of punch was finished, I rose, and was near the door, in my way upstairs to bed; but Coirechatachan said it was the first time Coll had been in his house, and he should have his bowl; and would not I join in drinking it? The heartiness of my honest landlord, and the desire of doing social honour to our very obliging conductor, induced me to sit down again. Coll's bowl was finished; and by that time we were well warmed. A third bowl was soon made, and that too was finished. We were cordial, and merry to a high degree; but of what passed I have no recollection with any accuracy. I remember calling Coirechatachan by the familiar appellation of "Corry", which his friends do. A fourth bowl was made, by which time Coll and young Mackinnon, Coirechatachan's son, slipped away to bed. I continued a little with Corry and Knockhoe, but at last I left them. It was near five in the morning when I got to bed.

SUNDAY 26 SEPTEMBER. I awaked at noon with a severe headache. I was much vexed that I should have been guilty of such a riot, and afraid of a reproof from Dr. Johnson. I thought it very inconsistent with that conduct which I ought to maintain while the companion of the Rambler. About one he came into my room, and accosted me, "What, drunk yet?" His tone of voice was not that of severe upbraiding; so I was relieved a little. "Sir," said I, "they kept me up." He answered, "No, you kept them up, you drunken dog." This he said with good-humoured English pleasantry. Soon afterwards, Coirechatachan, Coll, and other friends assembled round my bed. Corry had a brandy bottle and glass with him, and insisted I should take a dram. "Ay," said Dr. Johnson, "fill him drunk again. Do it in the morning, that we may laugh at him all day. It is a poor thing for a fellow to get drunk at night, and skulk to bed, and let his friends have no sport." Finding him thus jocular, I became quite easy; and when I offered to get up, he very good-naturedly said, "You need be in no such hurry now." I took my host's advice and drank some brandy, which I found an effectual cure for my headache. When I rose, I went into Dr. Johnson's room, and taking up Mrs. Mackinnon's prayer-book, I opened it at the twentieth Sunday after Trinity, in the epistle for which I read, "And be not drunk with wine, wherein there is excess." Some would have taken this as a divine interposition.

Not a very violent or damaging lapse by 18th-century, by Highland, and particularly by later Boswellian standards. But, since Boswell's own pen and frankness have made it into something of a classic occasion, it is I hope permissible (while avoiding the fashionable tendency to treat the poor man as a resurrected psycho-analyst's casebook study) to pause for a moment to consider it.

Boswell had said of himself, "no man is more hurt by wine than I am." He was, however, no dipsomaniac in the modern sense. His body and nerves did not constantly crave for alcohol. When things, as they so seldom did, were going happily and easily with him he could do without or with little liquor. When he was excited or depressed or needed to bolster up his courage or wanted to cut a figure, he flew to the bottle. I see him coming into the farmhouse at Coirechatachan on this return visit, cold, tired, hungry. The memory of social successes, where he had conducted himself so well in higher circles at Raasay and Dunvegan only recently, was still in him. There was also the memory that some three weeks earlier in this humbler farmhouse where Johnson had been at ease, he, Boswell, despite all the friendliness, all the warmheartedness, had felt a little out of it. Well, here he was, and here was a chance to set that to rights. His mentor had gone up to bed. A social night was just beginning. He, Boswell, the London spark, the Edinburgh lawyer, the descendant of a "long line of Scottish Barons", could drink as well as any Highlandman, or at least he'd try to. Dawn must have been breaking before the attempt ended, and it was high noon before he admitted defeat to himself. It is characteristic of one of the better qualities in Boswell, a quality that makes him so essentially readable, and like-able, that he admits, long afterwards and in cold blood, not only to this night of excess but to the indignity of its failure and consequences.

Poor Boswell was much laughed at for all this after his Journal was first published, and, in a footnote to subsequent editions, tried to protect himself by saying that he had recorded the incident merely to throw light on Johnson's character:

> My ingenuously relating this occasional instance of intemper-ance has I find been made the subject both of serious criticism and ludicrous banter. With the banterers I shall not trouble myself, but I wonder that those who pretend to the appellation of serious critics should not have had sagacity enough to perceive that here, as in every other part of the present work, my principal object was to delineate Dr. Johnson's manners and character. In justice to him I would not omit an anecdote, which, though in some degree to my own disadvantage, exhibits in so strong a light the indulgence and good humour with which he could treat those excesses in his friends, of which he highly disapproved.

There may be an element of truth in this; and the report of Johnson's reaction on the morning after may well have been the reason for Malone (Boswell's invaluable adviser on the published version) agreeing to the inclusion of the incident. But it is equally likely that the passage in the printed version is only one more example of Boswell's incurable ingenuousness.

We who come so long after him may feel grateful that Boswell never lost this ingenuousness. Is there any other writer in English in the 18th century who brings the fact of that century more alive to us than Boswell? Apart from his great gifts as an observer, his industrious talents as a chronicler and his conscious and sustained literary artistry, his pure ingenuousness plays its part in what he has to give us. But it must have been an uncomfortable quality to possess. He could not see that when he told what he believed to be the truth about someone else it might give offence, or when he admitted the truth about himself it might make him ridiculous.

Lord Macdonald, Mrs. Thrale, Fanny Burney, Sir John Hawkins, Lady Diana Beauclerk ("the woman's a whore, and there's an end on't") and a score of others who may have felt personally angry about what Boswell wrote of them in the Journal and in *The Life* are now not only beyond offence but beyond anyone being offended on their behalf. And as for Boswell himself, he has reached a place in literature where we no longer laugh at him but smile, sometimes irritably, sometimes sympathetically, across the century and a half. But it must have been uncomfortable for him at the time, and he must often have wondered why, and never have found the answer.

The result of Boswell's bout was to leave him with fretted nerves; and he never fully recovered his composure at Coirechatachan. Johnson, on the other hand, seems to have taken to the farmhouse life with greater ease, and nerves or no nerves, Boswell has left us with an unforgettable picture of the great man of Fleet Street in these improbable surroundings where he dominated the scene even more than at Raasay. At Coirechatachan Johnson had no fears as on the island that "we have not been able to entertain *them* much":

> I had a good cup of coffee this afternoon. Dr. Macdonald's wife, "Mrs. Dr. Roy" (i.e., red Doctor), as Malcolm MacLeod toasted her, was a neat, pretty little girl. She sat down upon Mr. Johnson's knee, and upon being bid by some of the company, put her hands round his neck and kissed him. "Do it again," said he, "and let us see who will tire first." He kept her on his knee some time, while he and she drank tea. He was now like a *buck* indeed. All the company laughed in great glee, and they were all pleased to see him have so much good humour. To me it was a very high scene. To see the grave philosopher—the Rambler!—toying with

a little Highland wench! There was a coincidence of opposed ideas. But what could he do? He must have been surly, and weak too, had he not behaved as he did. He would have been laughed at, and not more respected, though less loved.

Johnson's spirits rose at Coirechatachan while Boswell's did not so much decline as remain quiescent.

Mr. Johnson was this morning for going to see as many islands as we could, never minding the uncertainty of the season, which might detain us in one place for many weeks. He said to me, "I have more the spirit of adventure than you." For my part I was anxious to get to Mull, from whence we might almost any day reach the mainland.

There may have been a number of reasons for this. Johnson had a private, or nearly private, room to which he could retire. Boswell was always with the crowd and sometimes overcome by it. To Johnson, whose childhood had been spent in humbler and more constricted circumstances than had Boswell's, this farmhouse life may not have seemed so oppressive. There may also have been another reason, and I have sometimes allowed myself to speculate on its possibility. It is simply this: it is possible that Johnson was able to perceive a quality in the spirit of loyalty which he found at Coirechatachan which eluded Boswell. To mention this, even in passing, it is necessary once more, and for the last time in these pages, to touch on the subject of Jacobitism which most certainly occupied so much of the travellers' thoughts on Skye and which made its final, and as I see it, its most human and most natural appearance on the stage at Coirechatachan.

Such Jacobitism as remained in the Highlands and Islands as late as 1773 had come from two sources. There had been the Jacobitism of the chiefs, some of it inspired by genuine loyalty to an idea, the House of Stuart or to a person, some of it by opportunism, the feeling that it might be a good thing to back a popular and possibly winning cause at the earliest stages. There had also been another kind of Highland Jacobitism amongst the humbler classes. It was the kind that had moved the clansmen of Skye to disobey their chiefs, Macdonald and Macleod, in 1745, and for many of them to leave Skye to join the Prince's army. It was a Jacobitism that had little to do with dynastic politics, with opportunism, or what is now known as romance. It sprang from Gaelic patriotism, from a feeling for race. And though that feeling may, as the campaign proceeded through achievement and then to disaster, have become mingled with a personal feeling for the young Prince himself, its origins were in the Gaelic past.

For centuries, as Gaeldom in Scotland had been driven further and further back more deeply into the hills, more remotely into the islands by the Lowland forces and by the Sassenach-speaking Southerners, there had existed a legend that a fair youth would come from overseas to lead the Gaelic forces of Scotland to victory and to the reclamation of the lands which they had once owned. The arrival of Charles Edward Stuart in 1745 set alight the belief in this legend amongst the ordinary Highlanders, and there is no doubt but that many of them joined in this the last struggle of the Scottish Gaelic people led by this vision.

Macdonald of Kingsburgh, some of the tacksmen, and some of the rank and file of the Highland army, were thus animated, and not even the defeat of 1746 completely extinguished their hopes. Mrs. Mackinnon, Coire-chatachan's wife, who was Macdonald of Kingsburgh's own daughter, in 1773 bears witness to this. Here is Boswell's account:

> She told us a very extraordinary dream which she had during her first marriage. She saw the late Sir Alexander Macdonald; but recollecting that he was dead, she asked him if it was not so. "No," said he, "I am not dead. I am alive." Said she, "You

mean, sir, that you are alive in another state—in heaven" (or
"happiness"). "Yes," said he; "and I'll tell you anything that
you'll ask me." "Why then," said she, "Sir, will you tell me
if this unfortunate man will ever be restored to the throne of
Britain?" "Yes," said he. "He certainly will." There was something so generous in her making this her first question—in her
loyalty going before her concern for her family and everything
else—that I was touched in a most sensible manner, and took
hold of her hand across the table, shook it eagerly, and made her
health go round. She had then nine children, and the smallpox
of a very fatal kind was raging in Skye. She asked how her children
would come off. He said she would lose but two; and those that
survived would be a great comfort to her. This has exactly happened. She asked if Lady Margaret would marry again. He said,
"No." She asked what kind of man Sir James would be. He said,
"He'll be the best man you ever had, while you have him";
which meant that they would not have him long. She said that
everything else which Sir Alexander told her in this dream has
turned out so exactly that she had a firm faith in the restoration
which was also told.

This Mrs. Mackinnon was now a matron in middle life,
but it is not the first time that she comes into the Jacobite
story. Those who are familiar with the detailed account of
the Prince's dramatic day and night when he was in refuge
at Kingsburgh will have met her as Mrs. MacAllister—a
young married woman scarcely more than a girl, who was at
this fateful time staying with her parents. As Mrs. Mac-
Allister she makes in 1746 a brief but unforgettable appearance, second only for vividness and courage to that made by
her father, old Macdonald of Kingsburgh. Her first husband
died some time after the events of 1746, and she then
married the son of Mackinnon of Coirechatachan to re-
appear if not in history at least in English literature during
the visit of Boswell and Johnson to her husband's farm
in 1773.

Just before the travellers left Coirechatachan we hear
the last of this daughter of Kingsburgh in a scene which is

one of the most evocative that Boswell ever recorded in all his writings about Johnson. In reading and re-reading this scene again I have sometimes wondered whether the great English Samuel Johnson, with his warm heart as well as his Tory youth behind him in the mist of vanished years, was not more in accord with the last glow of humble loyalty he found at the farmhouse at Corri than was his more "romantick" and younger Lowland Scottish disciple:

> While we were at dinner, Mr. Johnson kept a close whispering conference with Mrs. Mackinnon about the particulars that she knew of the Prince's escape. The company were entertained and pleased to observe it. Upon that subject there was a warm union between the soul of Mr. Samuel Johnson and that of an Isle of Skye farmer's wife. It is curious to see people, though ever so much removed from each other in the general system of their lives, come close together on a particular point which is common to each. We were merry with Coirechatachan on Mr. Johnson's whispering with his wife. She cried, "I'm in love with him. What is it to live and not love?" So she humoured our merriment. At the same time, she was really most heartily taken with his conversation. Upon her saying something, which I did not hear or cannot recollect, he seized her hand keenly and kissed it.

How that woman lives for one across the years! She makes this short appearance upon the crowded, brilliantly lit stage of the tour for these few moments, but her image remains, and the tones of her voice sound in one's ears long after those of other greater, more important, more lengthily described characters have faded—"I am in love with him. What is it to live and not to love?"

I knew this description of the last dinner at Corri almost by heart. As I wandered round the ruins of Coirechatachan I repeated to myself as much of it as I could remember. The storm, if it had not yet completely abated, was now beginning to blow itself out, and I could walk and wander in comparative comfort. The burns and little rivers were

The red Cuillin above 'Corri' which lies just round the corner of the hill

(Courtesy of the National Library of Scotland)

'The Ruins of Iona' as Johnson saw them
(Courtesy of the National Library of Scotland)

loud in spate, but, apart from their chattering, there seemed a promise of peace. The great purple slope of Beann na Caillach (the Mountain of the Old Woman) which sweeps up directly in front of Corri shook itself free of its clouds and, unchanged from 1773, looked serenely down on the ruins and upon this modern and solitary traveller who was wandering in and around them. It looked down as serenely as it had done upon the evening and the night and the morning of poor Bozzy's great bout, and later upon the happy scenes between the great English traveller and the farmer's wife in Skye.

Apart from the changeless mountain and the glen it was, however vividly the description of the scenes of 1773 might have lingered in one's mind, strangely difficult to associate these scenes with the pathetic and crumbling ruins that remained. In my own lifetime I had seen those ruins decay from neglect. Unless some pious society or individual troubled to preserve them a few decades more would see them gone. They would certainly not last the century out.

I do not usually approve of doing such a thing, but with the thought of this almost inevitable decay and disappearance in my mind I determined to keep for myself some tangible memorial of a house which for years had haunted my imagination. I picked up a small stone, not out of the wall of the farmhouse, but one which had obviously been a part of the walls and had fallen on to the ground. I put it into my pocket to take away with me.

By now, the sun in a rather watery fashion was beginning to come out. I could see that I was completely alone in the glen. My mood of reaction from sentiment had quite left me. It was more than I could resist. With the stone in my pocket and in my hand, I shouted out Mrs. Mackinnon's words up the purple slope of the mountain and over the empty glen—"What is it to live and not to love?"

IX

COLL AND THE CATHOLIC ISLANDS

WHAT might be described as the episode of the Island of Coll provides one of the most extraordinary adventures of the whole Hebridean tour undertaken by Boswell and Johnson. They had no intention of going there; and indeed there could have been little in advance in Coll to attract their attention. Neither large nor small, undistinguished by any unusual natural features, Coll had no historic or romantic past. At one time agriculturally fairly prosperous, it had remained one of the least disturbed, least known about, of the Inner Hebrides. Today its agriculture has declined and its population shrunk. Holiday visitors seldom go there. Coll is one of the most neglected, least sensationally obvious of Scotland's remarkable islands. Yet wherever the English language is read with any pretentions to scholarship, the name of Coll is now remembered. It is remembered because a storm in 1773 washed Dr. Samuel Johnson and James Boswell on to its rocky coast and kept them there for ten days.

The name of Coll is also remembered in a more personal way. The young laird of Coll, Donald Maclean (known in both Boswell's and Johnson's descriptions simply as Coll), is one of those characters who, for no reason that one can name, leaps out of the pages of memoirs or descriptions, never to be forgotten. There must have been something unusual about this courteous, kindly, athletic Highland youth; for though they do not repeat many of his remarks nor describe much of his appearance, he instantly caught the affection and respect of both Johnson and Boswell.

And, in some indefinable way, that affection and respect is transmitted to us. Johnson in his *Journey to the Western Islands* paid a few measured but obviously kindly tributes to him. They were not anything out of the ordinary, yet something of the old man's feelings must have displayed themselves in what he wrote. For when it was learned by the large English public that greeted Johnson's book that young Coll had been drowned at sea as the proofs of the book were actually going through the press, young Coll was mourned in London with, as one critic put it, "a sense of personal loss".

"Coll does everything for us. We'll erect a statue to Coll . . ." "He is a noble animal. He is as complete an islander as mortality can figure. He is a farmer, a sailor, a hunter, a fisher; he will run you down a dog. If any man has a tail, it is Coll. He is hospitable, and has an intrepidity of talk, whether he understands the subject or not." We know from Boswell's Journal that these were some of the spontaneous tributes which Johnson in his warmest-hearted manner did not so much pay to the young Highlander as throw out at and about him in his conversation. Literary London had not learned of these opinions at the time of the appearance of Johnson's book, for Boswell's own Journal was still unpublished, nor, when it did appear some years later, did Boswell include the "noble animal" quotation as shown above. Yet literary London had somehow had its fancy so taken by the image of Donald Maclean, the young laird of Coll, that it felt his untimely death as a "personal loss".

Literary, and to a certain extent social, London must certainly have gathered round the great man of Fleet Street upon his return from his Island wanderings, and have bombarded him with questions about what must have seemed at the time one of the most improbable of expeditions. It is quite possible that, in his talk in London, Johnson may have expressed some of his personal feelings about the young laird upon whose island he had been driven, and who had acted as so hospitable a guide to the two travellers. This may, in part, have accounted for a temporary and fashionable reputation in the smaller London of Johnson's circle in the 1770s, but it does not account for the vivid figure which Donald Maclean of Coll still presents to us. No, this likable young Highlander who, almost accidentally, steps across the path of Dr. Johnson and James Boswell in 1773, must have been a remarkable fellow to make so remarkable an impression, and, accidentally or not, he has earned his place in 18th-century English memoirs.

The episode of the Island of Coll in the Hebridean Tour, unexpected as it is, is introduced by, is indeed the result of, what is surely one of the most remarkable lesser sea voyages described in our language. The travellers, having left Coirechatachan and Ostaig at the Southern end of Skye, had been intending to make for Icolmkill or the sacred island of Iona, which Boswell had set his heart upon visiting. When they reached Ardnamurchan, that rocky point which thrusts itself out from the West coast of the mainland of Scotland, the wind turned against them and there was much indecisive tacking before the skipper realized that it would be impossible to make the Sound of Mull. The storm rose, and it became obvious as night fell that the boat would have to try and take shelter under the coast of Mull or be driven back upon one of the lesser islands of Eigg, Canna or Coll. No one on board knew the harbours of Eigg or Canna, and the storm and night were now so advanced that even the young laird of Coll was uncertain of being able to guide the boat into the harbour of his own island. Dr. Johnson who throughout this increasingly terrifying storm had been lying below, at first seasick then "in philosophick tranquility with a greyhound of Coll's at his back to keep him warm", heard that there was some doubt as to the course to be set. He then uttered the now famous dictum "Coll for my money". And Coll, by what seems to us now a miracle, it was.

This stormy voyage, that so nearly ended in tragedy, and so nearly deprived posterity not only of both of the accounts of the tour but of Boswell's *Life of Johnson*, is so superbly reported by Boswell that it would be an impertinence even to quote from that report here. It should be read in full. One or two comments, however, may be permissible. The first is to suggest to the reader who wishes to enjoy the full force of Boswell's description that he should consult the fuller version in Boswell's private Journal. The second is to draw attention to a fine example of Boswell's ingenuousness. He admitted and put down in his private Journal that in order to soothe his nerves and his fears he begged Coll to allow him to do anything to help. Coll gave him the end of a rope which was fixed to the top of a mast and bade him hold it until he was commanded to pull. Boswell was fully aware that "this could not be of the least service but kept me out of their way who were busy working the ship". This is a most human and Boswellian thing to have done and most characteristic of him to have recorded it in his private Journal. What is remarkable is that even his ingenuousness should have allowed him to print it.

The third comment is on the behaviour of Johnson. He had gone below in this very small boat when sea-sickness overcame him. Boswell has it that "he knew nothing of the danger we were in". Boswell had been dissatisfied with Johnson's own account of the storm in his *Journey to the Western Islands* and in his comments on the book which he sent to Johnson said: "You treat the storm too lightly. Coll and the Islanders thought we were in real danger." It is difficult to follow Boswell entirely here. Admittedly, upon deck and in the company of the small and agitated crew shouting in incomprehensible Gaelic, he would be more physically face to face with the danger. But, on the other hand, anyone who has been below deck, recovering from sea-sickness in a cockle-shell of a boat in a high storm, knows that there is another kind of terror that can seize one.

We shall never know the truth. I do not think that

Johnson can have been so ignorant of nor so apathetic to
the danger as Boswell (possibly to excuse his own fears)
makes out, or indeed as Johnson himself, long after the
event, hints in his letter to Mrs. Thrale. If Johnson had
in fact some greater idea of the peril they were in, it is to
me, who loves his memory, some consolation to think that
he who feared the thought of death throughout all of his
life, faced it calmly upon two occasions—upon his death-
bed in 1784 and in these Western seas when he was as
near to a violent end to his life as at any time in all his
seventy-five years.

For the rest, there is no comment needed. The rising
storm, the black mountains of the mainland, the shouting
in Gaelic, the steering of the one-eyed sailor, the waving of
the glowing peat to give light as darkness fell, Boswell's
prayers fortified by the memory of quotations from Ogden,
his characteristic recollection of his wife, Coll's cry "Thank
God we are safe". All is there in Boswell's prose written
down in the last leaves of his Journal before he acquired
(Heaven knows how) some fresh sheets in a shop in Coll.
Here is as fine a piece of reporting as Boswell ever put on
paper, and incidentally as clear a portrait of himself as he
has given us. Here is no introspection in a moment of
gloom or excitement, but a flashlight picture of the man
himself emerging from the darkness with Boswell's own
hand igniting the flash and catching the image of himself
on the photographic plate of his written page.

There are no boats today that sail from Skye to Coll,
and as the winter was coming on in real earnest, after my
departure from Coirechatachan, I returned to Edinburgh
to make my notes upon this the first part of the Boswellian
and Johnsonian Journey through the Highlands and
Islands. It was indeed more than merely the first part, for
I had covered on horseback, on foot and by boat, all the
mainland Highland tour, Skye and Raasay. There now only
remained for me the Inner Hebrides. These I decided to

keep till the Spring, and, with the coming of an early season in the West of Scotland, almost as beautiful as the long-lasting Autumn of the previous year had been, I set out for Coll in the first flush of the year.

This was not the first time I had seen this little-visited island. As a boy and as a youth, upon my journeys to the Outer Hebrides, I had waited in the little steamer in the calm of the bay by Arinagour (known to Boswell as Locheirn) and had seen the open boat which used to meet us rowing into the harbour carrying mails, furniture, beasts and passengers. On stormy days, the passengers used to help with the oars. Long, low, flat, subtly coloured in grey and brown, with here and there a touch of Summer colours from the wild flowers in June, Coll had remained in my memory over the years. It was so different from its grander, more precipitous neighbours. Its very lack of grandeur and distinction made it memorable. And even then as a youth I had read, just read, Boswell's tour, and the name of Coll had stayed with me.

Now when I came back to Coll with my mind fuller of what I had read in Boswell and Johnson about Coll, I looked upon the island with a fresh and lively curiosity. The old rowing boat of my younger days had disappeared and a motor-vessel chugged out from the little pier at Arinagour to meet our steamer. But the freight was the same kind that had been carried twenty years earlier. There were the mails, some calves, and the furniture of a whole small household that for some mysterious reason was moving back to this humanly shrinking island.

I landed at the pier and walked by the row of little white-washed cottages that forms the only street of the only real village on Coll, and went up to the one little inn on the island. Already the past seemed to be lapping all around me. But it was not the past of the 18th century when for ten days the immortal travellers had been stormbound here. It was the past of an island, a

o

fruitful agricultural island that throughout the last half of the 19th century had been dying.

There was a melancholy in the air that did not so much depress me as drive on my inquisitiveness to find out for myself about Coll. It was a melancholy that for all its prevalence in the air of the island was almost defeated by the Gaelic gaiety of the gallant old Highland woman who keeps the inn.

For a week to ten days I stayed upon Coll, wandering on foot, fishing its hill lochs, and, in the evenings, reading and re-reading Boswell's Journal by lamp and candlelight. I have said in various other places in this account of my own disjointed wanderings in search of this book which I am writing that I have strongly felt the fact and presence of Boswell and Johnson in the air in various unexpected spots. I felt them during the Autumn storm when we were riding over the old disused hill track from Fort Augustus to Glen Moriston. I felt their presence, or perhaps wished for it, in a place where they had never been, at South Uist, where I met and spoke with the descendant of "the little woman of mild and genteel appearance" whom they had met at Kingsburgh. The longer I stayed and wandered in this island of Coll from which the tide of humanity has so quietly receded over the centuries, the more clearly did I become aware of the fact that Boswell and Johnson had been here, the nearer did their presence become; as the days went by, and only the more recent did their departure appear.

Coll has for the island-lover an enchantment all its own. The highest hill upon it is a little over 300 feet. It is about ten miles long; but the flat or undulating road does not go all round by the coast and it would be possible to circumambulate (if one may use so Johnsonian a word) the island easily in one day. The East coast is rocky. The West coast declines to the borders of the Atlantic in some of the most beautiful beaches in all the Hebrides. The celebrated silver and gold of the Western island sands is here mingled with the very faintest pink colour which only catches the tail of the eye as you glance at it at first, and then disappears when you look at it steadily. The seas that wash these infinitely delicately coloured bays are, upon a sunny day, peacock-blue and green, dotted here and there with the heads of inquisitive seals. The land between these two coasts is rich, green and potentially fertile, with, only upon the slight uplands, gneiss-rock coming through the surface. Only upon these slight uplands too is there heather, and amongst this heather there are tarns and lochans full of eager, active brown trout. Its climate is sunny and peaceful. The great clouds from the Atlantic do not often gather over its flatness, but blow in and on to the mainland and to Mull to coagulate there and to burst on the mountains. It is an island for dreaming away days of sunshine in Spring or high Summer.

Yet at the back of those dreams it is impossible not to feel the note of melancholy that fills the scene of this peaceful island. A hundred years ago there were 1400 inhabitants. After the first world war there were 400. Today there are 200. Why? Here are no great sporting properties, no romantic glens to be turned into tourist attractions. There are sheep and cattle, but not enough to turn away humankind as in the desolate parts of the North West of the mainland. This is a fertile green garden-land of an island from which humanity has ebbed away. The first impulse in the early part of the last century had been eviction; emigration had followed on its own. The population of 200 may now remain static, but there is a sense of emptiness, needless emptiness. One is living in a green shell of the green past from which life has gone.

How little the outward aspect of the island of Coll must have changed since 1773! And it is perhaps the thought of this that brings the image of the storm-bound 18th-century travellers so clearly to mind as one wanders upon

Coll today. A few buildings, a church here, a schoolhouse there, have been added to the island since 1773, but these, and one or two restorations or modern cottages by the roadside, are all. The old sheilings of the 18th century are either still standing, having been repaired, or are decaying stumps languishing not so much into the heather as at Coirechatachan in Skye, but into the green turf. The appearance of Coll must be as it was when they came here. Only the people have gone, almost gone. But even amongst those 200 that remain there are descendants of those who saw Boswell and Johnson on Coll. They have no traditional tales handed down to tell you about them. But it is something to know that they are here, and it gives an added touch to the illusion that the travellers have not long left the island. It may have been that, owing to lack of any other reading matter (Coll is not so well supplied with books as it was in 1773), I read over and over again from the Journal, and as I wandered on the island I became more and more conscious of the way Boswell and Johnson seemed to have impressed themselves on to the air of this island. In the curve of every sandy bay, behind every little hill or glacier-scarred rock projecting through the turf, and in every one of the lush green valleys in the centre and on the West side, I expected to come upon them again.

Coll is the island of the Hebrides that Johnson and Boswell have made their very own. No one else has written about it, and they wrote about it at leisure. Having been forced to stay upon it for ten days they had nothing to do but to observe, to talk and, for Boswell, to write in his Journal.

And how easily that Journal flows during these days of enforced isolation! Instead of recounting "romantick" adventures or telling of the meetings with distinguished Highland chieftains and ladies, Boswell has here a scene, not dull, but of quiet subtle colours, to set before us. He does this at ease; and this is one of the reasons why Coll

remains so persistently in the mind of the reader of the
Journal when other and more spectacular events and
stopping places on the tour occasionally get a little out of
focus. That is perhaps the word for the Coll episode in the
tour. Coll is always in focus. The images are clear.

Dr. Johnson sitting up in bed on the first morning
on the island and replying to Boswell's repeated wonder-
ment at the two men actually finding themselves in the
Hebrides, "Sir, people may do anything almost by talking
of it"—surely one of the great man's most comforting
sayings!—and then going on to lay plans for further visits:

> "I really believe I could talk myself into building a house on
> Island Isay, though I'd probably never come back again to see it.
> I could easily persuade Reynolds to do it. There would be no great
> sin in persuading him to do it. Sir, he'd reason thus: 'What will
> it cost me to be there once in two or three summers? Why,
> perhaps £500, and that is £150 a year; and what is that in com-
> parison with having a fine retreat to which a man can go, or to
> which he may send a friend?' And he'd never find out that he
> might have this within twenty miles of London. Then I'd tell
> him he might marry one of the Miss MacLeods, a lady of great
> family."

"Sir, people may do anything almost by talking of it."
And one wishes they had talked a little more on this
particular plan.

And then the conversation, if so it can be called, between Johnson and the aged minister of Coll on Bayle and
Leibnitz when the two men, each hard of hearing, talked
together at the same time. Despite argument in duet,
Johnson liked the old minister for his firmness—"At his
age" (he was seventy-seven) "it is too late for a man to be
asking himself questions on his belief."

Then later there is the stay at "the tradesman's box",
by which name Johnson at first called Coll's neat 18th-
century house, so accustomed had he grown to the feudal

grandeur of Dunvegan; Johnson's antiquarian researches, his views on the "little house" or retiral closet for the stool, when Coll promised to add such an amenity to his own house soon. This is omitted from the published tour. But what an inoffensive yet characteristic touch it adds to the pages of the discovered Journal!:

> If ever a man thinks at all, it is there. He generally thinks with great intentness. He sets himself down as quite alone, in the first place, I (Boswell) said "a man was quite happy there too". Mr. Johnson said he did not know that. I was for having books and prints. He did not insist for that. He told me he knew of a gentleman who had a set of the *Spectator* in that place.

Johnson standing listening to the bagpipes with his ear close to the great drone. Johnson strutting about the room "with a broadsword and target". Johnson wearing a large blue Highland bonnet which Boswell had taken the liberty of putting on his head. Johnson with the flaps of his hat tied beneath his chin while he waited underneath a great stone for Boswell and Coll, and presenting an "eremetical appearance". Boswell's discoveries of the old papers at Coll's house, including the Jacobite and anti-Jacobite letters which he omits from his published version. The conversations night after night as the storm-bound travellers waited for their boat. All these and other events upon Coll are in focus in Boswell's photographic pages upon Coll. His observations are set down night after night, not in excitement, nor depression, nor in late recollection, but daily as they go along. To stay upon the island of Coll for a week, wandering and fishing, talking to the few Highlanders left there, and in the evenings to turn over the pages of the Journal is, in my experience, as near as a man can come to the feeling that he has just missed seeing Dr. Samuel Johnson and James Boswell.

Before I left Coll I experienced a coincidence which, coming as it did at the end of my stay on the island, brought me even closer to the memory of one of the two men who had been here in 1773. On the last day of my week on the island, I climbed a small hill by Arinagour bay on which there is a stone monument looking out to sea. On it is written in Gaelic and in English a memorial to another son of the clan MacIan, but this time spelt in the Scottish way with a "t". It is to John Johnston, born 1846, died 1928—"A friend of the Gaelic people and of the Gaelic language." He was what was known in our grandfathers' day as "a land agitator". When he was born on Coll the last of the Macleans of the family who had entertained Boswell and Johnson still owned the island, and the population was actually a little larger than when the travellers had been there. By the time of John Johnston's death, the figures had sunk to nearly 300. Looking at this stone memorial which gazes out across the bay from which so many of the sons of Coll have sailed, the modern traveller can pay it no more than the passing tribute of a sigh. How angry the futility of that sigh would have made the Scottish, the Coll-born John Johnston who struggled and went to prison for the land of his people! How contemptuous of that sigh would have been the great English Johnson! One can imagine his growl of indignation:

> To hinder insurrection by driving away the people, and to govern peaceably by having no subjects, is an expedient that argues no great profundity of politics. To soften the obdurate, to convince the mistaken, to mollify the resentful, are worthy of a statesman; but it affords a legislator little self-applause to consider that where there was formerly an insurrection there is now a wilderness.—*Pacem Appellant.*

The fascination of this island of Coll, which Boswell has made his own and Johnson's, remained with me after my visit to it. I had been unable to take a boat from Skye direct over their route to the island. But I spent some of the Summer sailing between the islands upon which the travellers had nearly been driven, and, in calmer weather than they had enjoyed, endeavoured to recapture some of the circumstances of the voyage they had made. It was upon a fine June day, while I was passing between Canna and Eigg that I allowed myself to wonder what would have happened if the winds had been stronger or in different directions upon that Autumn day and evening of 1773.

If the storm on the 3rd of October, 1773, had whirled about, as it so often does in these western seas, if it had blown a little harder from the South, even the fact of Coll's knowledge of his own island would not have been enough inducement for Mr. Simson, the captain of the small vessel, to make for Coll, and the boat would have had to head for Eigg or Canna. If the wind had come in from the West they would have been driven in to one of the many long sea lochs on the mainland by Moidart, Morar or Knoidart. A strong wind from the East would have foiled even these plans, but it would have driven the boat out into the Minch, and from there the only land at which it could have touched in this latitude would have been at Barra, Eriskay or South Uist.

All these islands and those districts of the mainland were at the time, and still remain, strongholds of Roman Catholicism presenting then and now, in a country more strongly given over to the Reformation than any other in Europe, one of the most extraordinary instances of the survival of that Faith in the West. Anyone interested in the history and character of Boswell, anyone whose attention has been caught by the two men's account of their tour in Scotland, does not need to be a Catholic, a Scot or a Highlander to realize what we have missed by this accidental omission of these remarkable districts from Boswell's and Johnson's visit to the Highlands and Islands.

Before speculating upon what would have been the effect upon the two travellers of seeing for themselves the survival of Catholic Christianity in these Celtic districts, it may be as well to reflect on what they would have seen there. And to do this it is necessary to say something about a side of Scottish religious life which has been very little written about, but which, from that very fact, offers an interesting study whatever one's own religious views may be. I refer to the indigenously Highland and Hebridean Catholic districts.

The survival of Catholicism in the, geographically speaking, quite large areas of the Western Highlands and Islands of Scotland was different from the post-Reformation Catholic survivals in rural England. There Catholicism, in so far as it lived in country districts throughout the 17th and 18th centuries, did so only by the fidelity of old Catholic land-owning families. These old Catholic families would have co-religionists amongst their servants, who would be allowed and, where trusted, encouraged to attend the highly dangerous celebrations of the Mass in private houses; but even the most courageous of these English Catholic land-owners never attempted to proselytize the districts in which they lived. They knew that such efforts, if openly conducted, would not only be useless but would lead to the suppression of even the small privileges which they were allowed. The Faith would, by such rash actions, have been imperilled. They sent their sons to be educated abroad. Where they could not marry amongst families of their own kind, they married Continental Catholics, and, though they most certainly considered themselves as Englishmen and patriotic Englishmen at that, they were forced into a position of being looked upon as foreigners and often traitors by the rest of their nation.

In the Highlands of Scotland, on the other hand, the Catholic Faith was retained by a few land-owners and chieftains, but, for the most part, its survival was the product of the will of the people, supported by the Celt's remarkable tenacity and long memory. When Gaelic-speaking missionaries arrived in the Barra islands in the latter half of the 17th century, they found that though there had been no priest there for over ninety years the people had preserved the memory of the Faith and had resisted the efforts of Presbyterian missionaries who had then left them alone. They had retained a few Latin prayers, had continued to baptize their children, and ask for blessings on their enforcedly priestless espousals. The ardour with which they welcomed the first priest after nearly a century was extraordinary and pathetic. They besieged him for re-baptism, for the marriage rites, for Confession, the Mass and Communion. Their thirst for the Faith was such that through the pathos of it there creeps a slightly comic note. When their first visiting priest wished to go North on his mission to Uist, they threatened to detain him by force, and only let him go on promise of return or of the immediate visit of one of his colleagues. They said that they so longed for the return of a priest that when he did come they might actually keep him with them under peril of his life, thus adding a fresh danger to the Catholic missioner's life in Scotland. If he had escaped the persecution of the Kirk of Scotland, he might suffer death at the hands of his too ardent flock.

Catholicism then in these fairly comprehensive districts of the Highlands and Islands was not an aristocratically or even politically preserved remnant of an old regime. It was maintained, in the face of danger and difficulty, in the hearts and in the practices of the people. Moreover, it was very much not regarded by its adherents as something foreign, even to the Scotland in which they lived. As Celts they looked upon themselves as the true and original Scots, their language as the true language of Scotland, and the Catholic Faith, which they preserved amongst them, as the traditional Faith, not only of Europe, but of Scotland. Indeed, in so far as their religion touched upon their patriotism, they regarded the preservation of it as, amongst other things, a patriotic duty, a guard against the tendency, believed by them to be shown by their southern Sassenach Lowland neighbours, to be swallowed up in British Protestantism. Apart from this, they did not think of the Faith as an element in political struggles. While it is true that nearly all Catholic Highlanders would naturally feel sympathetic towards the Jacobite cause, as one which would guarantee them freedom of worship, it should be remembered that the majority of actual fighting supporters in the two risings of the '15 and the '45 were Episcopalians fortified by a considerable number of Presbyterians.

The present writer is a Roman Catholic Scot of Highland origin, some of whose forbears originally came from Highland Catholic stock. He feels it necessary to admit or, as he would prefer to put it, to proclaim this fact before he goes on to speak of the qualities of these Highland Catholics, qualities which they have displayed in the past and still preserve. There is about these people a peculiar sweetness of demeanour and character which has been remarked by those who have known them, whether of their own Faith and race or not. It is a quality which they have today and which they displayed in the past. Their ardent preservation of their religion did not in them breed a sense of persecution leading to fanaticism. It has been a remarkable fact that for the century and a half during which they have been increasingly at liberty to practise their Faith, their relations with even the strictest of their Presbyterian Celtic and Highland neighbours have been cordial to the point of offering an example to the rest of Christendom.

Today visitors from all over Great Britain constantly remark on the friendliness that exists between these Catholic Highlanders and these Highland Presbyterians. It may be that this sweetness of demeanour possessed by the Highland Catholics has made it impossible for their neighbours to quarrel with them; it may be that the sense of a common race and common language has overridden religious differences (a rare achievement!); or, more charitably, it may be just Christian charity on both sides. But this is no recent development, springing, as some might cynically suppose, from a general modern indifference to religion. Time and again over two centuries it has been remarked upon in testimony from both Protestant and Catholic sources. Two years before the visit that Johnson and Boswell made to the Western Highlands, the priest in charge of the large Catholic district of Moidart, Father (or after the Highland custom Mr.[1]) Austin MacDonald, writes in his annual report to Rome in 1771 of the admirable relations between his flock and the Presbyterians. Such are and were the qualities of the Catholic Highlands. In letters, in memoirs, in poetry, even in song, and in a hundred different minor testimonies, these qualities have been noted, preserved and handed down to us.[2]

How much Johnson and Boswell knew about the qualities of the Highland and Hebridean Catholic districts is uncertain. Amongst the reasons Johnson gives, in a passing sentence, for regretting that he did not visit them is the fact that in "Romish districts" old customs tend to be preserved, and that he and Boswell might have indulged their researches into old customs with even greater success on Eigg, Canna or Moidart, than on Coll and Skye. Apart from this somewhat prosaic reason it is possible that both Johnson and Boswell regretted this omission on their tour on other grounds. Johnson throws out a remark of sympathy

[1] It has been suggested the Scottish Catholics used "Mr." at the time of the persecution to avoid the dangerous word "Father" in public, and that the custom survived. It is more likely that Mr. is an Anglicization of the Gaelic "Maighstair", by which word priests in the Highlands are still addressed. Maighstair is very much a term of respect approximating to the Italian "Don", and, as in Italian, used before the priest's Christian name.

[2] This same Mr. Austin MacDonald in another letter to Rome, having mentioned that he had 500 communicants, goes on to pay tribute not only to their faithfulness in duty but to their innocence of character, which he had "not seen equalled in any other Catholics". 182 years later the priest in 1953 in charge of the same parish paid his people a similar tribute when speaking to the present writer. "Every priest," he said, "when he leaves here tells his successor that he will never find such Catholics as in these glens. The successor always takes this with a kindly pinch of salt, but when his turn comes, he too tells the same to the priest who comes after him; for it is true."

about the "Romish missionaries" to these remote islands. Boswell remains silent.

Had they been driven on to the mainland whose dark mountains just before the storm broke had been inspiring Boswell with such romantic reflections, they would have struck the very centre of the largest and most flourishing Catholic district. They could scarcely have avoided meeting one of the two priests, Mr. Austin MacDonald or Alexander Macdonald, "the priest who worked so hard that he loved fatigue" and who was in charge of Morar for fifty years from 1747 to 1797. They would probably have been taken to see the remains of the recently burned down Catholic Seminary on the island in Loch Morar, which had been destroyed in '46 when Lord Lovat was captured. Had they been, as they so nearly were, compelled to put in for Eigg or Canna, they could not have avoided meeting, and would probably have been entertained as guests by, the priest Alexander Kennedy, whose parish contained some 500 Catholics and no Protestants—Mr. Kennedy who was to die late in that very winter of 1773 when Boswell was back in Edinburgh and Johnson in London. Had the storm been more severe and had it driven from the East, Mr. Simson's little ship would have been cast upon the not so very distant Outer Hebrides at the Barra Islands or Uist. Here they would have seen the Catholics living contentedly at Barra, but at Uist under the persecution of their landlord, Macdonald of Boisdale.

They would have seen the Mass-houses, no more than large crofts or barns, in which in these remote places the entirely Catholic populations of the islands were at liberty to worship. They would have seen the doors of these Mass-houses open to the West, or as near as was possible to the West. They would have seen the rows of worshippers, who could not get into the Mass-houses themselves, kneeling outside on the grass, and the turf of the machair, the heather or, in autumnal Hebridean weather, the mud. They would have seen them kneeling, watching and waiting for the elevation of the Host by their island priest, and hearing however distantly amidst the winds and the seas, the sound of the sacring bell.

They would have visited the caves both on the mainland and on the islands in which, until quite recent times, the Catholics had to gather to hear their Masses. They would have heard from Mr. Kennedy, the priest of Canna and Eigg, how in the previous year he had been forbidden to visit his flock on the island of Muck by the very same laird whom Boswell and Johnson had met but recently at Dunvegan, and how, with the example of Boisdale of Uist before him, the laird had thrown the priest into prison for as long as he could for merely landing on the island. But they would have heard also of the better conditions that were everywhere allowing the Faith to be practised by such Catholics as were not being evicted from the Highlands. And, perhaps most interesting of all, they would have met in the persons of the priests and the upper classes of the Catholic Highlanders, Scottish Celts who were Europeans as well as Scotsmen, who had been educated in the languages of France, Italy and Spain, as well as in their native Gaelic and English.

One looks at the unsurpassed portraits of 18th-century Highlanders which Boswell has given us in his descriptions of Malcolm Macleod, Macdonald of Kingsburgh, his wife Flora, the landlord of Anoch, the old woman in the hut by Loch Ness, the deaf old Minister of Coll, and half a dozen others. One hears the sound ringing in one's ears which he has evoked for us over the centuries, from the dancing at Raasay, the "strange howl" of the women at the wauking of the cloth, the Gaelic singing, merrymaking and storytelling at Coirechatachan, concluding with the very accents of "What is it to live and not to love?" still haunting the ruins of the all but vanished farmhouse. Then one can only mourn the loss of what one has missed from Boswell's pen in a presentation of the sights, sounds and personalities of the 18th-century Catholic Highlands and Islands. The loss is made all the more sad by the fact that, owing to the remoteness of these districts as well as to the lack of curiosity on the part of the few travellers of the time, or their reluctance to visit them, there is very little that has been written that can evoke for us the *feel* of the past of these places. Boswell and Johnson suffered from no such lack of curiosity or reluctance. No one better than Boswell could have made them live for us again. And as for Johnson's observations and comments, though they would have been delivered in a more stately manner, how revealing they might have been!

And what would have been the effect on these two curious, inquisitive and highly individual travellers, whose path in the 18th-century Highlands posterity has followed so intently, if they had landed on Canna, Eigg, Barra or the large mainland districts of Morar and Moidart?

Johnson, though he was careful to guard himself against the suspicion of being credulous of its "superstitions", was, as we know, far from being unsympathetic to the "Romish religion". Most of the Roman Catholics whom he met in London, however, were Frenchmen or Italians, and his sturdy John Bull attitude towards their foreignness affected his view of their Faith. There are, however, indications that he was more tolerant of Irish Catholics, and that he had a generous sympathy for them on the score of the religious persecutions they had to endure. What he would have said, how he would have reacted if he could have come out of the Calvinist Highlands into the Catholic districts and seen the ardour with which their Faith, still in the face of some persecution, was sustained, it is impossible to say. I, for one, cannot believe that his generous heart would not have been moved, and that we would not have been left without some memorable accounts of his experiences and his views.

Boswell's beliefs, or as some would say, his fluttering and vacillating superstitious whims, have been the subject of much analysis and dispute. No particular Church seems anxious to claim him as her own. This is understandable; the poor man, not because of his sins and his weaknesses, but because of overwhelming frankness about them, a frankness that seems able to embarrass posterity as well as his own contemporaries, has offered himself as a particularly unsuitable advertisement for any Faith or philosophy. Nevertheless, he touched them all. He hobnobbed with atheists, deists, philosophers, Calvinists, Catholics, Anglicans and even Quakers. By each and all of them he was, if only transitorily, affected. Despite this, one thing remains certain. He was born a Christian, died a Christian, and throughout his turbulent existence he struggled to be by fits and starts a practising Christian. He made his Communion according to the rites of the Church of England at St. Paul's, worshipped in the Presbyterian Kirk in Scotland, and, whenever he could, stole off to Mass at the Bavarian Chapel in London. It was in this Chapel that he began one season of Lent by receiving the blessed ashes on his brow. And, with the mention of that secret ceremony which has emerged for us only in the pages of his private Journal, we come to one other certain fact: in his youth, James Boswell was received into the Catholic Church.

Writers on Boswell have for a hundred and fifty years known about the possibility of such a ceremony. They have guessed about it, speculated about it, wondering how complete it was, and have concluded by noting that the "inoculation", if it did happen, left its mark, but did not, as we say about other inoculations, "take". Now Professor Pottle has set our doubts at rest. In his introduction to Boswell's *London Journal 1762, 1763*, he says this:

What can be stated with certainty is that Boswell made the journey from Carlisle to London on horseback in two days and a half, riding night and day; that he took lodgings in the house of a Roman Catholic wig-maker; that he went promptly to the Bavarian Chapel and saw mass celebrated; that he was immediately received into the communion of the Church of Rome; that for a very brief time he played with the notion of going to France and entering a monastery.

Until the papers on which Professor Pottle bases this definite statement are made public, we can know very little about Boswell's reception. It is possible that the ceremony took place in the Bavarian Chapel, or by night in that haunt and refuge of London "Papists" in the first floor of the Ships Inn or Lincoln's Inn Fields with a watcher at the door to guard against spies. Or it may have been celebrated in one of the cellars near Ely Place, or in a farm-house in what is now a London suburb. The ceremony itself would be short, no more than two witnesses would be required; and Boswell would have had to give no more than an avowal on declaration of his fulfilment.

Despite this, and despite our lack of knowledge about where it occurred in London, and about the officiating priest, it is important to remember one thing. Reception into the Catholic Church for a person who was not in danger of dying was, then in the dark underworld of Catholic London, just as deliberate an affair as it is today. Boswell would have had to convince the priest first that he knew what he was doing, second that he was sufficiently grounded in Catholic dogma, third that he was sincere in his wish to become a member of a then dangerously outlawed society; and this last condition would probably have been in the circumstances and date (1759) the most difficult to fulfil. Who was this young Scot, the son of a Whig Presbyterian Judge of the Northern kingdom, who appeared in London and wanted to be received into a communion so much at the mercy of judicial spies? Boswell would have needed all the evidence he could produce not only in his own actions and demeanour but from other sources,

P

possibly from the priest at the chapel in the Saltmarket at Glasgow, which he may have been attending for some months while a student at the University, to answer the inevitable question.

However, it was answered, and with what effect we now know. James Boswell, after what must have been a short period of practising the Faith, which he had adopted, returned in public to outward Protestantism for the rest of his life. The inoculation did not "take". Those who blame this failure on the weakness of the vaccine or on Boswell's constitution, bringing it forward as one of the most glaring examples of his instability of temperament, should pause to consider before they completely condemn.

If this Scottish youth, who fled from home and country to London to seek admission into this persecuted society, had persevered in his new-found Faith, he would have committed social suicide. He might not at the time have bothered his head about that, but what would have been more serious is that he would as a British subject have been cast upon the world an outlaw in material things. He could not have been an officer in the army, or navy, entered for the law, or followed any profession save that of medicine. He would have been automatically disinherited, and even if he had acquired possessions, he would not have been able to leave an estate. In London, in which town he was to begin the practice of his new religion, he could only have attended Mass by going to some foreign Embassy chapel, or haunting some forbidden meeting-place, under peril of severe penalty. It is in this context odd to reflect that in all Britain the only places where he might have worshipped as a Catholic and fulfilled his religious duties in comparative safety and without molestation would have been in the remote Catholic Highlands and Islands of his own nation of Scotland—those islands and remote mountainous districts by which he was to be blown in the October storm of 1773 fourteen years later.

Whether these and many other crippling and alarming disadvantages too numerous to mention here weighed with him soon or late, whether the knowledge of them only fully came home to him after he had taken the secret step in London, we cannot say. Whether the subsequent three months' reckless plunging into the pleasures of the town under the skilful guidanceship of Samuel Derrick, and a subsequent and even deeper initiation into debauchery at the instigation of his father's friend Lord Eglinton, was the cause of his flight from his Catholic vows and intentions, or whether it was the anodyne by which he sought to forget them, we do not know.

This strange and pathetic incident with its immediate and pathetic sequel had its effect. For the rest of his life Boswell appears to have remained haunted by his youthful action and youthful apostasy. Only a few of his contemporaries knew what he had done, and these, including his father's friend Sir David Dalrymple, later Lord Hailes, remained silent. The only record up to date which we possess that in after years he told anyone was when he admitted to Rousseau that he had been received as a young man into the Catholic Church. Throughout his association with Johnson he was continually, and with varying success, "drawing" the older man for his views on the "Romish religion", but he never admitted even to this intimate, and what might have proved sympathetic, companion this secret of his youth.

What would have happened if the Autumn storm had blown the travellers into the mountains or islands of remote Catholic Scotland and had left them there for days? What would have been the result of the meeting of James Boswell and Samuel Johnson with the priests of Moidart, Knoidart, Morar, Arisaig, Eigg and Canna, and possibly the Outer Isles? Would Boswell who could seldom resist the appeal of the Mass and of Catholic ceremony, even in a great town, have stayed away on an Atlantic island where he and Johnson had been isolated for days on end and where there was no other religious ceremony, no other Faith practised? And if he had not stayed away, what would he have said to Johnson about it? Would he at last have told him of the secret ceremony of 1759?

It is as idle to speculate as it is irresistible. Only one gleam from the future, from what was to come, gives the faintest illumination as to what might have happened. The travellers never touched upon Scottish soil where the Catholic Faith was a living thing, but within a week or two they were, at Boswell's earnest instigation, to visit Inchkenneth and Iona where the ghost of a great and sanctified past hung in the air and seemed to animate the very stones of the ruined crosses.

"*Sancte Columba, Ora pro me*"—these were the words Boswell prayed to the long-departed Saint in an agony of supplication as he knelt before the cross on the little island of Inchkenneth. But he had stolen away in the darkness to kneel before the cross and to pray, and his old friend and companion did not know what he was doing.

X

THE HOLY ISLES

BEFORE following them to Mull, Iona and Inch-kenneth, I allowed these divagatory speculations on Boswell, Johnson and the Catholic Highlands which, with some hesitation, I have placed before the reader, to divert me in my own wanderings. In the early season of 1953, and before a wet and stormy June and July had broken, I moved upon summer seas between the islands of Eigg, Canna, South Uist and Barra, and upon the coasts of Moidart and Morar. It was an enchanted period of what might be described as half off-duty in this following of Boswell's perambulations and sailings. I kept myself, however, to the rule of proceeding as much as possible under my own efforts. I sailed, or rowed, rather than went by steamer, and only took to the steamer on the deeper waters to avoid the aeroplane. I walked wherever I could, and put my leg once again over a Highland pony on some of the steeper hill tracks.

I rode, walked, fished, talked with priests, ministers and laymen of both Catholic and Protestant religions and to laymen of no religion, with sailors, crofters, commercial travellers, a Greek, a Spaniard, an Italian, two French people, some English and one monoglot Gael, but always I kept the tail of my eye on my object. Iona and Inchkenneth were never very far away. In the end my conscience, if it needed any assuagement, found it when, by hazard, I met, as I have recounted, Flora Macdonald's great-great-grandson in Uist; and with that chance meeting to prompt me, I turned back, and by a roundabout way reached the Inner Hebrides again.

The travellers had landed on Mull with some relief after their long isolation on Coll, and their spirits rose somewhat at the prospect of movement. I did not, however, stay long on this large island, for there is little that remains there in the way of atmosphere nor anything beyond the wild and romantic but often cloud-obscured scene to remind one of 1773. Moreover I shared something of Boswell's desire to reach the islands of Iona and Inchkenneth which, despite the fact that I had roamed much amongst the Hebrides, I had never before visited. Boswell and Johnson went first to Inchkenneth and thence by what was probably the easier passage, by sea, to Iona. As I had an invitation to stay at Iona, and, as I was impatient to arrive at this, one of the most famous islands in Western Europe which I had so unaccountably neglected, I went there direct. As I traversed the almost desolate mountain land of Mull, I recalled Johnson's annoyance at losing on this island his valuable oak stick which he had used since 1766 and which he had brought with him from London. When Boswell tried to persuade him that it had not been stolen, he said, "No, no, my friend. It is not to be expected that any man in Mull who has got it will part with it. Consider, sir, the value of such a *piece of timber* here." Mull, though considerably denuded of human beings since 1773, is now slightly better wooded. It pleased me to cut myself a staff in memory of Johnson's jibe and to take it away with me. The stone from Coirechatachan, the stone from the top of Dun Cann in Raasay and this stick are the only tangible and physical things I brought back with me from my own tour of the Western Islands.

So often in this book have I had the melancholy duty of chronicling my visits to ruins which were once standing and inhabited buildings, and to deserted glens and islands which in Boswell's day were full of humanity, that it comes as a relief to record a very different state of affairs on Iona. Today the island still retains some of its indigenous Hebrideans who, though they share that restlessness which nearly all other Islanders, save those on South Uist, possess, live in considerably greater prosperity than did their forefathers in the 18th century. The island, without being vulgarized, is a holiday resort; and most important of all, is the centre of a flourishing religious community.

In 1773 Iona, or Icolmkill as it was then more popularly known, was not only neglected by the Church authorities and such antiquarians as existed in Scotland, but did not support a native population of crofters of the same size as those on the neighbouring islands. It certainly bore no relation to the prosperity of Coll which the travellers had recently left. Indeed Boswell says that all the inhabitants, except a few shepherds, lived close to the ruins of the Cathedral in what must have been a huddle of small and primitive "black houses".

This desertion of Iona (which must have begun at the Reformation) had, in its way, a beneficial effect. While it is true that the Cathedral and old ecclesiastical buildings were allowed slowly to decay, the stones were not, as so often happened in other parts of Scotland, much despoiled or taken away to be used in other buildings. When Boswell and Johnson arrived there on the island they received a considerably less "horrid" impression than that from which they had suffered at St. Andrews where the lapse of time, the rage and zeal of the reformers and the utterly careless behaviour of succeeding generations had combined to give a real effect of savage desolation to the Cathedral ruins. Boswell, who had been looking forward to setting foot on this sacred isle throughout the whole tour, was not disappointed at his first encounter with it, as described in his private journal:

I then saw the tower of the cathedral just discernible in the air. As we were landing, I said to Mr. Johnson, "Well, I am glad we are now at last at this venerable place, which I have so long thought that you and I should visit. I could have gone and seen it by myself. But you would not have been with me; and the great thing is to bring objects together." "It is so," said he, with a more than ordinary kind complacency. Indeed, the seeing of Mr. Samuel Johnson at Icolmkill was what I had often imaged as a very venerable scene. A landscape or view of any kind is defective, in my opinion, without some human figures to give it animation. What an addition was it to Icolmkill to have the Rambler upon the spot! After we landed, I shook hands with him cordially.

Boswell's feelings upon this landing in the darkness were largely animated by prepared sentiment, but that sentiment was not dampened by the discomfort of the primitive accommodation with which he and Johnson had to put up with.

On the first night Sir Allan Maclean (whom, though Iona now belonged to the Duke of Argyll, the people still acknowledged as chief), and Johnson and Boswell all had to sleep together in a barn on a bundle of hay. The servants slept at the other end of the barn and a wind blew through the broken door all night. Boswell happily describes it as an "encampment". Nowhere else on the whole Highland journey had the two men to pass a night in quite such circumstances. Even the filth at Glenelg was enclosed in an inn where something could be bought for food and comfort. Yet neither Johnson nor Boswell appear to have been in the least put out. No doubt the presence of Sir Allan, who upon this his first visit to Iona for fourteen years, was accorded a feudal welcome of the kind that had elsewhere disappeared in the Highlands after the proscriptions of 1747, gave them some support and sense of comfort. But the main thing surely that kept their spirits up was the simple thought of where they were, the thought that they were on St. Columba's island. At the back of that thought, just as behind and above the barn where they lay the Cathedral tower still stood, there was the knowledge that what the Saint had achieved here centuries earlier still stood and triumphed in Western civilization.

Nor were Boswell's eager sentiments to suffer when on the next morning daylight discovered the island, the Cathedral and the remains of the ecclesiastical buildings to him. He wandered both in company and alone, revelling in his antiquarian and his genuinely religious emotions. He gives a slightly fuller and more pleasantly Boswellian account of what he did in his original journal than in the published one. When he came to put his reflections on Icolmkill before the world, one cannot help feeling that he was writing a little under the shadow of Johnson's celebrated passage beginning "We were now treading that illustrious island which was once the luminary of the Caledonian regions" and ending "That man is little to be envied, whose patriotism would not gain force upon the plains of Marathon, or whose piety would not grow warmer among the ruins of Iona."

By the time that Boswell's book came to be published, this Johnsonian passage had already achieved fame. Almost as if to protect himself from the faint possibility of echoing it in any way, Boswell quotes it in full in his own publication, adding for good measure and in a footnote the information that "The present respectable President of the Royal Society was so much struck on reading it that he clasped his hands together and remained for some time in an attitude of silent admiration." When Boswell quoted Johnson's Iona paragraph in his book he could not resist putting the whole of the first word into capital letters, "WE were now treading . . .", a delightfully ingenuous and wholly innocent attempt to "climb on to the band wagon", as the modern phrase has it, of a classic piece of prose by underlining the fact that he, Boswell, was there too.

At Inchkenneth, as I have already mentioned, Boswell had been deeply stirred in his religious emotions before he reached Iona. He had, however, saved up some of his expectation for St. Columba's own island, and his account in his original notes makes pleasant and grateful reading. The cry from the heart that came from him in the darkness on the lesser island three days earlier is not quite so audible, and the introduction of the inevitable Ogden gives the scene a slightly comical effect in modern eyes. But it is pure Boswell.

> I then went into the cathedral, which is really grand enough when one thinks of its antiquity and of the remoteness of the place; and at the end, I offered up my adorations to God. I again addressed a few words to Saint Columbus,[1] and I warmed my soul with religious resolutions. I felt a kind of exultation in thinking that the solemn scenes of piety ever remain the same, though the cares and follies of life may prevent us from visiting them, or may even make us fancy that their effects were only "as yesterday when it is past", and never again to be perceived. I hoped that ever after having been in this holy place, I should maintain an exemplary conduct. One has a strange propensity to fix upon some point from whence a better course of life may be said to begin. I read with an audible voice the fifth chapter of St. James, and Dr. Ogden's tenth sermon. I suppose there has not been a sermon preached in this church since the Reformation. I had a serious joy in hearing my voice, while it was filled with Ogden's admirable eloquence, resounding in the ancient cathedral of Icolmkill.

I too stood with gratitude and emotion within the walls of this venerable building now no longer a ruin, but repaired by the piety of succeeding generations and crowned and filled by regular prayers of those today who have made it a place of Christian worship after so many empty centuries. Some fifty years ago the proprietor of the island, the then Duke of Argyll, restored the fabric of the Cathedral; and recently the Iona Community, under the leadership of Dr. George MacLeod, has made it the Mother Church of one of the most ardent and certainly most

[1] Boswell always spelt the saint's name in English in this way.

hopeful and vital of the movements within the Kirk of Scotland.

Most people of serious intent in Scotland today are aware of the work that the Iona Community is doing in the country and in the cities of Scotland. No visiting holiday-maker to the island, not even the most transitory passenger put ashore by the steamer for the afternoon and then taken away again, could fail to feel inquisitive about this novel brotherhood which has grown up within the Church of Scotland with St. Columba's island as its headquarters. And certainly anyone of whatever Faith who has had the curiosity to follow the footsteps of Boswell and Johnson as far as this place, which provoked from each of them such memorable reflections, must feel a curiosity about those who in the 20th century are attempting to make the "ruins of Iona" live again.

MacLeod of the Iona Community. (How proud is that surname when it stands alone! Dr. somehow gives it a faint touch of pomposity, wholly uncharacteristic of the man, and to call him George in public print offends my taste.) Mac-Leod springs by ancestry from these islands. Indeed Boswell and Johnson stayed with his great-great-grand-uncle Mr. Neil MacLeod, the minister on Mull, just over the Sound from Iona, on their way when they were leaving the island. Johnson paid him the tribute of calling him "the cleanest-headed man he had met in the Western Islands". Some 19th-century editors have boggled at the epithet cleanest, and, on the grounds that in Boswell's handwriting his "n's" and "r's" are often identical, have preferred clearest. Let them boggle! Boswell passed cleanest through three editions, and, as the admirable Carruthers points out, one of Johnson's own definitions of clean was "elegant, not unwieldy, not encumbered with anything useless or dis-proportioned". To clinch the matter, the Reverend Neil MacLeod's own descendant prefers cleanest; so do I.

MacLeod in coming to Iona in middle life has returned

to the roots of his being, but in doing so he has travelled in his ancestry and in himself by various routes. His grandfather, a famous Glasgow minister and preacher, his father a rich 19th-century Glasgow business man, himself a soldier, then a minister of the Church of Scotland and a popular preacher, then an ardent worker in his own slum parish on the Clyde, he has now come to the mountains and the shores of his ancestral country and to that island of the past hard by it whence his eager restless spirit seeks to reanimate the church of his fathers in this century.

What would the 18th-century travellers make of MacLeod if they could meet him on Iona today and see his work there? Johnson, though he might not admit it, would probably be puzzled and might erect some barriers of defence against MacLeod's enthusiasm. He might find it strange that a man brought up in the "civilizing" and highly Anglican atmosphere of Winchester (though he would be the first to admit that he had not been, as was Sir Alexander Macdonald, "tamed into insignificance by an English education") should reject Episcopacy not from ignorance nor because he had not seen it at its most attractive and practised fervently and with faith, but simply because he preferred the simplicity of his native Presbyterianism. He would moreover be puzzled by the intent as well as the form of that Presbyterianism as preached and practised by the Iona Community on that island which once so stirred his own religious sentiments.

All this would puzzle Dr. Johnson. In a cantankerous mood he might well talk about confusion of thought, about the lack of a guiding principle to direct these eager 20th-century spirits amongst the well-defined tenets of Rome, Canterbury and Geneva. But again, who knows what Johnson would now think or say? His bursts of generous feeling and expression were as unpredictable as were his moods of obstinate objection, and, for all that he might be puzzled, I do not think that his large heart would be impervious to the enthusiasm of those who work and worship in the Iona of today, nor that his spirit would fail to perceive the genuineness of their religious convictions. And I cannot believe that his piety would grow any the less warm if he were to find himself not "among the ruins of Iona" but within the walls of its rebuilt Cathedral now once again a house of prayer.

Boswell's voluble spirit would, I feel, be much more susceptible. MacLeod's ardent nature, his patent belief, his very impatience, and not the least his ready flow of talk and wit, would attract him. The sincerity and devotion of his younger followers would interest him. And I mean no disrespect to the Iona Community when I say that Boswell, who had worshipped at the altars of Rome, the St. Paul's of Wren and the village kirk at Auchinleck, might feel that in the Iona of today he had found something that for the time being would satisfy his many-sided and restless religious aspirations. But the operative words are "for the time being". In his pathetically persistent search for goodness and for God, he, more than most men, longed for Authority to guide his most erring, most erratic if forever hopeful footsteps: and who am I to say that he was wrong? Authority in religious matters was not intended for James Boswell alone.

I stood with MacLeod in the nave of the rebuilt Cathedral and thought of Boswell who had stood here alone. I told MacLeod how our famous compatriot had preached a sermon of Ogden's to these bare walls long ago. I recommended to my host the faded apologetics of this almost forgotten 18th-century Divine. "He has a cool logic," I told him, "which once comforted one of the most uneasy of our fellow countrymen." MacLeod with that fanciful acquiescence which is so much a mark of his character promised to consider preaching from Ogden some time in Iona Cathedral. I begged him to let me know so that I might be there to hear.

Later in the morning I wandered by myself in the North and West of the island where Boswell himself had walked and investigated. The Western sands of Iona are, of course, celebrated, and I doubt if anywhere in the Hebrides is that famous peacock blue made by the combination of the silver sand and the blue Atlantic so green or so blue. It lacks, however, that exquisite and elusive hint of pink which is to be found in Coll alone. I talked to a few crofters and heard tales of the evil eye, one of the few manifestations of Highland uncanniness which Johnson with his avid curiosity for this sort of thing did not come across in his tour.

In the afternoon I went with MacLeod and another of his guests to the South end. Our object was the little bay or cove where St. Columba landed when he came from Ireland. Our companion was a young American Divinity student from Texas. With all the inquisitiveness of youth and the pertinacity of his countrymen he kept MacLeod and myself under a running fire of ceaseless questions on Religion, Faith and Morals.

When we reached the bay where St. Columba had landed, it was all that I could have expected or have wished for. Its very smallness touches the heart. A mere thrust of the sea, scarcely a hundred yards inland, it was obviously chosen, not very skilfully, as the first place on the island in which the Saint and his followers could find some kind of shelter. Boswell too had come to this place and had mused as I was now musing. Now, however, for the first time upon my own Boswellian Highland Jaunt, all thoughts of Johnson and Boswell were driven out of my head by deeper reflections on something far more important than their journey in the Highlands and Islands, something far more important than anything that happened in Scotland in the 18th century, something that had happened long before.

Boswell had knelt upon the shore of this bay and had "offered up a short prayer" (a fact again omitted in his published book). In the circumstances I felt too shy to

follow his example. MacLeod was silent too. The three of
us sat down upon the shingly beach and looked out at the
silver sea, silver under the high white clouds, and gazed
south-westwards towards the invisible coast of Ireland
whence had come to Britain nearly two millenia ago the
greatest tidings in the world.

The silence was eventually broken by the young American, eager as ever for information. "Would you say," he
said, "that the Celtic Church of St. Columba was more
akin to the Roman Catholic Church or to the Presbyterian
Faith of today?" MacLeod the Presbyterian and I the
Catholic looked at each other in silence, and if we did not
good-humouredly groan it was not because the question
was too immense for us but because the million little sea-
smoothed stones moving under the long wash of the waves
on the beach groaned for us. Eventually he said: "You first."

"No, no," I replied. "You."

But neither of us spoke. We smiled at the eager young
man with expressions of what I hope were Christian charity
and let the sea and the restless stones and the winds and the
cry of the sea-birds answer for us.

The next day I moved backwards along the coast of
Mull to Inchkenneth, whence Boswell and Johnson had
come on their way to Mull. Inchkenneth was the island
which Johnson had liked the best of all that he had visited
on his tour. Indeed he appears to have fallen in love with
the place, and said that the Sunday evening he spent there
was "the most agreeable that he had ever passed in his life".
He was much taken too by the company he found there—
Sir Allan Maclean, a Highland landlord of the old school,
somewhat polished by travel, and his two young daughters.
He really lets himself go when paying tribute to their
hospitality in his book:

> Romance does not often exhibit a scene that strikes the
> imagination more than this little desert in these depths of Western

obscurity, occupied not by a gross herdsman, or amphibious fisherman, but by a gentleman and two ladies, of high birth, polished manners, and elegant conversation, who, in a habitation raised not very far above the ground, but furnished with unexpected neatness and convenience, practised all the kindness of hospitality and refinement of courtesy.

Boswell at last seems to have been seriously influenced by Johnson's continual exhortations to buy an island, for he said that he was "really resolved to have it for an elegant retreat for our family during a month or two in the summer". When Boswell said his brother David "always talked of purchasing an island", Johnson characteristically gave away his own sentiments on this subject, so often repeated on the tour, "so does almost every man till he knows what it is". In this short jocular sentence thrown off in conversation is summed up much of the great man's philosophy of life. Later on he and Boswell walked by the shore. Boswell broke and ate an oyster to prove that he could support life by living here alone on shell-fish. There is also a charming description in the private journal of Boswell and Johnson gathering little yellow shells as a memento of their visit. Boswell's, rather surprisingly, were intended for his father, Johnson's for Mrs. Thrale's little daughter.

It is in the published Journal of *A Tour to the Hebrides* that we learn from Boswell that Johnson's delight in the island expressed itself in the composition of Latin verses. *Insula Sancti Kennethi* is almost the only poem by Johnson in which there is no undertone of melancholy.

> Quid quod sacrifici versavit femina libros,[1]
> Legitimas faciunt pectora pura preces.
> Quod vagor ulterius ? Quod ubique requiritur hic est;
> Hic secura quies, hic et honestus amor.

So run the last four lines of a short sigh of pure content. The verses were not addressed to anyone in a letter, nor

[1] The first two lines are a reference to the fact that at an evening service in Sir Allan's house the lessons had been read by one of his daughters.

intended for publication. They were spontaneous. If I owned this beautiful little island I should have them carved upon a rock by the landing place and just above the water, crystal clear as it always is in these western seas.

Well as I know the clarity of these enclosed reaches of that part of the Atlantic that lie between the Inner Hebrides, I do not think that I have ever seen it to such perfection as in that quarter of a mile of sea that separates Inchkenneth from its parent island of Mull. You come along the road from the north of Mull or down the steep mountainside due East and walk or stumble out over the stones to the nearest rock to which a boat can draw. From there onwards out to the minute harbour of Inchkenneth you seem, if you have the luck to make this short voyage upon a fine day, to be floating on air. Nowhere is the water much more than thirty or forty feet deep, and all the way across you can see the ocean floor below you, the sand, the rocks, the scuttling crabs, the flash of a mackerel's side and the green, the gold and maroon of the long fronds of the seaweed moving and waving delicately under the influence of the tides. The sail from Mull to the island of Inch-kenneth contains the quintessence of all that is loveliest in cruising amongst the Western Isles.

Inchkenneth is about a mile long and half a mile broad. It is emerald green, save where the wild flowers of summer dot the rich grass with pink and blue and purple. It is neither flat nor hilly, but gently undulating; and its pasture-land is fruitful. It is like a meadow moored just off land in the sea. If someone were to offer me as a gift one of the 787 Scottish islands, I should make my choice from the Hebrides, and the one I would take would be Inch-kenneth.

In the days of St. Columba it contained a minor and subordinate religious foundation under the rule of St. Kenneth, a favourite friend of Columba's who gave this

Q

little jewel of an island into his keeping as a special mark of his favour. The ruins of the chapel still stand; and nearby is a slender Celtic cross in an almost perfect state of preservation. Close by the chapel and the cross is the burial-ground of the family of Maclean, of which Sir Allan Maclean, host to Boswell and Johnson, was the chief in 1773. The burial-ground, the roofless chapel, the cross, indeed the whole island, must be almost exactly as they were in the days of Boswell and Johnson, save in one respect.

Sir Allan and his family lived in what Boswell calls "a commodious habitation, though it consisted of but a few small buildings only one storey high". It is probable that Sir Allan, when he eventually settled down upon Inchkenneth after returning from his military service abroad, did not build himself a new house. He probably restored and cleaned out the interiors of a number of farm buildings and crofts and made the whole into a kind of private village for himself, his family, his dependants and servants. In place of this agreeable arrangement there is now an ugly tall house, built in the style of a small block of modern flats in the suburbs of Glasgow. As if to add the last touch of outward ugliness to this blot upon an island paradise, the colour of the walls is pale khaki. It says much for the beauty of Inchkenneth and its surroundings, as well as for the charm of the lady who now inhabits this house and who has so tastefully decorated its interior, that one has not been on the island for half an hour before one is able to expunge this unfortunate excrescence from one's mind.

Johnson, as I have said, fell in love with Inchkenneth and the hospitality of its Highland chief straight away. Boswell too liked the island and relished the company there. He seems, however, to have been strangely quiet in his demeanour. It is so easy to see through Boswell when he is "putting on an act" for his readers, or even for himself, that one realizes that there is no touch of priggishness in him but a genuine expression of his feelings when he says:

I was agreeably disappointed in Sir Allan. I had heard of him only as an officer in Lord Eglinton's Highland regiment, and as a great companion of the Earl's,[1] so I apprehended that I should find a riotous bottle companion and be pressed to drink; in place of which, the Knight was as sober after dinner as I could wish, and let me do as I pleased. And what surprised me still more agreeably, though he swore, as Dr. Campbell does, he was a man of religion like Dr. Campbell.

When Boswell later danced a threesome reel with the younger of Sir Allan's daughters and Coll, while the elder girl played the harpsichord, the dance was proposed by himself, but he says: "This was making the most of it. As I have formerly observed, my exertions as a dancer are all forced by a reflex desire to promote lively good humour." Again I do not think that this was any priggishness on Boswell's part. When he was in his gay moods he liked drinking, talking, showing off, and generally peacocking about, but dancing seems to have been one of the social accomplishments of which he was least fond. Perhaps he was not very good at it.

But, however well or ill Boswell acquitted himself at the dance, whether he enjoyed himself or not, the scene is a charming one to recall in the eye and in the ear of fancy. Young Coll, the tall Highlander, full of spirits and gaiety, Miss Sibby, the younger daughter, Boswell himself, possibly a little stiff and correct, setting to at the reel while the tinkling music of the harpsichord under Miss Maclean's fingers sounded out some traditional Scotch tune. And there by the fireside Johnson and the old Highland soldier, Sir Allan, looking on approvingly, now beating time to the quick rhythm of the repeated melody, now lending the murmur of their own deeper voices to the general pattern of sound as the dance wove its own pattern long ago on the remote little Hebridean isle.

[1] Lord Eglinton was the nobleman who was set upon Boswell by Lord Auchinleck to make him forget his Catholic vows. This he did by introducing Boswell to the debauchery of the town in 1759 on his first visit to London.

Boswell's unusual and reflective calm upon Inchkenneth was almost certainly due to the fact that he had been looking forward for a long time to visiting with Johnson these holy islands off the coast of Mull. Ever since Skye he refers to his expectations of them and in his private journal says, "I have always had Icolmkill as a capital object in my mind since we first talked of visiting the Hebrides." He clearly drove Johnson on to include these islands in the tour; and Johnson more than once refers to his companion's anxiety that they should not miss Iona.

Ever since Johnson's letters to Mrs. Thrale were published, not long after her death, we have known that Boswell one evening on Inchkenneth stole away from the company at the tea-table, the talk, the harpsichord and the dancing, to be by himself amongst the ruins of the chapel. It was not, however, until the discovery of the private journal that we have known what passed on that solitary occasion when James Boswell was alone and on his knees before the little Celtic cross on St. Kenneth's island:

> I walked out in the dark to the cross, knelt before it, and holding it with both my hands, I prayed with strong devotion, while I had before me the image of that on which my Saviour died for the sins of the world. The sanctity of venerable Columbus filled my imagination. I considered that to ask the intercession of a departed saint was at least innocent, and might be of service. I indulged my inclination to what is called superstitious prayer. I said, "*Sancte Columbe, ora pro me.* O Columbus, thou venerable Saint, as we have all the reason that can be to believe that thou art in heaven, I beseech thee to pray God that I may attain to everlasting felicity."

If I have in these pages dwelt more than once upon what has seemed to me one of the most important traits in Boswell's character, his recurring and irrepressible outbursts of faith, his unquenchable hopefulness, his longing for goodness, it is because this side of him is so often neglected.

When it is not neglected, it is equally often referred to in condescending if not even disparaging terms as examples of Boswell's constitutional instability. Boswell has made his name in the public eye as a biographer of genius, a tireless and talented observer of the social scene in which he lived, and also as an entertaining fellow who never bothered to conceal the truth about himself. It has been well said of him that while other chroniclers, other writers of memoirs, have left portraits and sometimes even photographs of themselves to the world, James Boswell has given us an X-ray presentation of Boswell.

When a man turns himself inside out before the reading public it is perhaps asking too much of human nature to expect that public not to dwell upon precisely those things that they would be the least likely to reveal in themselves. It is only natural then that as each succeeding batch of Boswell's private papers comes out his reputation as a fornicator, a drunkard, a toady and something of an ass in social matters, should grow and increase. He was all of these things; and so, as we shall learn upon the Day of Judgment, have been, are and will be many others, both those better known and those more obscure than James Boswell. It would be hypocritical of me to pretend that I have not laughed over Boswell's follies and smiled sometimes rue- fully, sometimes sympathetically, over his own accounts of his sins. But my heart lifts, and my task, as a compatriot chronicler of this great chronicler upon his tour with Samuel Johnson in Scotland, becomes shot through with pleasure and with hope when I transcribe passages such as the one I have quoted above.

The cross before which Boswell knelt is still as he describes it. Whether it has been deliberately preserved or recently repaired, I do not know, but its slender shaft, rising like the stem of a flower from the bright green grass of the island, is remarkably undamaged. Nearby is the ruined chapel; and the burial place of the Macleans is as desolate as are all such cemeteries in the West Highlands: only the cross stands unravaged and serene.

I stood before it for some time, examining its beauty and the delicate markings upon it, marvelling at their survival through the centuries of storm and wind and rain. Then, touching it with my hands as Boswell had done before me, I too knelt and said a prayer for his departed soul.

The next stopping place that Boswell and Johnson visited, and the last one in the islands before they returned to the mainland, was the Castle of Lochbuie on the island of Mull. The Lochbuie incident has always been a favourite of mine on the whole tour, and I cannot understand why it is so often neglected in commentaries on the Scottish journey. It was, even in the published version of Boswell's journal, lively, humorous enough, even bordering on the farcical, but now that we have the full account as rescued from the croquet-box, the episode could go almost untouched as a scene (a pretty broad one) into an 18th-century Scotch comedy—if such things exist.

The Castle of Lochbuie, in Gaelic the yellow loch, so named from the yellow-tinted hill which protects the arm of the sea on which the old building stands, was an old fortress of one of the branches of the Macleans of Mull. Today it has been repaired, renovated and rebuilt, but lovers of the Lochbuie episode in the Highland jaunt can see the remains of the old keep and cellars and the primitive but feudal establishment in which the travellers of 1773 were entertained.

Maclean of Lochbuie was a fantastic character, an eccentric who, even in his own time, had gained a reputation in the Highlands and Islands. Boswell says: "We had heard a great deal of Lochbuie's being a great roaring braggadocio, a kind of Sir John Falstaff both in size and manners. . . . Coll says he was quite a Don Quixote, and that he would give a great deal to see him and Mr. Johnson together." He later admitted that rumour "had swelled

The Chapel on Inchkenneth and the stone cross before which Boswell knelt and prayed

(From a print in possession of the author)

Inveraray Castle and town about 1770
(*Courtesy of the Edinburgh Public Library*)

him up to a fictitious size and clothed him with imaginary qualities" and that "the truth was that Lochbuie proved to be only a bluff, hearty, rosy old gentleman of strong voice and no great depth of understanding". Even so he was remarkable enough, and comes to life in Boswell's pages like a cross between a Hogarth and an Allan Ramsay.

His wife, Sir Allan Maclean's sister, was much older than he and "behaved like the landlady of an alehouse". Sir Allan, who had seen something of the world, was compelled to apologize for the pair of them, saying that "they were just antediluvians". Miss Maclean, their daughter, "was as wild as any filly in Mull, at least had as little notion of good breeding. Mr. Johnson tried to talk with her. But it would not do. The poor thing knew nothing." Lochbuie lived in a kind of out-of-date feudal squalor. The dining-room in which the travellers ate had two beds in it. Though he was a comparatively rich man he had no spit for roasting and only one pot in which all meals were stewed. Characteristically, however, he had a fine cellar of which he was very proud, full of admirable port.

The clearest glimpse that I get of the laird of Lochbuie, however, is in his meeting with "the great cham of English literature, the sage of Bolt Court, the great lexicographer" or whatever popular phrase or *cliché* one prefers. Upon being introduced to him he bawled out "Are you of the Johnstons of Glencroe or of Ardnamurchan?" Whereupon Johnson gave him a "curious look" and said nothing. A day or two later on, when Johnson was examining the old Castle and the policies around it, Lochbuie roared out that he had excellent cellars in the vaults. Johnson, according to Boswell, "was offended at being disturbed in his antiquarian researches, or rather meditations, and said, 'I don't care about cellars'." He and Boswell, however, did view the pit or dungeon in which a few years earlier Lochbuie had calmly taken it upon himself to imprison a number of people who had offended him on the grounds that it was his

prerogative as a Highland Chief. For this piece of "ante-
diluvian" arrogance he had been fined by the Court of
Justiciary, on which incidentally Lord Auchinleck had sat.
He was so little affected by this that he jested over the
matter with Boswell, and, when he showed him the dungeon,
said, "Your father knows something of this."

It was when I read this recently that the image of this
preposterous old-fashioned Highland laird, old-fashioned
even in 1773, leapt most clearly to my mind. Not long before
I had been re-reading for adapting for the wireless my old
friend Sir Compton Mackenzie's not only highly entertaining but extremely life-like Highland farce *The Monarch
of the Glen*. In this book, as a large number of the reading
public knows already, there is an equally preposterous
figure of a modern Highland chieftain called MacDonald
of Ben Nevis. Students of Mackenzieana are divided on
Ben Nevis. Some claim to spot him as a portrait of a real
man; others claim that he is a pure invention of this most
fertile of modern fiction writers. He is, of course, neither.
Anyone who knows anything about novel-writing knows
also that it is next door to impossible completely to invent
a character, to pull him out of the air as it were. At the
same time, and especially when writing about so small a
society as that composed of modern Highland chieftains,
it would be most improper, and to say the least of it un-
professional, to draw a portrait from the life. Ben Nevis,
as are all other memorable characters in fiction, is partly
pure imagination, partly compounded out of observed
characteristics in other people.

But what Mackenzie most certainly did not do was to
make his Ben Nevis do things that real people have done or
even behave in the way they have been known to behave.
Now those who have read *The Monarch of the Glen* will
remember that one of the crucial points of the novel is
when Ben Nevis, recalling the ancient rights of a chieftain,
locks up a group of hikers in his castle dungeons. They will

also remember that he has a bawling voice, and upon meeting anyone whose name has the faintest Scottish connection at once tries to establish their pedigree. Mackenzie, though he has read widely and voraciously, had long forgotten the existence of Lochbuie, if indeed it had ever made any impression on him. *Plus ça change* one can only tritely say *plus c'est la même chose*. And to add the final touch of coincidence to the whole affair an old Highland landlord, and a lover of Mackenzie's books, told me that when he first read *The Monarch of the Glen* the only person in real life to whom he could fit Ben Nevis was a laird of Lochbuie in the last century whom Mackenzie had never met and, at the time of writing his book, had never heard of. The stream of Highland life and character flows on uninterruptedly—but not always in so exactly the same way and in the same channel.

It was with this farcical interlude at Lochbuie that the Hebridean part of the tour ended. For upon leaving the laird of the yellow loch the travellers left the island of Mull for the mainland, and in a few days after what might be described as a social grand climax at Inveraray, the seat of the all-powerful Duke of Argyll, the Highland Jaunt was over, and the Saxon lands that begin at the Lowlands claimed their own again. It may have been only a coincidence, but when reading Boswell's private journal I have sometimes wondered whether coming events did not cast their shadow on the last night at Lochbuie; for there was in Boswell's behaviour that evening more than a touch of the almost deliberately squalid escape from his better self which marked him in his least attractive moods.

Having polished off what must have been a considerable amount of Lochbuie's "admirable port" Boswell was, as he puts it, "seized with an avidity for drinking". A bowl of punch was produced which Boswell, so it would seem, did more than his share in finishing. Johnson, who was then retiring to bed, perceived his younger friend's inclinations coming upon him and, before departure, bade him in the Staffordshire accent which emerged in him in homely or intimate moments not to "drink any more poonch". Boswell in his private journal says that he was by that time resolved to drink more and adds, "I gave no answer, but slunk away from him with a consciousness of my being brutish and yet a determination to go somewhat deeper." The result of this determination was that Boswell vomited before he was able to do much with the second bowl and slept off the effects in the dining-room while Sir Allan and Lochbuie continued their evening's drinking and conversation regardless of him.

On the next morning Boswell was very conscious of his lapse, and reflected bitterly on how soon it had occurred after his resolutions at Inchkenneth and Iona. He also received something of a dressing-down from Johnson which contrasted with the badinage with which he treated the night's carousal at Coirechatachan. Johnson no doubt perceived the difference between the comparatively gay, if reckless, bout underneath the purple mountain on Skye when Boswell was doing no more than trying to keep his head up in a general gathering of Hebridean hospitality and this solitary slinking away under a "brutish inclination".

Alas! only too soon these brutish inclinations were to become more and more frequent as Boswell left the heights and uplands, not only of his native land, but of Johnson's company on the Highland Jaunt.

XI

THE END OF THE JAUNT

I T is an odd experience while waiting in the lounge of an hotel in that little modern West Highland cosmopolis which is the Oban of today to read Boswell's account of their arrival in "this small village, if a very few houses should be so called". Oban in the 1950s is in Summertime probably the most internationally congested of all Scottish towns. Not even in Edinburgh at the Festival season can you hear so many English, American and Continental accents. Of the Scottish voices the Glasgow one predominates, and only once in a while can you hear as a faint musical whisper the lilt of the true Highland which was once spoken here by everyone.

Oban, even in Boswell's day when it was a "small village", was the chief port to the Western Islands. Today it has become a junction for every kind of tour or jaunt in the West Highlands as well as in the Hebrides. The heavy Victorian neo-Gothic of the hotels, built when Oban was the centre of the Highland Games industry in the West of Scotland, is now almost pushed out of sight by the cafés, the shops, the cinemas and all the other 20th-century erections associated with a popular seaside resort. From morning till night, buses roll and roar into the centre of the town from all directions; and the bay is full of pleasure steamers, speed-boats and other vessels devoted to entertaining the visitor. In the shops, tartan souvenirs and comic Scotch postcards jostle with bottles of anti-midge lotions, detective fiction, buckets and spades, nylons, bottles of kola, and all the other paraphernalia to be found in Brighton, Blackpool or Rothesay. Loudspeakers blare out their instructions to the flocks of holiday-makers, travel touts stand at the street corners, and the colours of cinema posters insult the soft sunshine of the West. Once a year all this stramash attempts to raise its social level and bursts out into a bubble or binge of tartan Technicolor that it would be perhaps a trifle unfair to describe as entirely bogus—the Oban Gathering.

Meanwhile over and above and just behind this seaside resort, the coloured and changeless hills of the mainland raise their heads against the West Highland sky. Out to sea, and across the waters of the bay, the first of the islands lie dreaming in the still unstained waters of the Atlantic.

Not a hint of course of what was to happen to Oban was there when Boswell and Johnson arrived in 1773. The modern Boswellian traveller however may find in the present state of Oban something that may remind him of what happened to Boswell when he came to this point on his own journey. On the islands Boswell had been on the heights; never in his life was he to be quite so innocently and industriously happy again. When he reached the "small village of Oban" he was on the mainland of Britain once more, and, as he expressed it, "It was comfortable to be now *sure*" (his own underlining) "to get to any place in Scotland or England in so many days." A highly understandable sentiment, but with what we now know of Boswell's behaviour almost immediately after the Hebridean tour ended, there is a hint in what he says of longing for those somewhat less innocent and industrious pleasures and pastimes which he could be sure of on the mainland, but in nowhere on the islands.

Or is this being unfair both to Boswell and to Oban? Perhaps it is. But for one who has followed Boswell's wholly delightful wanderings in the still unspoilt and enchanted islands, it is a reflection that it is difficult to avoid as one comes from the peace of the Atlantic into the modern Oban.

When I came on to the mainland from the islands by Oban I went out of the town a mile or two to the Castle of Dunstaffnage which, as much as any building in the West Highlands, holds the history of Scotland within its magnificently thick but now damaged and all but deserted walls. This Castle, which has sheltered the Stone of Destiny, and in which Flora Macdonald was lodged upon her way South after her capture in 1746, stands proudly by the waters of the Firth of Lorne and at the mouth of Loch Etive. But a fire of a century ago has, without destroying the nobility of its profile, lent it an air of desolation. The present age, in its least agreeable form of an apparently aimlessly placed village of "prefabs" or converted Nissen huts, has crept up to its very fringes.

Campbell of Dunstaffnage, hereditary keeper of the Castle and holder of one of the proudest of Scottish titles, "the Captain of Dunstaffnage", lives hard by, preserving as twentieth of his line a guardianship from the remote past. His own house, to which his family removed after the 19th-century fire in the Castle, was itself destroyed by fire during the war years; and today Dunstaffnage, surrounded by such rich relics of his family's past as he was able to salvage from the flames, lives in a small house within a wooded corner of the policies of his estate.

I had not seen him since Europe had gone up in flames, since his own house too had been destroyed in flames, and since the tide of the 1950s in the shape of the "prefabs" had crept up to the walls of his centuries-old Castle. When I called upon my old friend and told him of the journey I was engaged upon, I reflected, though I did not say so, that it was a pity that the travellers of 1773 had not themselves called at Dunstaffnage when they had found themselves at a loose end at Oban. They had been given a card by Sir Allan Maclean to introduce them to the laird of MacDougall, but, from something that Sir Allan had said which Boswell does not reveal even in his private journal, they got the impression that the laird would be unwilling to entertain them. They therefore passed the night alone at an inn in Oban. If, however, they had called at Dunstaffnage they would have stepped as remotely into the past from their own date of 1773 as I did from my own year of 1953 when I sat amidst the salvage from the Highland ruins at Dunstaffnage and listened to the last of his line thinking aloud his own thoughts of the past. It is indeed a sad mischance that Sir Allan had not thought of directing the travellers' steps the few miles from Oban to the feudal survival at Dunstaffnage. Smollett in his *Humphrey Clinker* has, in a fictional form, an admirable description of the Castle and its laird about the same date. Boswell in a factual way would have been even more interesting.

If they failed to taste the remote past at Dunstaffnage, however, they moved forward in some style into the new Scotland and the coming age of the 18th-century Highlands when, two days later, they visited another Campbell, the great Duke of Argyll, at Inveraray. Always powerful in the West, the Campbells of Argyll had since the accession of the House of Hanover become the most important family in the Highlands, if not in all Scotland. The failure of the rising of the '45, and the utter extinction of the Stuart and Tory hopes, had finally settled the Argylls in their proud position. By the time that Boswell and Johnson visited Inveraray, the Duke had become not only the greatest of Highland chieftains and landlords, but a British statesman of power throughout the whole island and well known abroad.

In dining at the Duke's table and in sitting afterwards in the drawing-room, where the Duchess and her ladies held court, the travellers had moved, in one quick transition, from one world to another. They had left in the islands the last remnants of the feudal age of the Highlands and had passed into the then modern world of the late 18th century. That is a world the outward and visible signs of which are still to be seen in the noble buildings of the New Town of Edinburgh, in Dublin, in the architecture of much of what remains of London, in the palladian mansions of our great country houses throughout Britain, and in the manners and customs of a few old-fashioned ladies and gentlemen still alive. At Inveraray, the Highland Jaunt into the remote past which our two travellers had been undertaking ended.

It is not only for this reason that a comment on the ducal hospitality that they enjoyed at Inveraray is out of place here. The whole episode is so minutely described by Boswell and has been annotated by so many subsequent editors and essayists that there is little left to say, certainly in a wandering comment of this kind on the Highland tour. It is perhaps permissible to point out that in Boswell's admirable descriptions of his own snubbing by the Duchess and of his perky survival of it, of Johnson's expansive contentment within these spacious halls, and of the general scene of civilized high life, we get a foretaste of some of the best kind of writing that Boswell was later on to give us in *The Life*. Boswell's delight in the appearance of the ladies' maids "tripping about in neat morning dress", ever so slightly more warmly mentioned in the private journal than in the published one, is moreover an indication that his amorous proclivities after a long rest or suppression in the islands and in the remoter Highlands were beginning to make themselves felt again. Boswell always had a penchant for servant lassies, especially in uniform. He talks about seeing himself in the *rôle* of knight errant for these maids, but his footnote, in which he expresses surprise at the distance of several years that his "venerable fellow-traveller" should have read this passage (Johnson it should be remembered read Boswell's journal as it went along) without "censuring his levity", gives away the true feelings that were aroused in him.

The present Duke of Argyll, having heard of my "per-ambulations" and "equitations" in Boswell's footsteps, kindly invited me to stay at Inveraray, and I spent an agreeable few days wandering about the Castle and the policies, thinking on the past and tying together the loose ends of my own tour, taken so long after 1773. I had stayed at the Castle some twenty years earlier when the late Duke was alive, but my Boswellian interest was then quiescent, and I had scarcely given a thought to Boswell's self-satisfied way of dealing with Her Grace's glacial displeasure and to Johnson's delight in this Castle built, as he had put it, "with a total defiance of expense". Now in the 1950s, however, as at Coirechatachan, I found the sight of old half-forgotten scenes sharpened a new interest in me. As my host left me to wander as I willed and to browse away my leisure in his library, I made my final notes for this book in an atmosphere of pleasant appropriateness.

Inveraray Castle, for all the Dukes and Duchesses that have lived in it since 1773, has not changed funda-mentally since Boswell's and Johnson's visit. The eye and ear of fancy were free to reconstruct the well-known scenes which had occurred here and which I had read about so often since I had last been within these walls. Once, however, I did succeed in actually recalling, and with the assistance of my host, a genuine glimpse or sound of a Boswellian shade.

In his published version of the journal, Boswell mentions this incident:

A gentleman in company after dinner, was desired by the Duke to go to another room, for a specimen of curious marble which His Grace wished to show us. He brought a wrong piece upon which the Duke sent him back again. He could not refuse; but, to avoid any appearance of servility, he whistled as he walked out of the room, to show his independence. On my mentioning this afterwards to Dr. Johnson, he said it was a nice trait of character.

Whenever Boswell mentions "a gentleman" in an incident of a slightly humiliating character such as this, one tends to believe that he is referring to himself. There have been many who have thought that it was Boswell himself who had earned the Doctor's praise for so "a nice trait of character" in whistling as he carried the "curious piece of marble". In the private journal, however, we discover that the gentleman was Colonel Livingstone, Member of Parliament for Argyll, which is, for those who have liked to visualize the scene of Boswell showing his independence in this casual but characteristic way, disappointing.

Be that as it may, the ghost of Colonel Livingstone or Boswell or the unknown gentleman whistled again at Inveraray while I was there. My host knew the Boswellian account of the visit to the Castle almost by heart, and, when I reminded him of the incident, decided at my suggestion to revive it. He suddenly surprised the company as we were sitting at our wine after dinner one evening by asking me to fetch from the next room "a curious piece of marble", which he had left there. It gave me considerable satisfaction to take up my cue at once and without remark, but whistling both as I left the room and returned with an extremely ordinary lump of stone. I decided to make the naively Boswellian echo complete by setting it down on paper here.

It was at Inveraray, but at the town inn and after leaving the Castle, that Johnson delivered his resounding buffet to the Inveraray minister, Mr. John Macaulay, grandfather of Lord Macaulay. Johnson apparently took a dislike to Macaulay's manner of conversation and said after challenging him hotly "Mr. Macaulay, Mr. Macaulay. Don't you know that it is very rude to cry eh! eh! when one is talking?" Unfortunately a defect in the manuscript of Boswell's original journal does not allow us to know what the subject was upon which the minister was so hotly challenged. But we do know that later on in the same evening Mr. Macaulay said "he had no notion of people being in earnest in their good professions whose practice was not suitable". This was just the kind of remark that angered Johnson, who replied, "Are you so ignorant of human nature, sir, as not to know that a man may be very sincere in good principles without having good practice?"

How strangely prophetic are these contests which Johnson had with the Macaulay clan and with the fore-bears of the great Whig historian. As we have seen, Johnson had referred to Mr. Kenneth Macaulay, minister of Cawdor, brother to John Macaulay and grand-uncle of Lord Macaulay, as "the most ignorant booby and the grossest bastard". Some critics have seen in Lord Macaulay's savagely expressed contempt and dislike for Boswell a kind of posthumous revenge for the fact that Boswell had noted down his grandfather's humiliation at the hands of the great English Tory. This is unlikely. Boswell was just the kind of figure of which Macaulay was naturally contemptuous. Boswell's failings and follies were easy game for his cruel pen, and the gusto of his spiritual arrogance did not need the small incentive of this episode at Inveraray to inflame it. Nor can he have known about the phrase applied to his grand-uncle, "the ignorant booby and grossest bastard" (violent even for Johnson), for it was not discovered until Boswell's MSS. came to light in the 1930s.

There is another fact which Johnson did not know about but which Lord Macaulay must have known, though it certainly would not have affected his writings on Boswell. This same Mr. John Macaulay at Inveraray had been minister at Uist in 1746 and had been instrumental in promoting, indeed whipping up, the hue and cry for the hunted Prince Charles Stuart before he was rescued by Flora Macdonald. The Reverend John Macaulay's behaviour in this episode was not untinged with a desire for financial gain, and, whatever may be one's politics, cannot be looked

upon with much favour. Johnson obviously had taken a dislike to the minister on sight. What he would have felt if he
had known of his history on the islands one can only leave
to the reader's imagination.

The pleasant whitewashed inn at Inveraray has, only
a few weeks before writing these words, been partly destroyed by fire; but it was still standing when I was at
Inveraray. Late one evening I strolled down there from the
Castle to sit in the dark little room in which, by tradition,
Johnson delivered his rebukes to the Reverend John
Macaulay. I was alone in the room, and, as far as I could
gather, in the inn. Recalling that it was in this place that
Johnson had broken his rule about fermented liquor and
had his one solitary gill of whisky on the whole tour ("Come
let me know what it is that makes a Scotsman happy")
I too ordered my glass, and under its benign influence tried
to imagine the scene.

Most people are, I suppose, naturally Johnsonians
or Macaulayites, and I confess that I allowed my Johnsonian
affections to glow with the malt in me as I recalled, and
even went so far as to speak aloud to myself, the sentence
"Are you so ignorant of human nature, sir, as not to know
that a man may be very sincere in good principles without
having good practice?" And with this comforting thought I
clapped my glass to my lips and finished off my own gill
in a silent toast to the Doctor. In the act of doing this
another pleasant reflection came upon me which made me
smile. I recalled my father telling me that my own great-
grandfather had determined to break the Whig oligarchy
in his own time, if only locally, by unseating for Parliament
the Reverend John Macaulay's celebrated grandson at
Edinburgh. He had succeeded in doing so. "This calls,"
I said to myself, "for another glass," and having ordered
it and drunk it off, I said aloud, "Come, sir, you know
now what it is that makes a Scotsman happy."

After Inveraray the travellers came home to Edinburgh

by way of Loch Lomondside and Glasgow, then still a pleasant little city with the remains of its ecclesiastical past still about it, and with no more than the rich commerce of the "tobacco lords" to foretell its clanging, smoky, teeming and industrial future. From there they went out of their way to go to Boswell's home at Auchinleck where one of the most famous, but tantalizingly undocumented, quarrels in our literary history took place between Johnson and Boswell's father, Lord Auchinleck. Boswell, as all the world knows, could not bring himself even in his private journal to give us the details of this scene, and merely informs us that it sprang from a mention of Oliver Cromwell and Charles I with, of course, the ensuing contest on Toryism and Whiggery.

Walter Scott, who certainly was in a position to receive verbatim and living tradition from the Boswellian period, says that when Johnson challenged Lord Auchinleck to say what good Cromwell had ever done to his country, Auchinleck replied, "God Doctor! he gart kings ken that they had a lith in their necks" ("he taught kings that they had a joint in their necks") and that this precipitated the battle of the gods. This sounds more like an ingenious invention of early 19th-century Parliament House gossip than the truth. Auchinleck, however rough in his speech amongst his family and his immediate associates, would have been unlikely to have provoked his guest with so crude a jibe and would have been even more unlikely to have expressed it in the Scots tongue which Johnson could hardly have understood. It is more probable that Scott's informant was echoing a saying of Quin's, the actor, who had said that "on the thirtieth of January" (the day of Charles I's execution) "every king in Europe would rise with a crick in his neck".

From Auchinleck the travellers posted to Edinburgh, where they were received with such acclamation and congratulation on their successful voyage that Johnson was

almost put out and made a characteristic comment, the
kind of comment which no one venturing upon a pastiche
of the Doctor's conversation could ever have had the
happiness to hit upon: "I am really ashamed of the con-
gratulations we receive. We are addressed as if we had
made a voyage to Nova Zembla, and suffered five persecutions in Japan." From Edinburgh Boswell and Johnson
went to the inn at Blackshiels in Lothian where the Doctor
was to pick up the coach to London. On the way they
dined and stayed the night with Sir John Dalrymple at
Cranston. They undoubtedly treated this worthy, if
somewhat finicky, laird with casualness, arriving late for
dinner and departing for the inn early next day apparently
with no excuse. It is difficult to defend their conduct in
this matter, but it does not deserve the almost gloating
censoriousness which some recent critics have devoted to it.

At Blackshiels, Boswell saw his friend into the London
coach, and, beyond noting that the Doctor had with him
as a companion for the journey as far as Newcastle "the
worthy and ingenious Dr. Hope, botanical professor at
Edinburgh", makes no comment. He merely says that both
Johnson and the professor used afterwards to speak of their
good fortune in thus accidentally meeting.

Thus casually, rather than abruptly, almost as if it
had collapsed because of nothing to hold it up, the curtain
descends upon one of the most remarkable, vivid and
dramatically chronicled journeys in all our literature.

After Inveraray I too followed the travellers with
an impending sense of casualness, if not of actual anti-
climax, down Loch Lomondside into Glasgow and thence for
another look at the gracious façade of Lord Auchinleck's
fine Augustan mansion at the village from which he took
his title. I then returned to Edinburgh.

When I first had the idea of following Boswell in
Scotland, I had thought of seeing the two travellers in
imagination against the background of modern Glasgow

and the industrial Lowlands generally. Boswell's questions and Johnson's comments, on the modern Clydeside, on professional football, on 20th-century Scottish Nationalism, on dog racing, on hikers, on football pools, on the Edinburgh Festival and on a score of other developments of the 1950s in Scotland which they could never have conceived of in their day, would be worth hearing or even worth imagining. But I forbore even to imagine that I was hearing them. A large part of Johnson's glory is that he is inimitable, and a large part of Boswell's attraction for us, particularly in relation to his own country of Scotland, lies in the fact that he was unpredictable.

No, I stood at the very heart of the Glasgow of today, at the junction of Hope Street and the Central Station, upon a Saturday afternoon of unusual tumult and watched the football fans gathering to take their special trains down to whatever ground on which their game was going to be played. It was a lively and vivid scene, but I could not think what Johnson or Boswell have had to say about it. I decided then to leave their shades alone and where I could see and imagine them at their best—in the Highlands and Islands.

Feeling, however, that, if only physically, I must complete the tour thoroughly, I did not stop when I got to Edinburgh. Having paid my respects once again to James's Court, I walked out of the Capital down to the still minute Lothian village of Blackshiels. I located the farmhouse which was once the inn there, and I stood for a little in the farm courtyard where long ago the coaches had rested on their way between London and Edinburgh. Then, with the aid of a little enquiry, I found where the old road to the South merged with the new, and looked towards London and the South. After I had looked my fill, I decided that I had had enough of walking and took the bus back to Edinburgh.

.   .   .   .   .

The Northern Autumn in Scotland often lingers long and beneficently into the late year. The last week of November can more briefly, but just as beautifully, provide those hours of quiet but stimulating champagne-coloured and only slightly champagne-cold sunshine that further South are associated with the "season of mists and mellow fruitfulness" of September and early October. It was in the last week of November, 1773, that Boswell stood at the outside of the courtyard at Blackshiels and heard the rumble of Dr. Johnson's coach-wheels as his revered friend left him on his way home to London after the forever memorable Highland Jaunt.

The prolonged Scottish Autumn, lovely though it may be, ends eventually and abruptly in a winter, certainly in the East Lowlands, as disagreeable and as depressing as any season endured elsewhere in the British Isles. I have known an old Edinburgh eccentric who liked to hibernate in the Capital. "I love," he used to say, "the music of the winds amongst the house-tops, and when I am lying in bed at nights the crash of the falling slates makes me pull the bedclothes over my ears all the more comfortably." His, however, was an unusual, if not a unique, view of the outward temper of Edinburgh from December till April or even till May. For the rest of us, these months are the season of mud and windy melancholy. In Boswell's day this season was not even lightened or interrupted by the domestic felicity of Christmas; for in the 1770s that annual Christian festival was still suspect even amongst the least rigidly Calvinist Edinburgh homes. Only the pagan Saturnalia of the New Year's alcoholic debauch in the streets and taverns marked with its hectic flare an interval in the darkness between Autumn and Spring.

The winter of 1773–74 was no exception to this rule; and Boswell, who was always susceptible to his surroundings, seems to have set his mood to suit the weather. Scarcely had December begun and his revered mentor arrived in

London than he was seized with his constitutional melancholy, which at this time seemed to be more febrile than lowering. He plunged into a succession of debauches each one of which left him more saddened than before, but each one of which followed the last even more quickly. The three-year period of genuine reform, if not of complete tranquillity, which had followed upon Boswell's marriage in 1770 and which culminated in the happiness of the tour amongst the Western Highlands and Islands of Scotland with Johnson, was now at an end. And, like the Scottish Autumn, turning with the crack of a whip into the Scottish Winter, it ended abruptly. In all Boswell's private papers there is nothing quite so consistently saddening or degrading as this record of the Edinburgh months that followed the Highland tour.

His ineradicable hopefulness, however, his capacity for affection, love and not the least for industry, which was just as constitutional with him as was his melancholy, were able to rescue him sufficiently to give him twenty-one years more of activity. During these twenty-one bustling years of ups and downs, though he was to suffer much again and make others who loved him and depended on him suffer too, he was to make his eager way in the world to become, after his own fashion, celebrated in his own world. Finally he was to leave as a monument to an increasingly admiring and wondering posterity the inestimable gift of the greatest biography in the language, his *Life* of his revered and loved friend Samuel Johnson, LL.D.

During these twenty-one years he was to give up his practice at the Scottish bar and to fail at the English one. He was to succeed, however, to his ancestral estates at Auchinleck and was to achieve there (a fact which is often forgotten) the well-deserved reputation of being a kindly and painstaking landlord and husbandman who handed on to his son his land intact, his money well preserved, and the affectionate goodwill of the Auchinleck tenantry. He was to fall into near despair, and to return to his work, and to hope over and over again. He was to be liked, laughed at, envied, despised and occasionally respected; but on the whole, amongst those who knew him best, the sentiment he was most frequently to arouse was affection.

He left Scotland forever towards the end of his life. He preserved, as his spirits and his earthly hopes declined, only a tenuous connection with his paternal estates of which earlier on he had proved so faithful a guardian. Of his attitude towards his native country, I can only say this: it was compounded out of feelings which in youth were strong enough to be held in the phrase *Odi et amo*, but as he himself weakened, both his dislike of, and his natural love for, Scotland themselves weakened. To the end, however, he preserved, perhaps all unknown to himself, some of the characteristics and paradoxes of character possessed by many of his countrymen—eagerness and gloom, a pursy self-importance and a warm heart, a foolish vanity and a deep capacity for industry, a romantic susceptibility and a love of triviality, an essential likability, a strong taste for the pleasures of the flesh and an ineradicable hope for the eventual mercies of Heaven, and life everlasting.

He died in his fifty-fifth year on 18 May, 1795. Worn down by a mixture of success and failure, of respectable ambition and recurrent frivolity and debauchery, he sank into a deep yet never-despairing slovenliness of habit and body in his house in, of all places, Great Portland Street. Great Portland Street where today the motor salesmen ply their ephemeral trade under the great white bulk of Broadcasting House—Great Portland Street in London, the city he had once admired and loved so much.

Yet who knows even then, in his last hours in London, in what direction some of his fading thoughts may have wandered—perhaps even northwards. Perhaps for a few brief moments he heard again the wash of the Atlantic on the Hebridean beaches, heard the music of the reel when they rolled back the carpet at Raasay, and when Malcolm Macleod "bounded like a roe" and when Dr. Johnson sat back surveying the scene in great content, his deep rumblings of happy talk providing a bass accompaniment to the music and to the flying feet of youth. Perhaps there came to him as consolation the thought of himself upon his knees in the darkness of the October night before the cross on the island of Inchkenneth. And perhaps there recurred to his dying mind fading memories of that time in his turbulent, restless life when he was at his happiest and at his best and most truly at peace with himself and the world—when his foot was on his native heath and when he was in the Highlands and Islands of Scotland with Dr. Johnson. It is possible.

INDEX

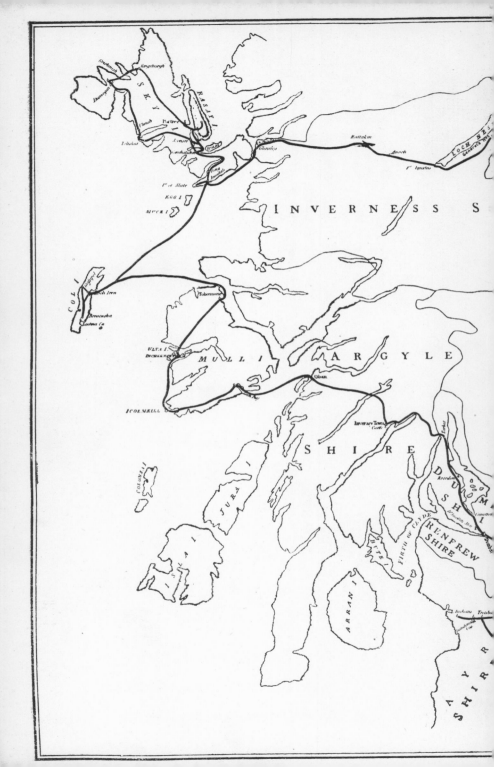